"[Coyle] snaps vivid shots of these fragile creatures who, in the instant of a dropped ball or a strikeout, plunge from heights of trash-talking cockiness to depths of finger-pointing defeatism. . . . Amusing, heartbreaking."
—*The New York Times*

"A gutsy reporting tour de force."
—Bob Woodward

"A painfully beautiful book. Though it reads like a novel, it provides a wrenching portrayal of real kids with real dreams. It is one of those rare books that is destined to affect the way we think about, and feel about, life in our inner cities."
—Walter Isaacson, author of *Kissinger*

"An eloquent, searing tale that is part *Brian's Song* and part Studs Terkel."
—Ken Auletta, author of *The Underclass*

"The crack of the bat heard over the sound of gunfire; a testament to the innocent courage of children, as well as to their ability to endure in spite of all, including the adults."
—*Kirkus Reviews*

"*Hardball* is no suburban, Little League feel-good yawner. . . . Coyle is a deft and sensitive writer and has crafted this, his first book, to perfection. . . . In the vernacular of Cabrini-Green, that Coyle guy whacked one to the gate."
—*San Francisco Chronicle*

HarperSpotlight

HARDBALL

A Season in the Projects

DANIEL COYLE

HarperPaperbacks
A Division of HarperCollinsPublishers

The author gratefully acknowledges permission to quote lyrics from "Cabrini-Green," by the Slick Boys, courtesy Slick Boys Inc.; and from "For What It's Worth," by Stephen Stills, © 1966 Cotillion Music Inc., Ten East Music, Springalo Toones & Richie Furay Music. All rights administered by Warner-Tamerlane Publishing Corp. All rights reserved. Used by permission.
Herbert Hoover's comments on Iowa are from Tom Weil, *The Hippocrene U.S.A. Guide to America's Heartland* (New York: Hippocrene Books, 1989).
Karen McCune's essay appeared in the *Chicago Tribune*, October 19, 1992.

HarperPaperbacks   *A Division of* HarperCollins*Publishers*
10 East 53rd Street, New York, N.Y. 10022

A hardcover edition of this book was published in 1993 by G. P. Putnam's Sons.

Cover photograph by Gary Crallé/The Image Bank

First HarperPaperbacks printing: February 1995

Printed in the United States of America

HarperPaperbacks, HarperSpotlight, and colophon are trademarks of HarperCollins*Publishers*

10 9 8 7 6 5 4 3 2 1

For Jenny

Whoever wants to know the heart and mind of America had better learn baseball, the rules and realities of the game—and do it by watching first some high school or small-town teams.

—JACQUES BARZUN, *God's Country and Mine*

AUTHOR'S NOTE

In the spring of 1991, I volunteered to coach in a new Little League being established at the Cabrini-Green housing project in Chicago, three blocks from where I was employed as an editor at *Outside* magazine. The following year, assisted by a leave of absence from work, I chronicled a season in the life of our team, from first practice to last pitch of the summer of 1992. Everything recounted in the following pages actually happened, although the names and identities of the Kikuyus players and their relatives have been altered to protect their privacy.

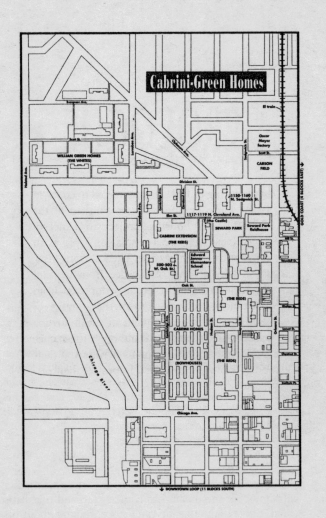

Cabrini-Green Homes

Evergreen Ave.

Scott St.

Larrabee Ave.

Cleveland Ave.

Halsted Ave.

El train

Oscar
Mayer
Factory

Sedgwick St.

Scott St.

CARSON FIELD

WILLIAM GREEN HOMES
(THE WHITES)

Division St.

Cambridge Ave.

Cleveland Ave.

1150-1160
N. Sedgwick St.

GOLD COAST (4 BLOCKS EAST)

Elm St.

1117-1119 N. Cleveland Ave.

Larrabee Ave.

(the Castle)

SEWARD PARK

Seward Park
fieldhouse

CABRINI EXTENSION
(THE REDS)

Hill St.

Wendell St.

Edward
Jenner
Elementary
School

500-502
W. Oak St.

Oak St.

Orleans St.

(THE REDS)

Walton St.

Cambridge Ave.

CABRINI HOMES

Hudson St.

Sedgwick St.

Locust St.

(ROWHOUSES)

(THE REDS)

Chestnut St.

Chicago River

Chicago Ave.

Oakley Pl.

DOWNTOWN LOOP (11 BLOCKS SOUTH)

PROLOGUE

Whenever the dream comes, Maurice falls out of bed. He doesn't fall very far, since his mattress rises only a few inches above the linoleum floor. Nor does he fall very loudly, because the bed is ringed by a thin but complete cushion of shirts, socks, underwear, and baseball cards that muffle the thump of a small body. The sound does not awaken Rufus, his younger half brother, who shares the mattress in the small apartment above the bar on Sedgwick Street. But his mother, who has lived in the neighborhood for twenty years, has her ears primed for trouble.

"Maurice, that you?" she whispers.

Nothing.

She tries again. "Honey, you okay?"

Maurice does not answer, because if he does his mother will know that the dream has come again, and that he is scared. She'll know that he can't stop thinking about his cousin Lonzo and how he looked there in the yellow light of the entryway, all laid out and bloated up in his head from the bullets and the blood. How his mother shoved her way through the police lines and cradled Lonzo's big head in her arms and got her good jacket so soaked they had to throw it away. How all the Cobras came to the funeral home in their Oakland A's colors, the white pinstripes that Lonzo used to wear. How they gathered around the coffin and kissed him on the cheek and curled his stiff finger in a Cobra C like *they* were his family, like they hadn't tried to keep him in the gang, like they weren't the ones who had gotten him killed . . .

"Mo-*reece*," his mother whispers. "You quit that movin' around and get back to sleep right now, you hear me?"

Maurice rolls back onto the mattress and says nothing. He nudges Rufus to give himself more room. Rufus, his lips wrapped tightly around his thumb, rolls over without making a sound. He's younger than Maurice by three years, and always sleeps peacefully. Maurice used to sleep like that, back when he was a shorty. Now he's grown up. Eleven years old—twelve in a couple of months.

Moving slowly so the mattress won't squeak, Maurice clears away a space and presses his ear to the floor. Music and voices drift up from the bar, faint and tinny. He hears the sound of glass breaking, then shouting, then music again. Nothing unusual. He can hear his brother breathing, soft and low. A small cockroach struggles up the wall, its carapace glinting bronze in the glow of the street lamp.

Maurice leans back. Mama always says to think of something nice when he can't sleep. He takes a breath and thinks of the blue house in Tennessee, and that summer a long time ago. He remembers how they spent every day on that big lawn, playing Wrestlemania and sock football, and how when it got too hot they lay on their bellies underneath the elms and let the sprinkler water fall over them. He remembers how they could go to the store, to the pool, to the movies by themselves, anytime of day or night. They'd go back to Tennessee someday, Mama told them, just as soon as they had a little bit of money saved up. That had been almost three years ago.

Time passes. Maurice rolls over. There's no chance of sleep, but that doesn't matter. It's almost morning, and the red haze over Sedgwick Street throws a soft glow on his baseball cards, so familiar after a winter of study that each outline immediately summons a name—*Shawon . . . Frank . . . Ozzie . . . Cal . . . Andre.* Across the room, leaned carefully against a paint-bald wall, a blue aluminum bat shines hard and bright. Maurice often has heard people complain about life in the neighborhood, but right now he wouldn't want to live anywhere else.

"It ain't really so bad, living here," he once explained to a friend. "In summertime, we play baseball."

APRIL

Play area should be inspected frequently for holes, damages, stones, glass and other foreign objects.

During warm-up drills players should be spaced so that no one is endangered by wild throws or missed catches.

At no time should "horse play" be permitted on the playing field.

—Little League Safety Code

ONE

Carson Field is 333 feet long and 290 feet wide, roughly the same dimensions as a Chicago city block. It is bounded on the north by the Oscar Mayer meat-processing plant, on the east by the elevated train tracks of the Ravenswood line, on the south and west by Division and Sedgwick streets, respectively, and on all sides by an eight-foot-high chain-link fence. There are two infields scratched out of its expanse, one in the northeast corner and the other in the southwest, each covered with blond dirt as fine as glacial silt and anchored by a well-dimpled backstop. Each infield is appointed with a pitcher's rubber and a home plate cut from thick pine slabs and tamped deep into the earth so that they don't move. Each infield has two fenced-in dugouts. There are no outfield fences. Balls keep rolling until they ring against the chain link.

The remainder of the field is covered by a thin skin of crabgrass, bluegrass, chickweed, knotweed, pigweed, dandelions, and European clover that was originally imported to the Midwest to feed livestock but which now thrives in jungly lots and sidewalk cracks. In some parts of the field, the many varieties of plants have grown together, blending into a sparse but adequate covering of dingy green. In others, however, the different colonies have remained stubbornly independent of one another, creating tufted kingdoms of leaves and stems bounded by narrow lines of barren earth. This pattern lends Carson Field a motley appearance, one vaguely resembling a color-coded world map. It also makes it tough to field a grounder.

"Man!" Jalen yelled, slamming his glove into a clump of dandelions. "Maaaan!"

First practice of the season, and Jalen was mad. That was the second ball that had bad-hopped past him, and it wasn't fair.

"Maaaaaaaaaan!" He aimed a kick at the offending flora with one of his Scottie Pippens, the new kind with the 33s stitched in silver thread across the heel, then thought better of it. Grass stains. He yelled instead.

"Look at this! This place *phony!*" Jalen held his empty hands out, crucifixion style, so his coaches and fellow players elsewhere on the field could better appreciate the tableau: him, the still-rolling baseball, the dandelion puffs blowing around him like snowflakes.

Jalen was eleven years old, but he could look fifty. He was tall and bone-thin, with charcoal eyes, an unsmiling mouth, and a brow that he wore perpetually crinkled, as if he were looking for something he had lost. Because of his light complexion, his parents had nicknamed him "Jiffy," after the peanut butter. When he was little, he hadn't minded so much. But now he was in fifth grade, too old for baby names. "Y'all getting on my *nerves,*" he would warn, shaking his head sternly. "I *ain't* no samwich!"

Across the outfield, a sharp-featured boy named Demetrius leveled an accusing finger at Jalen and sang in a piercing falsetto: "Bus-ter, bus-ter, Jay-ay-len a bus-ter." Now he danced to his chant, shaking his rear end to the beat. The other kids laughed. Jalen tensed, then shouted.

"You the *buster,* Demetrius."

"Bus-ter, bus-ter, Jay-*ay*-len . . ." Demetrius added a slow, taunting twirl to his repertoire.

"Shut *up,* Demetrius, you ain't nothin' but a crack baby anyway."

"Jalen!"

A new voice, a gravelly tenor, cut across the out-field. Coach Kevin used his fungo bat like a pointer, and enunciated each word slowly. "Pick . . . up . . . your . . . glove . . . right . . . now."

Kevin was aiming for firm, parental clarity, but to Jalen it sounded like an ultimatum. Disregarding the danger of grass stains, he booted his glove in Kevin's general direction and walked toward the backstop, splay-footed, stiff, determined.

"I quit!" he yelled.

"Jalen!" said Coach Kevin, but it was too late.

"Y'all a whole team of busters," Jalen called over his shoulder as he neared the gate. "Y'all gonna lose every game."

A muscular hand appeared on Jalen's shoulder, stop-ping him a few steps from the sidewalk. "Where are you headed there, chief?" asked a soft, low voice. Coach Bill. The head coach. He had been standing by the backstop, watching.

"Don't touch me or I'll *sue* you." Jalen's eyebrows rose threateningly."

Bill removed his hand, but shifted his substantial frame between Jalen and the gate. He changed the subject.

"Hey there, chief, what position should we put you at this year?" Not getting an answer, Bill talked on content-edly. "I could see you at third base, but then again, a line drive might break you in half."

To illustrate his point, Bill wrapped his forefinger and thumb around Jalen's biceps, then sighted through the re-maining space as if through a telescope.

Jalen pulled away.

· *"Maaaaan,* the field is phony an' Demetrius *playin'* too

much an' whatchacallit Kevin *yellin'* at me, an' I'm goin'
home an' watch *Fresh Prince of Bel-Air.*" He sucked a
breath. "An' I ain't no *buster.*"

Bill squatted down like a catcher, then leaned in close,
confidential. Bill made a rule of never yelling at his players,
no matter what.

"I have an idea," he said quietly. "Why don't you and I
walk out there, we forget about Demetrius, we pick up
your glove, and we have a catch."

Jalen looked up, apparently surprised. Their eyes connected. Bill, thinking Jalen would follow, stood up and
walked toward the field.

He was wrong. Jalen emitted an incredulous honk of
disgust, pivoted smartly, and he and his Scottie Pippens
disappeared down Sedgwick.

Bill watched him for a while, then walked slowly to join
the rest of the team. That was his other rule: Never chase.

Whenever he was on the field, Coach Bill carried a manila
folder. Over the course of the season, it would contain the
slow accretion of schedules, applications, and miscella-
neous organizational flotsam. On this first day of practice,
however, it contained only one page. As Jalen strode stiffly
away, Bill walked to home plate, opened the folder, and as
he would a thousand times in the next few months, looked
at the team roster.

Bill had assembled the document on his computer at
work, and had arranged it with his customary efficiency.
On top, centered and underlined, was the name of the team
and the age group to which its players belonged: FIRST CHI-
CAGO NEAR NORTH KIKUYUS (9–12). Beneath that were typed
the players' names, ages, birthdates, addresses, phone
numbers (when they existed), and the names of parents
and guardians. Farther down the page came the names of
the coaches, each assigned a specialty (infield, outfield, hitting, pitching), along with phone and fax numbers for
home and work. At the bottom of the page was the phone

tree, a many-branched assemblage of Linnaean efficiency representing lines of command and communication: from Bill to his assistant coaches, and from them, subsequently, to the players. But Bill knew this piece of paper was little more than a neatly tabulated illusion. "If we can get half of these guys to show up regularly, and pick up a few more as we go along," he said, referring to both players and coaches, "we'll be doing pretty well."

Bill knew because he had been here before. His experience dated back almost a year, to the infancy of the ground-breaking endeavor now known dually as the Near North Little League / African-American Youth League, Chicago's only Little League based in a housing project. His involvement, and that of most coaches, had been a simple matter—a phone call from an old lacrosse buddy with an intriguing report about a new baseball program in need of coaches. Bill had attended a meeting, and had come away greatly impressed by the caliber of people in on the venture: bond traders, stockbrokers, bankers, insurance men, real estate men, venture-capital investors, many of them, like Bill, recent graduates of Ivy League universities. He had been encouraged also by the unique partnership of the league's two founders, an insurance executive named Bob Muzikowski and a community worker named Al Carter, two men of considerable charisma and energy. Theirs appeared to be a perfectly complementary relationship: Muzikowski provided the corporate sponsors and coaches; Carter provided the players, the neighborhood expertise, and a focus on reinforcing the children's African-American heritage, which manifested itself in several ways, beginning with his proposal to name each team after an African people—Zulus, Bantus, and Maasai, for instance.

Carter told the volunteer coaches that their job would require a commitment of one or two nights a week as well as a fair degree of patience, since many of the children had never played organized baseball before. He had said not to worry about safety. The field would be secure, provided you didn't do anything foolish. And he gave more specific advice: "Do not extend your index and pinkie fingers in the traditional two-out signal," he announced at one of the first coaches' meetings. "This is a Disciple sign, and could provoke a shooting. Use the peace sign."

Everyone had muddled through the first season fairly well. The league drew thirty corporate sponsors and 250 kids, as well as the brief attention of the local and national press. Although things had been more than a little disorganized at times—in part because of Carter's and Muzikowski's strong, occasionally clashing personalities—any confusion was overshadowed by the simple fact that the games had been played; the league had worked. As for Bill's Kikuyus, they had made it through that first season with a similar balance of chaos and order. The team had finished the year in the middle of the pack at 9–6, failing to make the playoffs by one game.

Bill now went over the new roster, starting with the coaches: Kevin, Brad, Cort, Feets, Dave, Dan, Mickey. Kevin and Cort were Bill's roommates; the others were more distant friends and acquaintances. Despite Bill's attempts to find people who did not fit the complete description, all were white, college-educated young men with short hair, suburban backgrounds, and orthodontically corrected teeth. His strategy, employed successfully the year before, was to sign up a surplus of coaches and figure that on any given night only a few of them would be able to make it. "When you ask guys if they want to coach baseball for underprivileged kids in a housing project, the answer is always, Yes, sure, I'll definitely be there, a hundred percent," Bill said. "The reality is that people have to stay late at work, they take vacations, they can't make it for one reason or another. This works out so that all the coaches don't have to be there all the time."

While the coaches hadn't spent much time together as a group, any unfamiliarity was defused by their custom of addressing one another with the honorific "Coach." This, besides granting every exchange the ring of fraternal rapport ("Coach Brad, why don't you help Coach Cort with batting practice"), became something of an inside joke when it grew apparent that the coaches were virtually the only members of the team to use the title.

Then there were the players. Already the list was becoming familiar: Maurice, Rufus, Freddie, Jalen, Louis, Alonzo, Demetrius, Nathaniel, Calbert, T.J., Rickey, Otis, and Samuel. Thirteen players, all boys. Maurice, Jalen, Freddie, Louis, and Alonzo were veterans from the previous year's team. Others had filled out an application at school and had been assigned to the team by chance. Still others had just shown up at the field, and Bill had jotted their names on the roster. Technically, this practice violated league policy, which stated that new players were to be placed into a pool, then distributed by league officials among teams. But to Bill and most other coaches, that didn't make sense. If you were lucky enough to get a kid interested, you grabbed him, gave him a glove and an application, told him three times when the next practice would be, because you might not get a second chance. This wasn't suburban Little League, and that, as Bill liked to say, was the point.

Looking at the names, Bill couldn't tell how good this team might be. Not only had most of the previous year's key players graduated to the league's thirteen-to-fifteen-year-old bracket, but word had it that two other teams, the Pygmies and the Ewes (pronounced *ee*-wees), were already practicing five days a week and had paid regular visits to a local batting cage during the off-season. At the Ewes' first practice, Bill had heard, more than twenty-five kids had shown up, eager to play for the defending champs.

Bill scanned the field and did a quick head count—three coaches, including himself; six players, seven with the AWOL Jalen. The First Chicago Near North Kikuyus suddenly looked very small.

From Carson Field, it doesn't look like a big place. It isn't, really. Seventy-one acres, twenty-three highrises, fifty-eight two-story rowhouses. Seven thousand people, eighteen streets, seventeen liquor stores, five churches, two grocery stores, no banks. The entire development takes up an L-shaped chunk of land just seven blocks by five blocks, though it is tough to tell for sure, because many streets dead-end when they reach the boundaries of the development, effectively eliminating the chance that someone might wander in by accident.

From most angles, the Cabrini-Green Homes, the second-largest housing project in the United States, look staid. Boring, even. The dominant structures are the rectangular highrises, seven to nineteen stories tall, some red and some white, all dotted by small square windows and divided by long, dark swaths of screened-in stairwells. On the red highrises, white concrete separates windows from each other; on the white highrises, black stains of long-ago rainwater thread from the lower corners of windowsills. From afar, each building appears to have been formed out of a single gargantuan brick and shoved endlong into the earth. The only signs of life come from the windows, many of which display shades, greenery, or in a few cases, lace curtains. Many others, however, are burned out, empty, hollow. It is the empty windows, particularly those on the upper floors, to which the eye is instinctively drawn.

In Cabrini, gunfire is discussed like weather. *Better go shopping early, because they're gonna shoot tonight. They sure were shooting last night, weren't they? They was shootin' early this morning, but then it let up and I got to go to my grandmama's.* Outside the neighborhood, it is discussed in terms of war. One person shot a week; one person killed a month; double that in the summer. During a particularly active two-month period in 1981, Cabrini's toll was thirty-seven wounded and eleven killed. Its annual homicide count regularly exceeds that of most other Chicago housing developments, as well as that of several states.

The project's notoriety is magnified by the fact that Cabrini lies a mere four blocks from the Gold Coast, which ranks below only Manhattan's Upper East Side as the wealthiest city neighborhood in the United States. Once in a while, from the couches in their condominiums, Gold Coast residents can see the flash of gunfire in the dark windows of the project; at night, the police occasionally station themselves on Division Street, warning the mostly white passersby away from the area. Some pundits, noting the contrast, have termed Cabrini the worst housing project in the country, but that statement, most informed people agree, is an exaggeration fueled by Cabrini's accessibility to the downtown media and thus its higher profile than it would have were it sequestered to the south and west, as is the case with most housing projects in Chicago. The Robert Taylor Homes are more daunting; more drugs are sold in the ABLA Homes; the Henry Horner Homes endure more abject poverty. But when it comes to bullets, few projects can compete with the place they call the Green. "Gang-bangers from the South Side are scared of Cabrini," says Officer Eric Davis of Public Housing North, the special police unit based in the development. "They're like, 'Fuck Cabrini, why should I go up there and get my ass shot?' "

Though Bill and the other veteran coaches heard the shooting only now and then, they had gained a vague sense of the impact of this violence on the children in Cabrini. Some, the coaches had observed, seemed reserved and overly frightened of new places, almost like babies. Others were talkative, confident, and cynical far beyond their years, almost like old men. The coaches probably didn't realize the full extent of the violence (one study had found that by the age of five, virtually every child in Cabrini had either seen a shooting or knew someone who had been involved in one), but they knew enough to understand.

One afternoon the previous season, a Kikuyus player casually told a coach about something he had seen that day. The player, Henry, was a first baseman of Ruthian physique, a sweet-faced kid with a quiet, amiable manner. That morning, Henry had gotten ready for school, kissed his mother, walked downstairs, and in the breezeway of his building encountered a crew of maintenance men hosing brains and blood off the wall and floor. Henry inquired, and learned that the vitals had belonged to a nineteen-year-old man just released from three years in a juvenile detention center. On his first day out, the young man had returned to what he believed to be his gang's building; he didn't know that the building had switched over to another gang until he walked inside, and then it had been too late. Some people were already laughing about it. *Imagine the look on that boy's face,* they said. *He must have been mighty surprised.* As Henry told it, he stepped over the pool of soap and brains, careful not to get his sneakers wet, and continued on his way to school.

While Coach Bill stood at home plate looking over the roster, practice carried on around him. In the outfield, Coach Kevin was hitting fly balls to Maurice, Nathaniel, and Louis. More accurate, he was hitting fly balls *at* the three players, because the ground was catching most of them.

"I *got* it, I *got* it."

Maurice ran toward a ball, head up, extending the large flapping pancake of an original Ed Kranepool signature-model first baseman's glove. The glove had lain dormant in Bill's family's basement since the mid-seventies, and by the looks of it, had seen its share of action before that. The sun had bleached the leather to the color of driftwood; the friction of growing hands had left only loose straps for the pinky and thumb. Even on adult hands it swam like an oversize potholder. "The Finest in the Field," read the faded inscription on the pocket.

"I *got* it, I *got* it . . ."

Maurice levered the glove up and stretched his small body to its full length. The ball thunked against the grass six feet behind him. He jogged over to retrieve it, shaking his head in disbelief.

"That one tailed away from me at the last second, Kevin," his voice called in, firm and authoritative. "Hit me another."

Maurice always wanted another ball. He seldom caught

any, but something about him always made the coaches believe he would. He was short for eleven, with an athletic build and a loose, rough afro that would have been fashionable two decades earlier. Among all the close-cut fades, boxes, and intricate swirls, Maurice's untamed fuzz stood apart, enabling kids to spot him a hundred yards away and inspiring one coach to call him "Young Arthur Ashe." His face, too, was distinctive. It was handsome and oval-shaped, with crescent eyes the color of anthracite and a small mouth set in a natural upturn that seemed unable to bend into less cheerful curves. As always, he wore a plain blue sweatshirt, long black shorts with the Charlotte Hornets logo on the right thigh, and black XJ-9000 tennis shoes with black laces, untied, no socks. All the kids knew that XJ-9000s cost only $12.99 at Payless, but their teasing never got to Maurice. "I don't care about shoes," he said. "I'd rather have the money for more important stuff." He always was saying things like that, things that made him sound old and wise. The previous year, some of the coaches had wondered whether perhaps Maurice sounded a little *too* wise, whether he were mimicking an older sibling or simply sucking up to get playing time. They soon decided, however, that the question was moot. Whatever his motivations, Maurice seemed like a bright, insightful kid.

"You know," he had told Bill, during a game in which the coach had chosen not to let the boy pitch. "It really doesn't matter much if we win or lose the game. The important thing is that we play."

Now it was Nathaniel's turn to play. A lithe boy with a columnar haircut, and slightly bucktoothed, he twitched uneasily beneath Kevin's fly ball, which was heading right at him. Holding his undersize fake-leather Japanese-made glove in the tips of his fingers, he took a tentative step sideways and, eyes closed, waved at the passing blur like a champion matador.

"Get in front, Nathaniel," yelled Kevin in his sandpaper voice, dropping the fungo bat and pantomiming how he should center his body under the ball. "If you're not in front, you can't catch the ball."

Nathaniel looked at Kevin as if he were insane. Nathaniel was a newcomer to the neighborhood. He lived in what the kids called the Orange Doors, a well-kept apartment complex on Sedgwick. His dad had signed him up for the league because he wanted him to make friends. So far, it hadn't exactly been working. The first two practices, Nathaniel resembled a race-walker as he completed the fifty-yard commute from apartment building to Carson Field. He made no attempt to act tough. *I am a buster,* his every move seemed to say. *I have no money and no desire to take yours. If you punch me or kick me, I will cry. Let me pass in peace.*

Nathaniel ran to pick up the ball, then handed it to Maurice to throw back in. Maurice happily obliged.

"No, Nathaniel." Kevin caught the ball with his bare hand and shouldered the bat. "*You* throw it."

Nathaniel giggled.

"*Next* time, you throw it." Kevin turned to the third out-fielder. "Your turn, Louis."

A pause.

"Louis! It's your turn."

Still no answer.

"*Hey, Lou!*"

Louis sat next to the fence, picking dandelions and stacking them in his glove. Kevin's face glowed pink. The boy had been doing this all practice.

"Okay, buddy," Kevin said under his breath. He dropped the bat, wound up, and threw the ball toward the outfield, high and far, directly at Louis. "Your ball!" he shouted.

Louis turned his head, carefully gauging the ball's arc and speed. He remained seated, not wanting to give Kevin the satisfaction of a response. But as the ball neared, it became clear that he would have to move. At the last second, Louis stood up and took a slow, casual step away. The ball thunked against the ground, barely a foot from his glove. The dandelions shook. Louis yawned.

Louis was a puzzle. For starters, he looked different from most of the other kids. He wore matching pin-striped Bulls baseball-style jersey and shorts, white-and-red Nike Air Force sneakers, and stylish wire-rimmed spectacles. It was not an uncommon outfit in the neighborhood, except that Louis's, because both his parents worked, was brand-new. His shorts bore the tracks of an iron, his shoes were fresh out of the box. His face was just as fresh, with oval eyes above an isosceles nose and jutting chin, everything cut to movie-star proportions. His dark skin was well scrubbed, and so smooth it seemed the dust of the field would not adhere. He lived on Hudson Street, not far from several teammates, but he showed up for the first practice alone, walking in his usual straight-legged manner, a stiff new Rawlings glove tucked under his arm like a leather attaché. A few of the kids had given low hoots.

"Louis Buster got some new clothes," one had said. "But he still a buster."

"Man," another had complained, "Louis got Sega Genesis *and* Nintendo and a real computer, and he don't let nobody come over."

Louis had paid no mind, and tilted his head back slightly as if to prevent the voices from drifting in his ears. He had heard the talk before: how he thought he was better than everybody because he had good clothes, how he talked white, how he was the pretty-boy teacher's pet, how he wasn't any good at basketball or baseball or anything except Nintendo.

"I think I'll quit this year," he had announced to nobody in particular at the beginning of practice. "I'm going to be out of town a lot anyway."

"What are you talking about, Lou?" Kevin had asked, hitting him playfully on the arm. "You're twelve now— you're the veteran on this team. This is your year, buddy."

Louis had put on a little half-smile and made a pronouncement he was to repeat many times over the first months of the season: "You put me where no balls get hit, I'll be happy. Balls start coming my way, I'll get mad." Then he had tucked his glove under his arm and walked off toward the outfield, heel-toe, heel-toe, knees hardly bending, as if wearing a suit of armor. Nobody had to tell him what position he was playing.

Over in the infield, Coach Cort was hitting grounders to Calbert, Rufus, and Demetrius.

"Hey"—Cort pointed toward the heavyset player manning second base—"why don't you try putting your sandwich down."

Calbert wedged a stray flake of tuna into his mouth, unzipped his fanny pack, and pulled out a plastic container of opaque purple liquid. "Just a sec," he said. "Got to drink 'cause of my asthma."

Calbert had arrived at the field on a shiny silver Huffy, toting a sandwich, three Little Hug grape drinks, two prescription inhalers, two packs of Now and Later fruit chews, and several sourballs called Cry Babies. That looked to be an average afternoon's intake for this short, round eleven-year-old with expressive eyes and a mouth that was almost constantly in motion. After shaking hands, he had told Cort about himself.

"I'm not from around here, I live over at 70 West Huron, it's a highrise building and I live there with my mother— you can call her LaToya, but I just call her Mom or sometimes Mom-Mom and she calls me her little big man—and my brother—he's real cute, we call him French Fry—he's only two but he can go to the bathroom and wipe himself and everything. I got a job—yes, a real job—working over at the Subway across the street where I wipe the tables and refill the chip rack and put away the cups—that is, when I'm not in the hospital or something with my asthma." He took a breath. "I been in the hospital for it lots of times, so Mom-Mom says I got to take it real easy on the baseball field, and if I should have an asthma attack, you should take me to Dr. Morgan at Children's Hospital. It happened to my dad a couple months ago—he had an asthma attack plus double pneumonia. I never played baseball before."

"What happened to him?" Cort asked.

"Who?"

"Your father."

"He died," Calbert said, turning his eyes toward the ground. "Last month."

Cort waited a moment to check whether the boy was joking. He wasn't.

"I'm . . . I'm really sorry." Not sure of what to do, Cort put a hand on Calbert's shoulder.

"Thanks. Mom says I'm in the league to help me get over it and make some more friends." Calbert reached into his fanny pack. "You want a Now and Later?"

Now, as Calbert drained the last of his Little Hug, Cort shouldered the bat patiently.

"Ready?"

"Ready."

The ball skittered toward him, and Calbert deftly moved out of its path, dropped his glove, did a quick 180-degree turn, and started chasing with surprising speed. He caught up to the ball just after it stopped, then scooped it up and whirled toward home without pausing to aim. His throw, a good nine-iron shot by Cort's estimation, landed in the first-base dugout.

"That one got by me, Coach," Calbert panted as he ran in. "I'm a little short of breath, so I better use my inhaler and get something to drink. I have asthma, you know. Can't get dehydrated."

He sat down and unzipped his fanny pack. "Want some?"

"No, thanks," said Cort, turning his attention to the field. When he saw who was next, he choked up on the bat a few inches.

Rufus, Maurice's eight-year-old half brother, stood shyly at the edge of the infield grass. He was small and frag-

ile, and his cocoa skin shone with the soft patina of a baby.
He and Maurice wore the same sweatshirts and XJ-9000s,
but they appeared to possess quite different personalities.
At the beginning of practice, while Maurice slapped hands
and exchanged stories on the field, his mother, Mary, had
stayed near the sidelines. When the coaches had walked
over to say hello, they noticed an unusual lump under her
black nylon overcoat.

"Y'all got to make a man out of my shorty this year,"
Mary had said, pulling back her coat to reveal Rufus hug-
ging her leg. "Maurice's growed, but this one's still soft. He
always be wantin' to hide behind me, all the time."

Rufus had been a little embarrassed, but not so much so
to let go of his mother's leg. He had looked up at the
coaches, smiled bashfully, and puckered his lips as a signal
for his mother to kiss him. She did, and he toddled out on
the field toward Maurice, weaving slightly, as if the separa-
tion had affected his inner ear.

"Here we go." Cort swung, and the ball rolled slowly
toward second base. Rufus tiptoed toward it, holding his
glove as far from his body as he could. The ball rolled past
him. He looked at Cort, smiled, and ran to get it, setting his
feet gently on the ground as if he didn't want to disturb the
dust. He rolled the ball back to Cort underhand.

"Come on, Rufus, the ball isn't going to hurt you," Cort
said, bouncing a ball off his chest to show him. Rufus
shrugged and smiled again. Cort started to say more, but
stopped. It was hard to yell at Rufus.

Cort picked up the ball, glanced at the field, and rolled
his eyes.

"Demetrius!"

The third member of Cort's charges was in full stride
across the outfield carrying Calbert's asthma inhaler, the
owner trundling behind in failing pursuit. Demetrius
smiled and taunted the heavier kid, slowing down so he
could catch up, then springing ahead on long legs whenever Calbert came within an arm's length of him.

Demetrius was the fastest runner on the team, and he looked it. Every feature seemed sharpened, honed, pruned of inefficiency. His skin was raven-colored; his thin, Asian eyes revealed barely more than pupils; his cheekbones were set high above a triangular chin; his hair was clipped into a tidy box. His frame was all legs and shoulder blades, hung with sinewy muscle that he occasionally employed to spin off effortless runs of backflips and full-gainers.

"Okay, Demetrius, cut it out," yelled Cort.

"Okay, Demetrius, cut it out," mimicked Demetrius, holding the blue plastic tube where Calbert could see it. Rufus, standing nearby, giggled, and Demetrius heard him.

"Whatchu laughin' at, you nappy-headed buster baby?"

Rufus took to busily examining the laces of his XJ-9000s.

"De-*mee*-tri-us." Cort's voice rose. "That's enough."

Heads elsewhere on the field began to turn. Coach Bill watched but said nothing. He was interested to see how Cort would handle this.

"Demetrius!" a voice roared from behind the backstop. "Get your black ass over here."

It was Mary. She rattled her coat menacingly.

"You give that boy back his medicine!" she said. "He *need* his medicine!" Demetrius slowed and dropped the inhaler to the grass. Calbert wheezed over and started sucking noisily on the blue plastic.

Demetrius jogged up to his coach, seemingly contrite. "My fault—I was just playin'," he said. Cort towered over him, hands on hips, unsure of what to do.

"I know," Demetrius suggested after a brief silence. "You can have free hits."

"What?" Cort squinted.

"Free hits. You know, on my arm." Demetrius rolled up his left shirtsleeve, offering a slender shoulder and egging him on with a smile. "Come on."

"Don't worry about it," Cort said, tapping him lightly on the arm and turning away. As he did, Demetrius whirled and popped a sharp right fist into Cort's triceps just where muscle meets bone, twisting his little knuckles to make it hurt more.

"*Damn.*" Cort, who rarely swore, rubbed his arm. "Demetrius!"

He looked up, and the boy was already racing across the outfield.

Demetrius had learned to punch at the two-story brick fieldhouse at Seward Park, a block from Carson Field. The boxing coach, a massive man named Tony Seals, had stood behind him and held his shoulders in his giant hands, instructing him how to gain leverage, how never to give his opponents anything steady to hit, how to twist his hands as he punched. Tony was strict but fair, and he made boxing seem like something serious, something you had to learn and practice and improve at, something that, as he said, could make you different from all the sloppy-ass street fighters out there in the Green.

Demetrius had a friend named Anthony Felton, a wiry boy with a chronically runny nose who lived in a brick highrise at 500–502 West Oak Street. They met in the boxing room at Seward Park, and although they were in different weight classes, they drifted together because they both were faster than almost everybody else. They liked to spar together, and have contests to see who could hit the speed bag more times in ten seconds, and practice their backflipping on the blue mats. Sometimes they would ask Tony who could flip the highest. Tony always lied and said they were even, but in fact Demetrius was usually higher. Toward the previous spring, though, Anthony was drawing close.

One afternoon about a month before the baseball season started, Anthony was sitting in front of his building, waiting for Tony to pick him up so he could get his trophy. He had gone 5–1 over the season and had won second place in his weight class. The Seward Park fieldhouse was only a five-minute walk away, but Tony made a habit of driving his boys to and from practice. It was never a good idea to be walking across Cabrini alone; you never could tell when something was going to jump off.

It was a beautiful day, one of the first nice days of the year. Anthony bided his time under the oak tree next to the building entrance, the only good flipping spot because of the grass. People milled in the parking lot, peeling off their coats to feel the sunshine on their skin. Anthony waved to Charles Price, a building manager for the Chicago Housing Authority, who had promised to find out whether the agency had any money for gymnastics mats so that Anthony and other kids in his building could practice their tumbling. Mr. Price waved back, and Anthony did a flip for him.

Then three teenagers ran up from the south side of Oak Street. They stopped between two rowhouses, and one of them popped off a single shot with a .22 pistol. The crowd scattered, then returned to find Anthony lying under the oak tree. He died an hour later at Northwestern Memorial Hospital. That night, a winter storm rolled through the city, bringing forty-mile-per-hour winds and dropping the temperature to thirty-three degrees. Around 500–502 West Oak, they said it was because of what had happened to Anthony.

Three boys, two aged seventeen and the other thirteen, were arrested and charged with first-degree murder. Investigators found, not to their surprise, that all were members of the Gangster Disciples gang, and that the thirteen-year-old had been the shooter. This, too, was no surprise: a juvenile probably would serve a maximum eight years in a detention home, compared with life in a state penitentiary for a seventeen-year-old. By way of defense, the boys said that they were retaliating because some Vice Lords had been shooting at them earlier in the day. They hadn't meant to hit Anthony.

Anthony's grandma asked for his red boxing gloves from Tony and hung them on the wall of her apartment.

People wrote notes to the dead boy, and she attached them to the gloves with transparent tape:

"Love is special, but boxing is light. Love always, Lil Valerie."

"Be the best you can be in heaven. Love, Andrew L."

Demetrius didn't go to Anthony's funeral. He stopped going to Seward Park and concentrated more on his schoolwork. His Great-aunt Carol, with whom he lived, said he seemed not depressed, just a little distracted and hyper. He got into fights more, and he started picking on smaller kids. She didn't remember him ever doing that before.

End of practice. Coach Bill closed the folder. Three weeks to go before the first game. That meant six practices, tops. The Kikuyus needed a better turnout than this. Bill looked out at the highrises, knowing that the rest of the team was somewhere behind those windows and in the small bungalows and three-flats of the surrounding neighborhood. Alonzo. Samuel. Otis. Rickey. T.J. Freddie. Their phone numbers and addresses were typed neatly on the sheet of paper, but that was all he had, and right now it didn't seem like much. He would call them every night, at least the ones who had phones, and send out word through their friends, but he wasn't about to start walking around the highrises, knocking on doors. Not by a long shot.

At one of the first league meetings, Al Carter had given a talk about the kind of coach-player relationship he expected. "You will have to be a big white brother to these kids," he told the coaches. "You will have to go into their homes and see how they're doing. If a kid doesn't show up, it's because he's been threatened. You will have to go get him and protect him." At the time, Carter's words had made sense.

Bill spotted a gangly figure in a Kansas City Royals cap loping across the diamond. Coach Brad, Bill's former roommate. He worked at a magazine whose offices were a few blocks away, and he often was made late by deadlines. Brad looked worried.

"You hear the news?" he asked.

Bill shook his head.

"Something's going on in Los Angeles. The cops who beat Rodney King were found not guilty, and the city's going crazy. They're pulling people out of cars, beating them, burning the place down."

"Damn," Bill said. "Anything happen around here?"

"Not that I heard."

For a moment, neither of them said anything. That night, Cabrini would echo with volleys of gunshots that some police officers described as a reaction to the verdict; locals taking their guns up on the roofs and firing, telling the Gold Coast and the rest of white Chicago that there would be no peace until there was justice. Other officers, however, said it was tough to distinguish this night from any other.

"All right," Bill called, cupping his hands around his mouth. "Bring it in!"

TWO

One day in late April, Alonzo decided to go for a walk in the neighborhood with his best friend, J-Nice. There wasn't anything special going on. He just liked to look around.

Alonzo had woken up early, as he usually did, because of the bells. It was easy to hear them, since his bunkbed was next to the window, and the window was near the open-air walkway called the ramp, and the ramp was covered with a screen. This floor-to-ceiling mesh, made of fettucini-width steel crosshatched into a diamond pattern, had been bolted on, here and everywhere in Cabrini, by the Chicago Housing Authority to supplement the original chest-high screens a few years back, after too many children had tumbled over the sides. While even the CHA acknowledged that the screens weren't visually appealing, they did the job. Children stopped falling out, and the ramps were transformed from safety hazards to de facto cribs. Each morning, the toddlers of Cabrini-Green would run loose behind the screens, assaulting them with toys, spoons, and hands, and making them resound like the bells of a thousand churches.

On this particular morning, Alonzo could hear the bells more clearly than ever because there wasn't any glass in his window. He had broken it playing football in his room with J-Nice, and his mother had covered the opening with plastic wrap. She would have liked to replace the window immediately, but according to CHA regulations, tenants wishing to do so were required to bring the window frame and the broken glass to the maintenance office—proof that they hadn't popped it from the molding intact and sold it at the Maxwell Street market for fifty cents.

Even through plastic wrap, Alonzo's view was unmatched. Dead ahead, their edges made golden by the rising sun, were the glass-and-steel minarets of the Gold Coast, looming so near that their shadows slid across Alonzo's window every morning: first the monstrous Art Deco castle of the Bloomingdale's building, then the rising pyramid of the John Hancock Center, and finally the graceful sliver of Water Tower Place. Alonzo liked the view, and he didn't mind the shadows, at least not in summer. They kept things cooler.

Alonzo walked sleepily to his closet and dug out his Slick jeans with the painted leather patch on the knee, his Yankees jersey, his gray imitation-satin Three Musketeers candy bar jacket, and his Miami Hurricanes cap. He shooed Mouse, the white cat, off the dresser and dug his glove, a black Kirby Puckett autograph with Snap Action, from beneath a battered copy of *The Bobbsey Twins at Mystery Manor,* by Laura Lee Hope. Then, as he did every day, he checked on his zoo: three Night Train bottles half filled with dirt and inhabited by several grasshoppers. He held one bottle against the room's solitary light bulb and peered inside, marveling at the hedge-trimmer jaws as they sawed ragged ovals in the bits of leaves and grass he had placed inside.

He set the bottle down and stepped into his black Air Forces. Because of the floods, he always had to do this before venturing outside his room. They weren't real floods, he knew, for they came not from rivers or rain, but from wash water burping up the sink. But they were worth fearing nonetheless. Warily, Alonzo poked his head out the doorway. The floor looked waxy and dull—no flood. As his mother liked to say, the Lord had blessed them this morning. Of course, she gave the Lord a little help, with a sawed-off broomstick wedged beneath the kitchen cabinet to keep a rag stuffed in the drain.

His mother was still asleep in her room, so Alonzo grabbed a Fla-Vor-Ice frozen push-up from the icebox—they had bought a package of a hundred for $2.99 at Aldi's discount supermarket—and headed for the door on tiptoe. His mother usually slept late on Saturdays, because Fridays were card nights at her stepsister's. She'd often be there until three or four in the morning, playing pitty-pat and tonk, and some nights she'd win enough to pay a chunk of her son's fifty-dollar monthly tuition at St. Joseph's, the private Catholic school across the street. Alonzo's mother loved her card nights. Sometimes, after winning a few games and sipping a few Canadian Mists, she would tell her friends, "I'm sending my boy to private school on public aid, and he ain't never come home with anything less than a B." She sounded proud when she said that.

Alonzo swung the door closed behind him, then carefully locked it with the key he wore on a chain around his neck. J-Nice was already on the ramp waiting. Alonzo once heard a man from CHA refer to the ramp as a "gallery," but his mother had told him it was a ramp.

"I don't know why he be callin' it that," she had said. "This ain't no museum."

J-Nice—his real name was Jacques—was a scrawny nine-year-old, and Alonzo was his hero. Alonzo filled the role nicely. He was twelve, he was tall (five-foot-one, according to the nurse at St. Joseph's, but he and J-Nice were pretty sure he was at least five-six), and most of all, he knew about things. He knew karate, he knew how to catch grasshoppers and how to hit homers. The thing J-Nice liked best, though, was the way Alonzo walked. He looked straight ahead, he kept his arms down by his hips, and he got this real cool look on his face where his eyelids drooped and his eyebrows rose and his mouth got all slack and heavy, harboring words until they gathered enough energy to emerge as near shouts. When Alonzo got that look, it was as if nobody could say or do anything to bother him.

"I'm a *black* belt," Alonzo announced by way of greeting. "You can call me Sensei."

"Man!" J-Nice's little chest puffed out. "I a black belt, too."

Alonzo did not look at his friend. "You must *learn* the Hand of *Death*." Widening his eyes slightly, he raised his right hand and made a sudden slashing motion toward J-Nice's head. J-Nice flinched.

"I coulda pulled out your *eye*." Alonzo lowered his eyelids, returned his face to its usual imperturbable state. "*Consider* it a warning."

"Man!" said J-Nice, hopping up and down with excitement. A dribble of snot ran down his lip. He erased it with a sweatshirt sleeve already plasticized with mucus. "Whatchu fittina do?" he asked.

But Alonzo was already cruising toward the stairs, stepping around Big Wheels and babies with cool insouciance, an emperor among his chattel. "Come *on,*" he said, and J-Nice jumped to follow.

Alonzo did not like to spend a lot of time on the ramp. A couple of months before, Alonzo had been spending an evening at home in his favorite position, that is, watching TV from beneath the shelter of the coffee table, when he heard some shouting outside his door. He paid no mind; people were always fighting on the ramps, and besides, the movie *Major League* had almost reached the end, the part where the Indians' power hitter lays down a bunt to win the big game. Then Alonzo heard a gunshot. He didn't do anything for a long time—his mother was upstairs playing cards, and even if they had owned a telephone, he knew enough not to call the police. Finally, when everything seemed quiet, he tiptoed to the peephole and saw, in fish-eye distortion, a man's leg and a widening pool of blood. After a while an ambulance came, as well as maintenance workers with buckets of soapy water. Alonzo never heard what happened to the man, or who he was, but even now the ramp bothered him. He still could see a faint outline on the concrete where the blood had been. The man had been wearing Air Jordans, Alonzo remembered. Leaving J-Nice behind, Alonzo strode quickly across the ramp, down the six flights of stairs, and into the sunshine. He tore open the plastic on his Fla-Vor-Ice and gave it a lick. Grape.

"Where we fittina *go*?" J-Nice had caught up and was pulling at Alonzo's sleeve.

Alonzo cocked his head, as if listening to something in the wind. "Best stay clear of the Wild End today. They fixing to shoot," he declared.

"Man!" J-Nice repeated. "They fittina shoot!"

To Alonzo and J-Nice, the Wild End meant the cluster of pale concrete highrises in Cabrini's northwest corner, a place more commonly known as the Whites. Around Alonzo's building, the Whites were not taken lightly. As one boy put it, pointing toward the stained gray buildings, "They do some *killin'* up there."

The source of the fearsome reputation of the Whites, however, was a matter less of violence than of simple geography. As every child in Cabrini knew, the project naturally divided into three chunks of roughly equal size, each controlled by a gang or gangs. The area north of Division Street, the Whites, belonged to the Black Gangster Disciples. The red-brick highrises between Division and Oak, the Reds, were split up among Gangster Disciples, Cobras, and Vice Lords. The southern third, a mix of brick lowrises and rowhouses south of Oak Street where Alonzo and J-Nice lived, was the territory of the Gangster Disciples. Matters were complicated somewhat by the fact that the gangs were grouped further into two main alliances:

People, to which the Vice Lords and the Cobras belonged, and the more populous Folks, to which the Gangster Disciples and the Black Gangster Disciples belonged. That, of course, didn't mean that GDs and BGDs, or VLs and Cobras, wouldn't occasionally shoot at each other.

There was but one rule to negotiating this mosaic, and Alonzo knew it well: Don't cross boundaries. As a resident of a GD building, he was free to play video games in the Laundromat on Orleans, shop at the small grocery on Oak or at Hipp's on Orleans, and play in the lot next to his building. Most everything else—the basketball courts and baseball diamond at Seward Park, the youth club at Division and Clybourn, the stores on Sedgwick, the little mall on Larrabee, the YMCA at Clybourn and North Avenue—was off-limits. In his dozen years, Alonzo had never been to the Wild End; he didn't know that the children who lived there referred to his end of Cabrini by the same name.

"Where we fittina go, then?" J-Nice stamped his feet.

Alonzo crunched his Fla-Vor-Ice thoughtfully. "Sammy's," he finally decided. "I need a cheeseburger."

They shouldered their way past the decrepit squadron of cars parked in front of their building, nodding to the old man in the "Wayne's World" cap enjoying his morning cocktail from the pilot's seat of an ancient Cutlass. But as they neared the street, Alonzo froze and his eyes widened.

"Man," he said. "Check that van—it's Rat!"

"*Man!*" said J-Nice, leaping up and down. "*Rat!* Man! It's *Rat!* Something gonna jump off for sure."

"Shhhh." Alonzo put a finger to his lips. "*Quiet.*"

Four men stood in front of a blue-and-cream Chevrolet van. One of them, a trim man with small, dark eyes and a fastidious goatee, did most of the talking. He wore new Levi's 501s, a tan Orioles cap with a black brim, and a black-and-tan leather jacket that bulged on the left. It wasn't a gun, the boys knew, it was a cellular phone. Only a buster would run the risk of getting shaken down in broad daylight, and Rat, the regent for the GDs, wasn't no buster.

"Should we go inside?" asked J-Nice.

"Nah," said Alonzo. "Ain't nothin' gonna happen out here. Rat like everything nice and peaceful."

Alonzo was right. Rat, a quiet man who neither drank nor indulged in drugs, also bore a profound dislike of violence. It wasn't a matter of fear. It was a matter of business. Snipering, like rain, kept people indoors; if people were indoors, sales went down. At thirty-six years old, Rat understood business. That was why he was regent. That was why he called the shots.

His job was straightforward: Buy the quarter-kilo of raw powder from his West Side supplier; hand it off to a mule, who brought it into a Cabrini safe house to be cooked, cut, and bagged by Rat's lieutenants. Make sure the rocks got to each building in the Reds and the rowhouses, make sure the guns were in position at the safe houses, make sure everybody paid him so the process could start over again. Like most big dealers, Rat worked in both "girl," or cocaine, and "boy," or heroin, which was packaged in small foil squares and sold for ten dollars a hit. Heroin powder was less popular but recently had started to sell better in Cabrini, as it could be inhaled, shot up, smoked, or rubbed on the gums. The variety was good; it helped sales.

Rat hadn't always been such a businessman. Old-timers in Cabrini remembered when he sang a sweet alto in the choir at St. Dominic's Catholic Church. His nickname, given not for finkish behavior but for his sharp, perceptive qualities, was tagged on long before his first arrest, at age eighteen, for disorderly conduct. He followed that up with a modest fifteen-year string of petty crimes and small-time dealing that peaked with a few prison terms, the last a two-year stint at Vienna Correctional Center in downstate Illinois. During that sentence, however, Rat's life changed. A friend of his introduced him to Larry "King" Hoover, the Gangster Disciples' city boss. Hoover, who oversaw the gang's every move despite his own 150-to-200-year sentence for murder, took a liking to this quiet, ambitious dealer and brought him under his wing. After Rat was released in December 1991, he was made regent at Cabrini, given financial control over most North Side GD drug sales, and awarded a position on the Board, a loose group of twelve Disciples who supervised the gang's city operations.

"Hoover, he'll just lay back and watch you," said one veteran Disciple who was at Vienna during Rat's ascendance. "If he see that you carry yourself well, you know how to control things and such, he'll want you in his circle. That's how Rat got hooked up. Once Hoover seen how smart and organized Rat is, and especially how Rat don't drink or get high—Hoover *love* that part—Rat was inside."

It was impossible to guess exactly how much profit Rat's operation produced, but the math was dazzling. Each quarter-kilo cost him $4,000 to $5,000; it was converted into 8,000 to 10,000 bags of ready-to-smoke rocks of crack that retailed for $10 each. The bags, usually in packs of twelve, were distributed to building captains, who doled them out to street dealers on a consignment basis. For each pack the dealer received and then sold, he was to return $100 to the captain; part of the $20 that he kept was used to pay lookouts. Dealers who didn't return the $100 risked getting V'ed—violated—by the gang's enforcers, Cannon and Pug. Sometimes it was a beating; other times it was a point-blank shot to the leg, carefully aimed to avoid breaking any bones. Along with the dealers' monthly tribute payments, all the money flowed back to Rat, who used it to buy more kilos, bail fellow GDs out of Cook County Jail, and pay his own tribute to the family of King Hoover. Although he never wrote anything down, Rat had a reputation as a ruthless accountant, methodically tracking every penny in a business when many dealers lost rolls thicker than their fist.

Rat, however, was not Cabrini's only major player. A few hundred yards north, in the handful of red highrises occupied by the Cobras, another man called the shots. He went by several names: Baby Prince, Al-Jami Mustafa (his Muslim title), and just plain Emp, short for "Emperor." Some Folks bridled at the implicit one-upping of the GDs'

King Hoover, but few could declare the Emp unworthy of comparison. Physically unremarkable—a little over six feet tall, chubby enough to have been a frequent target of bullies in his days at Waller High School—the thirty-six-year-old Emp nonetheless had built one of the most tightly organized operations on the North Side. In contrast to the Gangster Disciples, a group large and scattered enough to suffer frequent clicks—intragang feuds—the Cobras were a tight society. People in his buildings proudly testified how the Emp didn't tolerate rape or robbery or other bullshit crime, how he made people feel as if they weren't just in a gang, but in the Cobra *nation*. The Emp had a special place in his heart for the shorties, it was said; he would occasionally emerge from his West Side hideout, park his National rental car in front of 1150–1160 North Sedgwick, and flip five- and ten-dollar bills at the kids like candy. Like Rat, the Emp didn't drink or take drugs. Unlike Rat, he had never spent so much as a night in jail, so skilled he was in the art of distancing himself from the product.

Rat's and the Emp's natural enemies were the Slick Boys, the twenty or so police officers on duty in Cabrini at any given time. They were now and then effective in temporarily preventing dealing, but they could do little to stop it permanently. In a neighborhood this small and isolated, the Slick Boys rarely surprised anyone: their gray undercover Caprices flashed as distinctively as flags, and some dealers could recite the names and shifts of every cop from Public Housing North or the 18th District. ("*They* tell *me* when I have vacation days coming up," complained one officer.) Besides, like most people in the community, the police held a quiet appreciation for the way Rat and the Emp ran their businesses, and granted them the sort of respect rarely given to a gangbanger. When kids were hauled into the Public Housing North station for petty thievery or fighting, some of the Slick Boys lectured them, "If you're gonna be a criminal, at least get out of this bullshit and be a *good* criminal, like Rat or the Emp."

As hot weather approached, Rat was seen in Cabrini

more and more. This was to be his first summer as regent, and he wanted it to go well. After all, King Hoover had not assigned his prize pupil here by accident. It was part of the plan. Rat's sober, meticulous nature matched with the chaotic streets of Cabrini, which of all the Gangster Disciple territories was perhaps the least conducive to a profitable business. In Cabrini, there was too much shooting, too many gangs, too many young gunslingers willing to feud over petty turf violations, too few people who shared the Emp's and Rat's sense. In Cabrini, a good street-level dealer might clear $300 a week. In the peaceful projects, the ABLA Homes or Rockwell Gardens, for example, the *lookouts* were clearing that much. Out there, dealers didn't have to spend money on funerals and bail, and the only reason customers stayed away was rain. Out there, things ran clean, streamlined. Cabrini-Green, in the opinion of those who ran the area's only mildly successful business, could use somebody like Rat.

"Think he'll throw a barbecue?" J-Nice asked hopefully. Rat sometimes did so as a goodwill gesture to the people in the buildings he controlled. The practice was called "setting out money."

"Nah. He on business."

"They fittina smoke somebody?"

"Maybe. I heard . . ." Alonzo stopped and looked around carefully. "I heard the GDs gonna take back the Castle."

"Man!"

"Yop. I heard they fittina put shooters on the roof and sniper 'em. They fittina start soon."

Even J-Nice knew this was big. Strategically, the nineteen-story highrise at 1117–1119 North Cleveland was Cabrini's keystone. From the Castle's top floors, a sniper with a good rifle and a scope could hit anything from the Whites to the rowhouses. The flipside, of course, was that the Castle was among Cabrini's most frequently used targets, and thus had a well-deserved fame as the most dangerous building in the project. The danger did little to diminish its strategic value, however; after it was taken from the Disciples in the mid-eighties, the building had been controlled alternately or in tandem by the Vice Lords and the Cobras. Among younger Gangster Disciples, talk of reclaiming the Castle was renewed each spring; to police and older gang leadership, this impassioned teenage nostalgia was as inevitable as the bloom of dandelions.

"This a good time to take the Castle, too," added Alonzo, " 'cause the VLs is fighting with the Cobras."

"Wha . . ."

"The *VLs* is fighting with the *Cobras,* man," Alonzo said impatiently. "It's a People thing."

"What about?"

"My auntie say the VLs used to store guns for the Cobras, and the GDs paid some crackhead girl who was a girlfriend of the Vice Lords ten rocks and two hundred dollars to get them a rifle, an Uzi, a Tec-9, and a couple of pistols. So now the GDs got all the fire, and the Cobras think the VLs tricked on them."

"Man! That girl a fool."

"My auntie say she moved to the South Side. They wanna smoke her."

"Man!" J-Nice's hand wiped his nose, then pointed. "Look! He fittina push!"

Their conversation finished, Rat nodded to the men and stepped into his van. He could never stay anywhere long. He glanced around, his bright eyes flicking along the street for Slick Boys. He didn't look menacing. He looked tired.

Alonzo and J-Nice watched him pull away. There was no thumping stereo, no squealing tires. Rat drove slowly up the street, put on his blinker, and carefully entered traffic.

"Let's go," Alonzo said. "I need that cheeseburger."

Sammy's Red Hots and Liquor Store was an unusual choice for Alonzo and J-Nice, as it was on Division Street by the

El, close to Cobra territory. Getting there meant walking east on Oak until they were out of Cabrini, then north on Wells, and then west along Division; the U-shaped path kept them a safe distance from the Emp's highrises.

"I'll teach you my karate moves," said Alonzo, casting a meaningful glance toward his friend. "That way no one can mess with you."

"I already know karate," J-Nice lied.

"*Toad* Belly." Alonzo arched his back and walked directly into a parking meter. "Stick out your stomach and everything bounces off."

J-Nice gave it a try, leaping into a meter.

"*Snake.*" Alonzo stepped toward a lightpole, then turned his body at the last instant so he brushed past. He cast a meaningful glance toward J-Nice.

"I use that one when there are a dozen men against me." He paused. "Make that *two* dozen."

J-Nice ran full-bore at the lightpole, but forgot to turn and did a Toad Belly instead. He fell into the gutter, sprang up, and ran to catch his mentor. Before he had taken three steps, though, Alonzo had stopped and was pointing back at the pole.

J-Nice's eyes narrowed, then widened as he realized he had violated the neighborhood superstition against walking on the street side of a lightpole. While the consequence of such a misstep could conceivably take any form, most kids regarded the outcome as a foregone conclusion: You would be the next to get shot. J-Nice scuttled back, swung around, and corrected his position in the universe. Alonzo nodded approvingly.

"*Red* Palm," he said, cupping his hand and putting it in J-Nice's face. "They see this and they get so scared they can't fight no more."

"*Rat* Balm," said J-Nice, jumping up in excitement. "Man!"

They worked their way down Oak Street, Toad Bellying and Snaking their way along the sidewalk, Alonzo giving vivid blow-by-blow commentary of his many karate fights.

Then, as they neared the corner, J-Nice saw them. Four Little Cobras, walking south on Wells. Alonzo saw them, too, and in an instant transformed himself. His eyelids drooped, his face took on a slack, bemused expression, his walk slowed until each step was pronounced, thoughtful. He didn't speak. Since they were now on neutral ground outside Cabrini, the Little Cobras wouldn't have any ready-made excuse to fight, but Alonzo wasn't taking chances. You never knew.

The Little Cobras drew closer. Despite the day's increasing heat, they wore an assortment of Starter parkas—Charlotte Hornets, San Francisco 49ers, Oakland Raiders—and two wore Oakland A's hats with the brims turned slightly to the left, a sign that they were People. The shortest one, obviously the leader, was in the center of the group. He had a beautiful Polynesian-looking face and wore a ratty white overcoat that brushed the tops of his Air Jordans. The boy looked to be nine or ten years old. Alonzo didn't know his name, but he knew who he was: the Emp's son. He and his friends were called Little C's because they weren't old enough to be real Cobras. The other gangs had them, too: Little VLs, Little GDs; loose-knit groups of wannabes, able only to go boostering, or shoplifting, to work as lookouts, fight, and play with fake money-rolls made of strips of paper towel and rubber bands, until they were thirteen, old enough to get V'ed. Alonzo knew about this. The exact method varied with each gang, but the gist was always the same: The leaders beat you to see how tough you were. Then you were in.

Alonzo and J-Nice kept walking. The Little C's stopped at the corner. The short one, the Emp's son, put his right hand in the pocket of his overcoat and slowly extracted a Butterfinger—probably from Jewel, three blocks away. The Little C's couldn't shop at Hipp's or the supermarket on Larrabee or down on Chicago Avenue. Those were GD—out of bounds.

Ten steps away. Alonzo and J-Nice began to edge toward the curb. Alonzo's face was now completely slack, and his eyelids so low he appeared to be sleepwalking. J-Nice stayed very close to him, shouldering himself slightly in front so they would take up less space. None of the Little C's moved. Alonzo and J-Nice were almost past when one of the others spoke.

"I know that boy."

Coolly, Alonzo checked over his shoulder. The boy in the white coat had the Butterfinger leveled squarely at him.

"Your daddy kilt that white woman, didn't he?" The Emp's son didn't say it as an accusation; it was just a question. Alonzo did not react.

"Yop," the boy in the white coat confirmed. "He go to my school, and my mama say his daddy kilt a old white woman and left her in the alley."

Alonzo turned away. He and J-Nice kept walking north on Wells until they were out of earshot. Then J-Nice tugged on Alonzo's sleeve.

"What he *talkin'* about?"

"Who?"

"That boy—what he say about your daddy?"

Alonzo looked straight ahead. His eyelids dropped.

"*Grass*hopper," he said, and jumped over a fire hydrant.

MAY

Little Sicily is a world to itself. Dirty and narrow streets, alleys piled with refuse and alive with dogs and rats, goats hitched to carts, bleak tenements . . . the occasional dull boom of a bomb or the bark of a revolver, the shouts of children at play in the street, a strange staccato speech, the taste of soot, and the smell of gas from the huge gas house by the river, whose belching flames make the skies lurid at night and long ago earned for the district the name Little Hell.

—HARVEY WARREN ZORBAUGH,
The Gold Coast and the Slum:
A Sociological Study of Chicago's Near North Side
(1929)

ONE

Twelve days before opening day, and several teams were preparing to practice on Carson Field. Things in Cabrini had been fairly quiet of late; most police attributed this to the unseasonably cold weather. The meteorologists on TV attributed the cold partly to the year-old eruption of a Philippine volcano, whose ash was now deflecting sunlight away from the earth and disrupting normal patterns of atmospheric circulation.

Outside the northeast backstop, a man of about sixty smoked cigarettes and watched. He was a big man, solid but not fat, with hoary muttonchops; he wore a blue baseball cap on which the word "Boss" had been stenciled in white letters. The man came to the field almost every evening, arriving around five-fifteen and departing precisely at five forty-five. His routine was always the same: he checked his watch, stubbed out his Tareyton on the backstop, checked his watch again, and strolled into the Oscar Mayer factory to go to work. While he looked on, though, he liked to give advice, sending out puffs of smoke through the chain link.

"Hey there, boy, you keep that glove down, you hear?" he said, his voice gently chiding. "That little-bitty ball can't hurt you none, so what you jumpin' all around for?"

"*Man,* whatchu be talkin' about?" Demetrius's nostrils flared. "I ain't gonna get myself whacked!"

The man in the blue hat didn't seem to hear. "You got to stay in front if you want to catch it," he continued. "You got to stay in front."

"Old boy be talking to hisself again," Demetrius told Jalen, who stood nearby. "I think maybe he got Al Kiner's disease, you know, where you can't remember nothing?"

Jalen nodded knowingly. "My great-grandmama had her some of that whatchacallit," he said.

Maurice was the first to see the car. "There Bill!" he yelled, and ran toward the corner, where a dented brown Audi was making the turn onto Scott Street. The others trailed, sneakers slapping down hard.

"First!" he exhaled, slamming a hand onto the hood, making it boom like a bass drum. The rest of the team piled on behind. Bill didn't mind—the car had cost $1,500 and was on its last leg. He opened the door and stepped out, and as he did, Maurice deftly slipped behind him and into the driver's seat.

"Get in, Bill," Maurice ordered, "let's go for a drive."

Bill took a step back and looked down at Maurice.

"Come on." Maurice grabbed the wheel, impatient.

"Maurice, how old are you?" The voice was deep; its tone vaguely ironic. Bill and Maurice both knew the answer. The birthdate was on the roster: July 14, 1980.

"I *know* how to drive," said Maurice, trying to anticipate the next line of questioning. "I drive my uncle's car all the time, and that's a truck." His right hand groped for the seat-adjustment lever. "Come *on,* we only got a few minutes."

Bill stood and waited until Maurice looked up at him again. Catching his gaze, Bill arched his eyebrows and folded his arms.

"Maurice," said that same imperturbable voice, "how old are you?"

Maurice got out of the car.

It always worked that way with Coach Bill. He never got mad, never raised his voice, never told people that they had to do what he said or else. Like a stern father, he got disappointed. When somebody misbehaved, Bill usually just looked and waited, with a seemingly infinite supply of calm, until the sheer weight of his presence took hold. It usually did.

Bill hoisted the heavy equipment bag easily on his shoulder and stepped toward the field, squinting in the bright sunshine. Next to the players, he appeared taller than six-three, more massive than 205 pounds. The sleeves of his white T-shirt were folded neatly twice over, revealing arms well veined from hours on the lacrosse field. His khaki shorts partially hid the wormy pink scar on his left knee, souvenir of an injury during his sophomore year at Princeton. The knee still pained him slightly, and kept him from running and cutting as he once had. With a characteristic directness, he would describe himself as "twenty-six, and washed up."

Bill's appearance was incongruous with his age. His face was small and vaguely avian, dominated by a large, delicately built nose not unlike Joe DiMaggio's. Around such a centerpiece, the rest of Bill's features—the narrow, alert blue-gray eyes, the high forehead, the thinning, conservatively trimmed brown hair, the even-lipped mouth—were crowded for space, a bit out of proportion. On another person, such a nose might have inspired self-parody and slapstick, but it simply added to Bill's quiet gravity.

It wasn't so much his face, however, that made Bill look old. It was how he carried himself. He moved slowly, efficiently, monitoring the location and placement of each limb with great circumspection. When listening, he would rest his chin in the cupped palm of his right hand; when speaking, he moved his arms like a traffic cop, directing his way through conversations with backhanded sweeps and an elbows-out, hands-on-a-basketball gesture to hold people's attention. He never seemed nervous or ill at ease, and he only rarely dealt in the usual discursive currency of nods and smiles. To fellow coaches and players alike, Bill was inscrutable. Once Jalen had tried to guess how old the coaches were. For most, he came reasonably close—twenty-five, twenty-two, twenty-seven. Then he came to Coach Bill. Jalen didn't hesitate.

" 'Round 'bout fifty."

Bill managed office and retail space at North Pier, a warehouse turned shopping mall along the Chicago River. He often deprecated his job; it "wasn't exactly brain surgery." But in truth, it was a position suited only for the type of person who can skillfully juggle the problems and petitions of two dozen clients, and track each with radarlike precision. Nobody was better at this than Bill. Whether in his office or on the baseball field, he had the air of an all-capable, all-knowing older brother, calmly checking on problems, choreographing solutions, in every action displaying an almost military orderliness of mind and spirit that bubbled up in his language. *You three over here, you three over there, let's move it. You need some water? That's a roger, chief—get it now.*

While possessed of an ironic sense of humor, Bill tended to keep a seal on his emotions. Friends described him as infinitely even-keeled, a rock. "I lived with him for a year, and we've spent a lot of time together," Coach Brad said, "but I don't really know what he's thinking or feeling a lot of the time. I like Bill, but I don't really *know* him." Hardly any of Bill's friends were even aware that as this summer began, his parents were in the last throes of a long and painful divorce.

Bill noticed a poker-faced kid in a gray jacket and a Yankees cap. He was a Kikuyu from the previous year, and he had missed the first two practices.

"Well, look who's here," Bill said. "Howya doin' there, chief?"

Alonzo nodded, his eyelids staying at half-mast.

"Fine?" Bill persisted. "Does that mean you're doing fine?"

"Yop."

Bill always tried to tease Alonzo out of his silences, and sometimes it worked. Bill knew from experience that Alonzo's eyes, sleepy as they appeared, didn't miss much.

"How's Molly?" Alonzo asked suddenly, referring to Bill's girlfriend, who occasionally had come to the games the year before.

"She's, uh . . . she's doing fine," said Bill, caught off-guard.

"Good." Alonzo smiled slyly. "Tell her I said hi."

"Will do, chief."

Bill set the equipment bag down and was instantly surrounded by a flock of kids combing frantically for the few gloves big enough or new enough to be desirable.

"Get your mitts and spread out." Bill's arms went semaphore over the ruckus. "Get in two lines and start playing catch. Half of you here, half of you over there. Let's go now."

Bill chose this exercise automatically. Calisthenics aside, playing catch in two evenly spaced lines has been the customary beginning to every Little League practice since time immemorial. It loosens up the arm, hones coordination, and in a game perpetually fractured into a thousand specialized tasks, is one of the rare instances when the entire team does the same thing at the same time. Done well, it also has a certain aesthetic appeal familiar to anyone who has ever played baseball: the volleys of easy, chest-high throws arcing over the infield grass, the nonchalant chatter, the syncopated *pop* of a dozen mitts sounding like grease cooking on a hot kitchen stove.

But here, it didn't work quite that way. Within seconds, the Kikuyus were scattered around the field, chasing baseballs, throwing mitts, and most of all, complaining.

"*Maaaan!*" Jalen slammed his mitt down and scowled at the ball rolling behind him. "I fittina *quit.* Calbert throw like a *buster!*"

"He got my glove! Make Demetrius give back my glove!"

"Maaaan! Why can't we hit? We always be axing you to hit, but you *never* let us!"

"I can't throw no more 'cause I'm too thirsty."

"This glove *phony!* How come y'all so cheap you can't buy us some good gloves?"

"Bill?" Calbert collapsed heavily at Bill's feet, fingers clutching his chest. "I can't play no more. I need some ice cream, *bad.*"

Between them, Bill and Brad, who had just arrived, attempted to keep things moving. It was no easy task. While some of the players possessed the skills to throw and catch, many of them didn't, and there hadn't been adequate time to go over basics in previous practices. So Bill and Brad waded into the swarm, trying to teach the newcomers to get in front of the ball, to keep their mitts up, to catch with both hands, to step toward the target as they threw—and at the same time trying to keep the other players from running amok.

"Step right to me now, Rufus—*Jalen, put down that bat and get over here, now*—all right now, step to me, real easy."

"Move those feet, Nathaniel, you can't catch it if you— *Demetrius! Leave Calbert alone*—you can't catch if you don't move those feet now."

Coach-player communication was complicated by the coaches' need to calibrate their ears to the words and syntax of Carson Field. *Buster. Fittina. Ax.* A little kid was a "shorty." A leather baseball was a "league ball." You didn't hit a home run, you "whacked it to the gate." The player who crouched behind home plate was a "backcatcher"; neighborhood men in their fifties could recall using the term, but without knowing quite why. "The catcher is going to hit a home run" translated thus to "Backcatcher be fittina whack it to the gate."

While it undoubtedly would have helped matters to have more coaches, there were none to be had. Kevin was in Spain on a business trip, Cort was at work, and although Bill had called the other coaches on the roster, they hadn't shown up at either of the previous practices. Things were shaking out pretty much as Bill had figured: of eight original volunteers, there were four regulars. Bill tried to make better use of his coaching resources and encouraged the veteran players to help instruct the rookies, but so far Maurice seemed to be the only one who would consent to associate with someone of lesser ability. He worked patiently with Nathaniel, teaching him how to get his glove down for grounders.

"Nice work." Bill gave Maurice a long nod. "Way to go."

Bill was counting on Maurice to step up this year. The team needed some leaders, and at this point the small boy with the big hair seemed the likeliest candidate. Confidence was no problem—Maurice already had inscribed "M-Smooth, All-Star 1992" on the bill of his worn baseball cap. But it was his quiet maturity, inherited no doubt from his ever-present mother, that Bill appreciated most. He had seen the way Maurice looked after Rufus, the way he eschewed Demetrius's trash-talking, and the way he always wanted more balls hit to him. Bill also noticed that whenever Maurice talked to a coach, he would step up on something—the dugout bench, a car bumper, whatever was nearby—and place a hand casually but firmly on the coach's shoulder, partly for balance, but partly so that he could feel like an equal. When Maurice put Bill's shoulder in his grip, Bill never squirmed or shrugged as some of the other coaches did. If Maurice wanted to feel like a coach, Bill figured, it was best to encourage him.

"Hey, Bill." Jalen walked up, followed by a wary-looking kid with big eyes and a lantern jaw. The boy, who was at least a head taller than everybody else on the team, wore an orange-and-blue Nike warm-up jacket zipped to the chin despite the seventy-five-degree temperature. The nylon fabric puckered at the shoulders, as if he had started to outgrow it since putting it on.

"This my friend Harold," Jalen told Bill. "He wanna play. He ain't no buster."

"Good," Bill said, extending a businessman's handshake. "Nice to meet you, nonbuster Harold."

"Nice to meet you too, Coach." Harold's tone was deferential; he even bowed his head as he talked.

"Are you twelve?"

"Yop."

"Why the jacket? It's warm out."

" 'Cause that's my *style.*" Harold said loudly.

"What position do you play?"

Harold looked around. He could tell the team was listening. His voice climbed a few notches.

"I'll play pitcher, first base, shortstop, all of 'em," he said defiantly. "I play backcatcher, too. I'm better than *all* these buster backcatchers."

"Okay," Bill said evenly. He pointed to a chubby boy in a White Sox hat standing on the pitcher's mound. "Why don't you go backcatch Freddie."

"Oh, maaaan." Harold's voice rose further. "Gimme somebody *real* to backcatch. That boy, he just a shorty."

Bill shot Harold a disapproving look, and the boy's deferential manner returned as quickly as it had left.

"I fittina do that right now, Coach," he said, nodding.

In point of fact, Freddie had just turned nine. He was four feet, four inches tall and weighed close to a hundred pounds, a result of his near-exclusive diet of French fries. He was also the finest young athlete Bill and the other coaches had ever seen.

"Hey, Freddie," Bill called. "Bring it in."

Freddie whirled at the sound of his name, an innocent grin creasing his face. When he was born, people in the neighborhood had told his mother that he was an angel. He still looked the part—round head, round body, perfect teeth, long eyelashes, little wrinklings of baby fat at his elbows and knees. Women always wanted to pick him up and hug him. Freddie frowned when they did that. He didn't like being called cute. He liked to play ball. Since he was old enough to walk, he had been playing ball—baseball, basketball, football, it didn't matter, it all came naturally. The year before, when he was four years younger than some other players, he had led the team with a .750 batting average and pitched them to several victories. He jogged in now, his arms swinging close to his body, feet slightly pigeon-toed, intentionally so. His eyes were on the ground, as if he knew people were watching him.

"Why don't you warm up with Harry here," Bill said.

"His *name* ain't Harry," Jalen yelled. "It *Harold.*"

"No problem," Harold said loudly. "I been a back-catcher all my life."

Wordlessly, Freddie jogged back to the mound. Harold, waving off Bill's offer to help him with the equipment, ducked in behind the plate. He looked uncomfortable in his crouch, steadying himself with his glove hand so he didn't tip over.

Freddie, his Nike Bo Jacksons disappearing into a hole in front of the pitching rubber, took his stance on the mound. The smile disappeared, and he put on his pitching face, a burning sidelong glare that was unnerving in one so young. Coach Kevin had taught him to take a breath before every pitch, so he did, cheeks blowing out once, twice. He rocked forward, then swung into motion. His form was flawless: weight back, hips and shoulders rotating, left leg striding aggressively, toe pointed, right arm cocked like a buggy whip. He looked fearsome. The year before, just after he turned eight, he had struck out a coach on three pitches in batting practice—though, as the coach repeatedly found it necessary to point out, from the forty-five-foot Little League distance.

Freddie let fly. Harold, seeing the ball lasering for his head, hit the dirt. The ball sailed to the backstop untouched, a perfect strike, and Harold was up in a flash, yelling at Freddie and Bill, accusing them of attempted murder. Calls of "buster, buster" floated in from the outfield, and Harold responded by challenging the entire team to a fight. Bill, arms folded, waited for things to calm down, for the moment glad that more kids hadn't come. Behind the backstop, the man in the blue hat began to chuckle.

TWO

A few days later, another team prepared for practice. They were gathered in a tight circle, each member on a knee, listening. In the center crouched a tall, rawboned man, his pate glinting in the setting sun. He spoke with a slight honk of Brooklyn.

". . . And Lord, help us to always play our best and always be our best, and not ever, ever to listen to those who say we can't do something, because with You everything is possible. . . ."

The Northwestern Mutual Life Pygmies were one of the best teams in the league. The previous year, they were upset in the semifinals of the playoffs; they had gone through the regular season without a defeat. This year, although many of their better players had moved up to the thirteen-to-fifteen-year-old bracket, they still were one of the early-season favorites to win the championship, if only because they had kept their greatest asset, Coach Bob

Muzikowski, the man who had helped found the Near North Little League.

". . . This we pray in your name. Amen."

"Now." Muzikowski raised his head and stared into the expectant faces gathered around him. "Let's kick some ass."

Bob Muzikowski was six-foot-three, thirty-three years old, and he always seemed to be tilting forward on the balls of his feet. What scant brown hair there was on his scalp was usually rubbed into an electrically charged frizz. His cheeks were dented with shallow pockmarks, and his skin, though it had been exposed to many hours of Carson Field sun, remained the purest shade of subway-rider white. His dark, intense eyes were underlaid by tiny crosshatchings too numerous to be accounted for by mere lack of sleep. It was a compelling but not particularly handsome face, one that could have belonged to an aging rock-and-roller. Only when Bob Muzikowski began to move did he look vibrant and young.

He strode out of the huddle, pushing players toward the field. As practice got into full swing, he was everywhere, wrapping his arms around a reluctant batsman so he could feel what it meant to extend his arms, toeing a line in the dirt to show runners how to veer outside the first-base line when they made a turn for second, briskly escorting a distraught strikeout victim to the sideline to receive confidence-restoring cream-puff pitches from one of the team's four assistant coaches, and, when two of his players started fighting, getting angrier than either of them.

"Hey," he said, grabbing both boys by the shoulder. "You gonna hit somebody on this team, you make sure it's me next time—there ain't no reason for you all to be acting like a couple of stupid-ass gangbangers." Flecks of spittle dotted the players' faces, but they didn't dare wipe them away. "You wanna screw around, or you wanna play baseball?"

Baseball, came the answers.

"*Act* like it." Bob's face softened. "Timmy, this is your

teammate Oopsie. Oopsie, this is your teammate Timmy."
The boys shook hands and returned to their positions. Bob
smiled for a half-beat, then moved on.

As he marched around the field, Bob was trailed by a
queue of coaches from other teams. They asked and he
answered, rapid-fire. Can't find space to practice on Carson? Try the Franklin school up on Wells. Can't find
your second baseman? Just saw him running up Sedgwick. Can't get a check from your sponsor? Let me give
him a call. Don't have enough gloves? Here are the keys
to my car—blue Taurus wagon, parked under the El—try
the trunk. Don't have enough guys? Go over to their
houses, call the schools, grab kids off the street, do whatever you have to do.

Among his hundreds of friends and acquaintances, Bob
was known as a clean-living, hugely energetic, profoundly
Christian person. After all, how else could one account for
the basement apartment in his home which he and his wife,
Tina, ran as a halfway house; his trips to missions in
Bolivia; and his donation of approximately a third of his
annual $150,000-plus income to dozens of causes and pro-
jects in which he was personally involved. To those who
knew him, the fact that Bob was helping launch a baseball
league in Cabrini-Green was not a surprise. It was expected.

"The man never met a cause he didn't like," said Tony
Cimmarrusti, a trader and Little League coach who had
known Bob for seven years. "It's amazing how much he
does. He's like a modern-day apostle—he changes everything he comes in contact with for the better."

Yet there was a curious aspect to Bob's passion that was
out of keeping with his saintly work, a harsh, frenetic quality that occasionally overflowed into a violent temper.
Once, during a playoff game the previous year, Bob had
with increasing irritation overheard a father's complaints
about the coaches of the opposing team, who had suspended his son for bad behavior. After a few minutes, Bob
exploded.

"I am *sick* of this black-white bullshit," he screamed through the fence. "You're the one who doesn't give a shit—you're the one who is too lazy and selfish to get out here and help us, to help your own fucking kids."

"You're the one who's throwing him off the team," the father had yelled.

Bob stepped forward, his voice dropping to soft, dangerous tones. "You want to fight me?" His index finger tapped his chest tauntingly. "Right now, let's go, let's get the gloves and go over to Seward Park and get in the ring. I was a fucking Golden Gloves boxer, man, I'll rip your head off."

The father, a muscular fellow who appeared to be more than Bob's match, looked around, not knowing what to make of this crazy, frizzy-haired white guy. In the dugout, Bob's Pygmies cowered, frightened by the eruption.

His close friends and family were used to these spells. "Bob lost it," they would say, nodding with the understanding and concern one might direct toward a colicky infant. It wasn't just his temper, either. They would worry also about his violent mood swings, his inability to relax, his almost frantic insistence to take on far more than he or those around him could handle.

"Bob is still, well, he's *dealing* with a lot," said a longtime friend and business assistant, Mary Lesniak. "When he's up, he's way up, but when he's down, look out. He can be a terror."

Nine years before this practice, almost to the week, Bob Muzikowski had been drunk in a Holiday Inn bar in College Park, Maryland. That night was different for him, because for once in a long time he hadn't done any coke. It wasn't completely an act of will—fact was, his stash was empty. He felt a little stupid about the way it had happened: he had fallen and sliced his hand on his freebasing pipe, then, in his umpteenth fit of paranoia and regret, flushed the coke down the toilet, blood from the cut swirling into the powder and water. A couple grand, gone forever. Now, in the bar, he wished for that cocaine back. His hand ached.

Still, he felt pretty good. What wasn't there to feel good about? He had just completed the greatest six years of his life at Columbia University, a time of unremitting intensity during which he attended fewer classes, played more sports, and got high more often than anyone he knew. Who else had made city semifinals in Golden Gloves and played for Old Blue rugby? Who else had been smart enough to buy full-size Donkey Kong video games, install them all over campus, and split the revenues fifty-fifty with the university? Who else had scored the $32,000-a-year job with the New York City Fire Department's labor relations board? Who else would roll out of a whorehouse at seven-thirty a.m. and make a cost-savings presentation in front of Mayor Ed Koch at nine—and still do three lines of coke in the bathroom just before?

"I was the Columbia whiz kid, I could do it all," Bob said later. "I'd drop an ounce of 'caine on the table for Super Bowl parties, two thousand dollars, just like that. I took women out to the best restaurants in town, made and spent a ton of money. When I look back, I guess my working-class roots were showing."

Bob didn't have many fond memories of his childhood back in Bayonne, New Jersey. His mother was bullheaded Irish, and hadn't been shy about showing her four sons and daughter the back of her hand. His father worked at a Westinghouse factory, punching out elevator parts. He was a quiet man who spent most of his hours at home watching television and smoking Chesterfield kings, three packs a day. Bob decided early on he wasn't going to be like him. He grew up tough, captained his high school football and basketball teams, scored 1400 on his SATs, and wore his hair in a crew cut. Scholarship offers fluttered in, and Bob chose Columbia. But after his father died of lung cancer during his freshman year, Bob dropped out and came up with a scheme to help his mother pay the mortgage. He emptied his $2,000 savings account and put a down payment on a semi truck with a friend, and the two started their own container-hauling company. The system was simple: one would drive until he got tired, and then the other would take over. There was only one problem: Bob had a hard time staying awake on the cross-country hauls.

One day shortly after Bob dozed off and tipped a truck carrying cooking sherry on the interstate, his friend showed up with a cure: amphetamines. A year later, Bob returned to Columbia with a cumulus-cloud afro, a Fu Manchu mustache, and a new appreciation for the energy-increasing power of recreational drugs. By the time he graduated, the last few years were a blur. "I tried everything," he remembered later. "I did every drug and sick thing that you could think of. I was still able to function pretty well, but when it came down to it, I was lucky I didn't kill myself."

Bob still doesn't know what started the fight that night at the bar in College Park. He might have said something, or pushed somebody, or been pushed. All he knows is that everybody was moving and yelling, and some big, sweaty guy he had never met was trying to brain him with a Heineken bottle. Reflexively, Bob blocked the bottle with his left hand and used a Golden Gloves roundhouse to smash a thick beer mug against his attacker's face. The man went down. Bob, his hand bleeding again, was arrested, taken to the county jail, and charged with assault with intent to maim. Bond was set at $100,000.

He used his phone call to contact a priest he knew in New York, and together they prayed for it all to end. And, after ninety meetings at Alcoholics Anonymous and several near relapses, it did. The charges were dropped, and Bob started a new life.

A few years later he was in Chicago, married to Tina, a lifelong Christian whose devoutness nearly matched his own. He had a job selling insurance for Northwestern Mutual Life, and he was setting office records in sales. His colleagues had never seen anything like it; they would work on somebody for six months, then Bob would run into the person at a dinner, talk for half an hour, and come away with the check. It was no coincidence that many of Bob's clients worked as traders at the Chicago Board of Trade, the corn-fed equivalent of a Las Vegas casino, a place filled with edgy, cash-rich folk not unaccustomed to the perils and pleasures of high living. When Bob started firing off stories about New York whorehouses and four-day benders, and telling people he had already done anything they had ever imagined doing, they listened. Sure, he had a religious spiel, but he didn't come off as a typical Holy Roller. They liked how he gave half his income away. They liked how blunt he was; how he spoke their language. People bought his policies, and they liked doing so. Business soared, and Bob began having more time to devote to his many extracurriculars.

One evening in August 1990, Muzikowski was jogging home from work. He lived on North Park Street, just south of North Avenue, and his route took him past a trash-covered baseball field at Division and Sedgwick, the one called Carson Field. Many of his neighbors thought he was a little touched, running so close to Cabrini-Green, but he didn't mind. It was the most direct way.

He had noticed the field before, of course, and had remarked to some friends how good it would be to get a base-ball league going there, and make it just like the Little Leagues in the suburbs. Bob's friends were accustomed to having such ideas fired at them fairly often. "Do you golf?" he might ask, not waiting for an answer. "This country should ban that sport for a year, just make it illegal, and take all the resources and money that go into it and put them toward something worthwhile. You could solve the homelessness problem like *that*." Or: "If every family in Chicago who called themselves Christian were to adopt one family from Cabrini, this place would be history. If we had some Christians with some balls"—he would grab at his crotch and give a squeeze—"these fucking walls would come tumbling down."

On this evening, however, Bob saw people on one of the diamonds. He jogged over. They were kids, dressed in an assortment of jerseys, wielding ancient-looking gloves and bats. A tall man in a black sweatsuit stood behind the plate. He was the only adult on the field, and he seemed to be acting as umpire, cheerleader, and coach for both teams. His loud, clear voice shouted the count, his quick hands waved players to different defensive depths, and his stare broke up fights that had not yet started. If a player dared to talk back, the man would put his nose up to that of the offender and invoke the names of mother and uncle, father and brother, and wonder aloud, as the boy shriveled, where in the hell he was going to end up if he had so little respect for himself as to behave like that. Then the man would rub his hand roughly over the boy's head and stalk back to the plate, the veins on his forehead standing out like ropes. He was handsome, with close-cropped hair and horn-rimmed glasses, and the muscles of his brow were tensed in a perpetual glare.

Bob watched until the game ended, then walked over to the umpire and introduced himself. The man said his name was Al Carter. He worked for the city's Department of Human Services in gang relations, but spent much of his time working with Cabrini kids through his own organization, the Al Carter Youth Foundation. This baseball tournament was his new project. Bob and Al kept talking, and soon Bob floated a proposal. If Al could provide the kids, he could locate the coaches and the sponsorship money. With that they could buy new uniforms, decent gloves, a scoreboard, "the whole show."

Al Carter hesitated. He told Bob that in his forty-eight years of living and working in Cabrini-Green he had seen many volunteers come and go. He told him that more than a hundred agencies received money in the name of Cabrini-Green, and that only a fraction of it found its way back into the neighborhood. He told him how a lot of corporate types got into this kind of work so they could get a halo from their bosses. But in the end, Al told Bob okay, to go ahead and see what he could do.

"Don't worry," Al said in parting, pointing at Bob to make sure he got the message. "I won't be surprised if I don't see you again."

Thus the league began. By the following spring, Bob had organized a field cleanup and secured commitments from Continental Bank, Morgan Stanley, Merrill Lynch, J. P. Morgan, and Kidder, Peabody and others. In March it was decided that Al, who had the neighborhood experience, would be president, Bob vice-president, and Tina treasurer. When Bob prepared to register the league at Little League Baseball headquarters in Williamsport, Pennsylvania, the question of a name came up. There was some disagreement: Al preferred "African-American Youth League," but Bob didn't like the idea. What if someone white or Hispanic wanted to play? Bob wanted to name the league after the neighborhood, and since he was the one who drove to Williamsport, that was what he did. The charter committee ruled favorably, and the Near North Little League became one of the more than 17,000 Little Leagues in America.

The first year went well, but the relationship between Bob and Al was somewhat rocky. Al played the gadfly, questioning coaches about their corporate mentality, reminding them that they weren't from the neighborhood, rebelling against agendas and meetings, and irking the mostly white volunteers—many of whom were the Muzikowskis' close friends—with his outspoken, bombastic style. In a *Chicago Tribune* article published a few days before the first game, Al wondered about the coaches' motivations. "It might be good to take your picture with a little black boy and run back downtown to show it to your CEO, but [this league] doesn't mean anything unless it becomes a long-term thing. I appreciate all that has been done. Everyone is sincere and dedicated, but if guys are looking for their halo, they ain't going to get it from me." Al rubbed

Tina in particular the wrong way, and the two argued frequently and emotionally. Privately, Bob and Tina started
referring to the "Al problem."

Discontent flowed both ways. Along with other coaches,
Al was disconcerted by Bob's religiosity and his talk of
sending the teams to what sounded like a Christian camp.
His frequent run-ins with Tina made him all but write her
off; and though he succeeded in getting the Muzikowskis
to include an African-American educational component in
the league, he got the distinct feeling that he was being hu-
mored. Most important, perhaps, Al felt overwhelmed by
the hurricane of change Bob Muzikowski had summoned.
From Al's point of view the small, simple game on Carson
Field had been transformed overnight into a many-
branched organization whose name he did not recognize,
filled with young, confident suits who knew next to nothing about Cabrini, who were far more apt to take their cue
from Bob than from him, and who, if history was any indi-
cation, might well be long gone when the next season
rolled around. Sometimes it was enough to make Al blaze
with righteous indignation.

"They don't understand that I've been here, I've worked
in this neighborhood all my life," he said late in the first
season. "Respect must be put out properly. A lot of people
gave to this neighborhood before Bob Muzikowski came
along. They can't be coming in for one summer and think
they're the savior, think they're solving everything."

Already in 1992, tensions had begun to flare. Two
weeks before Opening Day, Al called a coaches' meeting
and announced that he wanted the league to march in the
African-American Liberation Day parade the following Saturday. This immediately sent up a ripple of controversy, as
Bob had long before scheduled that date for a baseball
clinic held by a Christian-athlete organization. The ensuing
debate was loaded with broad implications on both sides:
Al pushing what many saw as his African-American
agenda; Bob pushing his Christianity; both causing

discomfort for most coaches. The difference, however, was that Bob knew how to sell his event to the coaches, while Al did not.

In periodic updates before the clinic, Bob emphasized the baseball aspect ("I've seen this, and they're great—major-league ballplayers, big-time all-stars, and drill stations teaching hitting, pitching, bunting, the whole show"). He failed to mention the mawkish revival meeting that took place afterward, in which two former utility infielders used new baseballs as rewards for children who shouted Jesus' name. Al, on the other hand, did not explain any aspect of the parade except to say that it would celebrate African-American heritage, and that it was mandatory. When he heard at a coaches' meeting that one coach had told a player that he didn't have to go to the parade if he didn't want to, Al erupted.

"What the hell did that coach mean?" Al said loudly, the cords standing out on his neck. "That is a *serious* message you are sending to that black child. Black children hold white people in very high regard, and you can't drive up here in your nice cars from your nice homes and tell them that they don't have to celebrate the holiday of their people! You cannot do that!"

"Wait just a second there, Al," replied Tony Cimmarrusti, Bob's friend who coached the Zulus, his voice rising. "What if their parents don't want them to go? What if they have something else going on that afternoon with their family? We're here to coach baseball, not to order these kids around. I mean . . ." He looked around the room in earnest disbelief. "I mean, this is *America.*"

"You feel that way, then why don't you take your Porsche and go coach in Winnetka or Kenilworth," said Al, naming two wealthy suburbs. "When you've worked here seventeen years and you've been shot at fifty or sixty times, then you can tell me how things work. I don't need this bullshit right now." He stopped for a second and stared contemptuously at Tony. "*America.* Give me a break."

"What the hell does he think he's doing?" asked Greg

White, the black real estate banker who was third in the league's chain of command behind Al and Bob. "You try to ask him about anything, and he plays the racial card right away: 'You're bad because you're white, I'm good because I'm black and I've been here.' If he's trying to alienate everybody, he's doing a damn good job of it."

In the end, the league didn't have to select one event over the other. Predictably, Bob's Christian baseball clinic brought out more than 150 players, while Al's parade, which began as the clinic ended, drew only twenty-two players and one coach. Nevertheless, both sides felt vindicated. Al had made his point, Bob had made his, and everyone, on the surface at least, remained friendly.

THREE

Five days before opening day, and the Kikuyus were taking infield practice. It wasn't typical to have an infield made up of two third basemen, two shortstops, two second basemen, and two first basemen, but there was no choice. With the season looming, Carson Field was crowded with seven teams, and the Kikuyus were restricted to one infield. Coach Bill stood at the plate, tapping out grounders with a twenty-eight-inch bat that he swung with one hand. Coach Cort and Coach Brad roamed about, issuing advice in the form of snappy couplets resurrected from their own Little League years.

"Be ready now, be ready."

"Alonzo, let's see dirt every time you scoop that ball, every time."

"Stay in front now, Rufus, right in front."

"Two hands every time, Nathaniel, two hands."

The last few practices had gone reasonably well, under the cramped circumstances. The coaches had been forced

to improvise a series of space-saving drills: rolling grounders, playing pepper, throwing infield pop-ups and playing
soft-toss, in which players batted underhand pitches into
the chain link. The team was showing considerable improvement. Nathaniel, he of the buckteeth and questionable coordination, had hit a line shot over shortstop in the
last practice. Maurice and the Ed Kranepool glove were actually catching a few pop-ups. Rufus, though he still hovered close under his mother's wing, was showing good
hand-eye coordination in the field, and Calbert now knew
that the batter should run to first, not third, after hitting the
ball.

   Best of all, however, was the addition of two new players
to the Kikuyus' roster, Otis and David. Otis was a reedy
twelve-year-old from the Whites with a tall box haircut and
a broad, cheerful face. He had been on the roster since the
start of the season, but his family's lack of a telephone had
made it difficult for the coaches to get in touch. Luckily,
Jalen had spotted him walking past Carson Field one afternoon, and though it was clear that he had hardly picked up
a baseball before, Otis had proved to be a smooth, capable
athlete, tracking down grounders and fly balls without displaying the abject fear of most first-timers. He also had a
gentle, straightforward manner that was sometimes dis-
arming. At the end of his first practice, Bill had asked the
new player if his parents would be attending Opening Day.
"My daddy's in rehabilitation," Otis said, pronouncing
each syllable carefully. "He don't live with us no more. My
momma might come, though, if she don't have to work."

   David, the other new recruit, had not been on the original roster. He simply had walked onto Carson Field one
day, a handsome, broad-shouldered boy wearing real baseball pants and carrying a thirty-three-inch Easton bat.
Coach Bill had asked him whether he had played before.

   "Yeah, about four years out in Humboldt Park. Made the
all-star team last year—pitcher and shortstop. My family
just moved here."

   Bill had tossed him a few pitches, and David had

blistered the ball to deep left field, farther than anyone on the team had ever hit.

"How old are you?" Bill had asked.

"Twelve."

"When's your birthday?"

"October."

A miracle. This was sixty days inside the Little League deadline of August 1. Bill had extended a hand. "Welcome to the Kikuyus."

In just one week with David, the team's dynamic had shifted for the better. He was a quiet, coachable kid, who, though sometimes frustrated by the abilities of his teammates, rarely took part in the cat-calling and complaining. His skill granted him instant cachet with the other players, who quickly buddied up to him and began to mimic not only his home-run swing but also his unassuming ways.

"I don't know if it's because he's not from around here or what," Cort said, "but this kid is too good to be true."

Now, at what would be the last practice before Opening Day, Bill ran through the infield a dozen times, hitting soft grounders to each position, and shouting out different situations so the players could learn to throw to different bases. As time wore on, however, the kids—even David—grew restless.

"Man!" yelled Jalen. "This *phony*. When you gonna let us hit?"

Indeed, that was the question. The Kikuyus had come not to field grounders or chase fly balls or learn how to run bases. They had come to hit. What's more, they possessed an unshakable, Nintendo-fueled confidence that they could hit a homer every time at bat. Bill, aware of this desire, ran the soft-toss drill time and again, but it just wasn't the same. They had to *hit* the ball, whack it to the gate, bid cool condolences to the unlucky fielders sprawled in its wake, touch home plate with a casual tiptoe and come back to the dugout with a stone-cold look. Bill was anxious for them to hit, too. Many of his players, accustomed to the friendler lobs of batting practice, would enter Saturday's game against the Morgan Stanley & Co. Mau Maus with no experience facing a hostile pitcher.

As the complaints magnified, Bill spotted an opportunity—a team in the outfield whose coach he knew. He turned the bat over to Brad, walked out, and a short time later returned with good news.

"All right, bring it in," he yelled. "Time for a scrimmage."

The team cheered. Their opponents were the Big Kikuyus, a team of the thirteen-to-fifteen-year-olds coached by Ron Swidler, an interior designer who also worked in North Pier. The Big Kikuyus, both coaches knew, would normally stomp the younger players, but things could be evened out by having coaches pitch for both sides.

The Kikuyus gathered around the bats, and started practicing their stances and home-run trots. "Yeah, boy," said Freddie, doing a pelvic-thrust dance. "Gonna *whack, whack, whack* their heat to the gate."

Bill jotted down a lineup on a scrap of paper. When he was done, he counted . . . nine names. He counted again, and made another list, this one of players who were missing. Calbert wasn't around, but he had an excuse: His mother's car had been stolen and he had no way to get to practice, since he wouldn't ride his bike at night and he didn't like to take the bus. T.J., Bill had heard through Alonzo, had moved to the South Side. Rickey? Somebody said that he had moved in with his aunt in the Henry Horner Homes.

And what of Samuel, that sad-eyed ten-year-old who had missed every practice thus far? Samuel had played on the team the year before, a chubby, husky-voiced left-hander who showed up for perhaps half of the games and struck out most every time. He had not turned in an application for this year, but Bill had put him on the roster anyway. Thanks to the phone tree, Samuel had been contacted before every practice, and he had always said he'd be there. Bill checked the address in his folder: 1117–1119 North Cleveland, otherwise known as the Castle.

He knew the building. Though he had no way of telling for sure, it seemed from the outside a worse place to live than the other highrises—more burned-out windows, no security guard, more sinister figures in hooded Starter jackets hanging around the entrance. Samuel didn't seem to like it, either. Whenever Bill drove him home, he rolled down the car window and yelled up to a fifth-floor window in a plaintive, loud voice. "Mama!" he would shout. "Ma-maaaa!" After a few long moments, his mother's voice would bellow down, telling him to get his fat ass upstairs, and Samuel, so slow and delicate on the baseball field, would leap out of the car, and race up a fenced incline, past the big hooded coats, up four flights of stairs and down the ramp, where his mother would have the door unlocked and ready to fling open.

"Hey, hey, Coach, let's get this thing moving." Bill looked up from his list. Ron Swidler was taking the mound, his defense arranged. He popped the ball in his mitt. "Let's play some ball!"

"All right, guys." Bill waited until everybody was looking at him, then continued. "This is just practice, so let's have some fun, let's get our cuts up there."

He knelt and stretched out his hand, palm down. The rest of the team stacked their hands on his—a pregame tradition from the last season.

"Ready . . . one, two, three, Kikuyus."

The game began with groundouts by Freddie and Demetrius. Then Nathaniel, swinging with spastic grace, lined a pitch to left, and Harold followed with a dribbler to third that went for a single. Then Calbert, who couldn't decide which side of the plate to hit from, drew a walk, loading the bases.

"Let's go!" Calbert shouted, energized by his success. "Whack it to the gate."

Jalen strode out of the dugout carrying his weapon: a coal-black thirty-four-inch, thirty-four-ounce wooden softball bat that he had purchased at the Maxwell Street market for five dollars. It was by far the biggest bat in the equipment bag. Its barrel seemed to stretch for several feet, and was scored by a series of yellow markings and three-inch-high letters that read "Rude Dude." When Jalen set the head of the bat on the ground, the knob almost touched his sternum.

"Hey there, chief." Bill curled his finger for a private conference. "Don't you think you might be able to get around on the ball a little better if you had a lighter bat?"

"Those bats is *buster* bats." Jalen's dark eyes shone angrily. "This here a home-*run* bat."

Bill thought for a moment. "Tell you what," he said. "You get a hit with that, and I'll buy you a slice of pizza. You strike out, and you got to use a lighter bat next time. What do you say?"

Jalen nodded, and they clasped pinkies to seal the wager.

Back in the dugout, Bill nudged the other coaches. "Watch this. That bat is too big for *me*."

Jalen's first swing was late.

"Is he batting or pole-vaulting?" asked Brad.

But on the second pitch, a medium-speed fastball, Jalen leaned back and started Rude Dude early, twisting his Scottie Pippens into the dust and levering the bat around with stiff arms—somewhat like a hammer throw. And he nailed it. The ball made a quiet, solid thump on Rude Dude's belly, the third baseman ducked, and the ball skittered down the left-field line for a three-run triple. Pulling into third base, Jalen smiled. He pointed to Bill, then to Chester's Pizza across the street.

"Make it pepperoni."

In the third inning, with the score Kikuyus 4, Big Kikuyus 2, one of Ron's players hit a hot smash toward Demetrius at shortstop. He put his glove down backhand, careful to hold it safely away from his body. The ball skipped underneath Demetrius and past a napping Louis in left field for a two-run homer.

"Hey, Demetrius," Bill called. "I want to see that ball bounce off your chest next time."

Demetrius's narrow eyes doubled in size. "You crazy. Thump off my chest, *right*."

By now, the two teams were alone on the field. From the dugout, the coaches checked the sun. Nobody liked to be on the field after dark, particularly at the corner closest to the highrise, where the teams were now playing. As Kevin once put it, it didn't take much work to imagine the cross-hairs of a rifle scope on your back.

As Brad went into his windup, low booming noises rang out from far across Division Street. Firecrackers were common in Cabrini, but this, though distant, sounded louder, deeper.

"That probably isn't a car backfiring, is it?" Ron asked nervously.

"That's a nine," said Alonzo, meaning a nine-millimeter semiautomatic pistol, which had recently become the weapon of choice in the city. One popular brand, the Inter-tec Tec-9, held thirty-two rounds in a single magazine, re-tailed for $260, and came with the option of Tec-Kote, a special finish that, said the company's promotional litera-ture, provided "excellent resistance to fingerprints."

"*Placka-placka-placka*," said Alonzo, steepling his long fingers and pointing them at Ron. The sound changed, and he cocked his head.

"Rifle," he said, switching grips on his imaginary gun. "*Doosh, doosh, doosh*."

"Oh, super," said Ron.

Perhaps more than the other coaches, Ron was well versed in Cabrini's potential dangers. A few days before, his mother had driven by Carson Field at dusk while Ron was coaching. She had never been to the field, and had wanted to see this team that her son talked about so much. She sat in her Volvo on Sedgwick Street for a few moments, then motioned to Ron to come over. She rolled down the window.

"Get in," she said. "I'm taking you away from this place."

"Okay, Mom," Ron said, prepared for such a reaction. "The neighborhood isn't great, but this field is safe and I don't take chances." This was true. After practice, he wasted no time getting to his car, which he usually parked facing the clean, well-lit spaces of Wells Street.

"Why are you doing this to me?" she said. "I can't believe I raised my son to come out here and risk his life in a war zone. Do you know taxi drivers won't go down this street? Do you know why?"

"No, Mom," Ron said.

"Because people *shoot* here," she said. "People get *killed* here."

"We're okay out here," Ron protested. "The league says we aren't in any danger."

"*The league says* . . . You don't know that. How can they tell you you're going to be fine when the police can't even stop it?"

Ron's mother finally let him go, and in the following days the story made the rounds among the coaches. Soon it was something of a parable, "The Complaint of the Volvo Mother," and it joined the ranks of similar stories and jokes the coaches told about the dangers of Cabrini—stories at once morbid and comic, acknowledging fears and dismissing them, spooky tales for people dealing with a world they didn't understand.

On this night, the coaches quickly agreed that they should call the game. Players on both sides protested mightily, but the coaches packed up the equipment and loaded it into their cars and gave rides to the kids who needed them. By the time the sun set over Division Street, Carson Field was deserted.

It was a warm July evening in 1970 when patrolman Anthony Rizzato and Sergeant James Severin started their evening walk. Like the other dozen or so Chicago police officers who had volunteered for the Cabrini-Green Walk and Talk program, they had no specific destination. Their objective in trading their squad car for walking shoes was to become more a part of the community they were policing, and thus slow a crime rate that lately had been on the rapid rise. The situation in Cabrini-Green was not nearly as dire as in other, poorer neighborhoods to the south, but this project received more attention because it was only a few blocks from the Gold Coast. The Soul Coast, people called it. Police had recently given it another nickname: Combat Alley.

At seven, about an hour before sunset, the two officers saw that a baseball game was being played at Seward Park, just south of Division and Sedgwick. This couldn't have been any surprise to them, for in those days baseball was the sport of choice in Cabrini, far more popular than basketball or football or anything else. Most every highrise in the development sponsored a team; at important games the crowds grew so large that the field had to be roped off to allow play to continue. As it happened, Sergeant Severin coached one of the teams, and it was partly because of the relationships formed through baseball that he felt comfortable wandering through the project. He and Rizzato now strolled to the field to see who was playing.

"These people are my friends," Severin had told a friend a few days before. "They won't hurt me."

The shots came from above. The first bullet went through Severin's arm and chest; the second through Rizzato's back. The players scattered. The officers fell near the third-base line, Severin grasping for his radio. He never got the call off.

The headlines in the next day's *Chicago Tribune* stood two inches high: "Snipers Slay 2 Policemen." The scene was depicted as a Vietnam on Division Street: three hundred officers lugging carbines, shotguns, and M-16s, ducking crossfire from unseen snipers in the dark windows above; helicopters providing cover as the police tried to retrieve their dead. *Time, Newsweek,* and other publications described Cabrini as a "chamber of social horrors" where "teen-age vandals roam the floors, terrorizing residents with the same impunity that allows them to snatch quarters from children in the playground." Three thousand mourners, including cadres of police officers from Baltimore, Washington, D.C., Wilmington, Boston, Philadelphia, Cleveland, and New York, attended the officers' funerals. The Walk and Talk program was suspended indefinitely.

In the aftermath, there was no shortage of people to blame. Police blamed the criminal element in the community; newspaper columnist Mike Royko blamed Mayor Richard J. Daley; others blamed the Chicago Housing Authority. The people of Cabrini, while they decried the killings, protested the subsequent police search of the project's apartments and what they alleged were the brutal beatings of two young men who refused to submit. A young activist named Jesse Jackson led a peace march through Cabrini, where he criticized Chicago police chief James B. Conlisk, Jr., for calling the snipers "animals." "The reign of terror must stop," Jackson said. "But it must stop on both sides."

The snipers, four young men between the ages of fourteen and twenty-three, were soon caught. They had, the press reported, walked into the bathroom of apartment 602 at 1150–1160 North Sedgwick, placed a board across the bathtub to stand on, removed the window screen, and fired two scope-equipped .30-caliber rifles. At the time, their motive was never made clear, though most of the press reported the four were gang members who had been at a party when they saw the police officers walk onto the field, and suddenly had decided to shoot them. *Time* called the circumstances "chillingly casual," and used similar words to describe the disposition of another person in the news that week, an accused murderer named Charles Manson.

Cabrini-Green's reputation, long suspected, was sealed.

"Everybody on both sides went crazy," remembered Al Carter. "People outside Cabrini didn't understand that the vast majority of the people here were just as angry and upset as they were. But from then on nobody trusted them. And you best believe that nobody in white Chicago trusted Cabrini."

"Trust" never has been a word used much to describe the rest of Chicago's relationship with the gritty neighborhood along the north branch of the Chicago River. First settled by the English even before Chicago became a city in 1837, the area was taken over by successive waves of newer, poorer immigrants in search of work in the many tanneries and factories along the river. By the late 1800s, the neighborhood had developed a considerable renown not only for its unparalleled filth and decrepitude, but also for its violence. Its streets were ruled by some of the day's preeminent Irish gangsters: Clabby Burns, Kid Murphy, and Cooney the Fox, whose deadly ruthlessness was faithfully and somewhat titillatingly reported to gentle readers in the exclusive and thriving Gold Coast half a mile distant. Policemen, the *Chicago Times* reported in 1865, were not "venturing to invade its precincts, or even cross the border, without having a strong reserve force."

By the early 1900s, however, the Irish and Swedes had been replaced by another immigrant group—impoverished and illiterate peasants from the rocky fields of Sicily. On arrival, each village staked out a street for its own: the people on Larrabee were from Altavilla, the people on Cambridge from Alimena and Chiusa Sclafani, Townsend was Little Bagheria. This community, poorer and more insular than any Chicago had seen, engaged in a decades-long series of gang wars and feuds that struck fear in the hearts of their Gold Coast neighbors and that, by 1929, boosted the area's crime rate to twelve times that of the rest of Chicago. The district dubbed "Little Sicily" became known by another name, "Little Hell." The corner of Oak and Cambridge—not coincidentally, the site of the neighborhood's largest Catholic church—saw so many shootings and stabbings that it was celebrated as one of the city's "Death

Corners." The press and police of the day attributed most of the killings to the Black Hand, and considered them mostly inevitable. As Chicago's then chief of police put it, "Oh, we've always had trouble up there. They never bother anyone but each other."

After World War I, and again after World War II, Little Hell was invaded by yet another group of new arrivals, this time from the American South, pushed by the introduction of the automatic cotton picker and pulled by promises of urban prosperity. Though the Sicilians banded together to keep the newcomers from acquiring property or attending area schools (as the Irish and the Swedes had done decades before), their resistance was short-lived. They rented their basements to the new arrivals, often at a premium over what they would charge their countrymen, and the face of the neighborhood began to change. This time, however, the Sicilians did not depart immediately, and the neighborhood became one of Chicago's few truly integrated slums.

In the early forties, great change came to Little Hell. In an attempt to revitalize the area, the city bulldozed the wood-frame shanties and erected a block of rowhouses, two-story homes of brick and concrete that resembled nothing so much as army barracks. On August 26, 1942, Mayor Edward Kelly dedicated the first of the Mother Frances Xavier Cabrini Homes, named in honor of the first American citizen to be made a saint, a woman who had given medical care to the Italian immigrants of the neighborhood in the early 1900s. The 581 families who moved into them reflected the racial mix of the surrounding neighborhood: seventy-five percent white, twenty-five percent black. Applicants were screened carefully to ensure two-parent, one-wage-earner households. Unseemly behavior such as littering or walking on the grass was punishable by fine.

"These homes, built by the Chicago Housing Authority, symbolize the Chicago that is to be," Kelly proclaimed. "We cannot continue as a nation, half slum and half palace."

With the infusion of government money and the 1950 announcement that more CHA homes were on the way, Little Hell became more livable. Residents could shop at the Del Farm supermarket, the A&P, or Greenman's department store. They could go to the bank on North Avenue and get a good meal at Flowers' restaurant. Children could play basketball at the new Lower North Center, roller-skate at Wells High School on Friday nights, and spend their allowance at Tom's Candy Store, where the owner was Italian and his wife was black. Mayor Richard J. Daley visited twice, attending the 1955 ground-breaking for the fifteen red-brick highrises of the Cabrini Extension, and the 1962 dedication of the William Green Homes, eight concrete highrises whose bleached appearance quickly earned them the name the Whites. Some were six, some nine, and some nineteen stories tall. They were clean, and everything in them worked, even the elevators. Limitations in federal dollars had prevented the building of more rowhouses, which the CHA felt were the best style of housing for families, but the highrises seemed a good solution.

"These new vertical neighborhoods," said Elizabeth Wood, then the CHA's executive director, "will compete with the suburbs for social desirability, especially for families with children." A 1957 CHA report noted that the galleries reduced inside corridors and provided open porches where children could play and adults could visit. This feature, the report said, "adds zest to living in the new home for some families who formerly had to come out of the basements to see daylight."

The buildings kept rising. In 1963 developers broke ground for Carl Sandburg Village, a private apartment highrise just east of La Salle Street; supporters hoped it would be a bridge between Cabrini and the Gold Coast. By the late sixties, Cabrini-Green had grown from its original sixteen acres and 1,500 people to a large-scale development of seventy-one acres and almost 20,000 people, eighty-nine percent of whom were black.

Back in Washington, D.C., however, Congress and the

Supreme Court were making changes that would shake the foundation of federal housing policy. First, a well-intentioned 1969 law fixed tenants' rents at twenty-five percent of their income. This quickly drove out the stabilizing force of the project: the working-class families who now found cheaper rents in private apartments. Furthermore, a number of suits by the American Civil Liberties Union severely handicapped the CHA's ability to screen its residents and evict troublesome tenants. Increasingly, the people who stayed in Cabrini were those who lacked the means or the desire to pull themselves out.

To make matters worse, the CHA was developing cracks after its initial successes. After a *Chicago Sun-Times* series in 1965, newspapers regularly ran stories on the danger and difficulties of life within housing projects such as Cabrini. In 1968, a presidential commission wrote how the sheer scale of such projects were "stultifying to the human spirit" and described their administration as "heavy handed." By that time, however, CHA director and real estate developer Charles Swibel was already well into what would become a nineteen-year reign of financial impropriety and political cronyism. Late in his tenure, a Department of Housing and Urban Development study would discover that only five of the CHA's nineteen project managers were "competent or knowledgeable to be managing projects," and that the agency never fired or laid off any of its 2,288 employees. Swibel's CHA, the HUD report concluded, was operating "in a state of profound confusion and disarray. No one seems to be minding the store; what's more, no one seems to genuinely care."

In April 1968, when Martin Luther King, Jr., was assassinated, the residents of Cabrini grieved in relative peace. It was not so elsewhere in Chicago. Great swaths of Chicago's West Side were burned in rioting, and thousands of people were displaced. Reacting swiftly, Swibel suspended all screening and distributed the refugees village style, moving entire blocks into vacant apartments. A decision was made to place fifty families in 1150–1160 North Sedgwick and fifty families in 1117–1119 North Cleveland, the Castle. Residents complained that the families had gang connections, but their objections were overruled. The people had to live somewhere.

Two gangs—the Cobra Stones, a branch of the notorious South Side Blackstone Rangers, and the West Side Vice Lords—soon made their presence felt. Fueled by the black power movement, they represented a new breed of gang: equipped with quasi-religious imagery, guns, drug-supply lines in some cases, and in the case of the Blackstone Rangers, enough shrewdness to win a $927,000 community grant for their work on the South Side from President Johnson's Office of Economic Opportunity in 1967 and, later, two tickets to President Nixon's inauguration.

To defend themselves against the newcomers, Cabrini youths formed two gangs, the Blacks and the Deuces Wild, the latter originally a baseball team. Lines were drawn. Fights became frequent, and life in Cabrini suffered. The sound of gunfire was heard every night. People were beaten up for living in the wrong building or walking down the wrong street. Drug sales took off in earnest. The Blacks and the Deuces Wild eventually aligned themselves with the Disciples, the burgeoning rival to the Blackstone Rangers on the South Side, and soon Cabrini-Green occupied a unique position among housing projects: while the Vice Lords controlled the western projects and the Disciples and Blackstone Rangers fought over the southern territory, Cabrini, thanks to the CHA and the riots after King's assassination, played host to all three.

In 1970, when Officers Severin and Rizzato were shot at Seward Park, Cabrini-Green became a national symbol of urban decay. Though it was not widely reported at the time, the incident was rooted in irony. Until a few moments before the shooting, the two principal gunmen had belonged to warring gangs. One, a seventeen-year-old Cobra Stone leader named Johnnie Veal, had lived with his family on the South Side until they were relocated after the April 1968 riots. The other, twenty-three-year-old George

Knight, from Cabrini, was a shot-caller for the Blacks. Accounts of the events leading up to the shooting were sketchy, but most agreed that Veal and Knight had shot the policemen to seal a pact between the two gangs, a peace treaty.

FOUR

The phone rang at seven-fifteen.

"Coach Brad?"

"Uhhh . . ."

"Brad, this Calbert. Are we gonna play today, because it's raining and misty and it's not very warm outside, maybe forty-five or fifty degrees, and visibility is not very good at all, and cold ain't good for my asthma—I got asthma—especially if it's raining and it look right now like it might rain all day." He took a quick breath. "My mama say that maybe you'd want to plan a little something else, like a movie or a video game arcade or maybe a picnic somewhere inside, and she can bring a cake or maybe some fried-tomato sandwiches. Now, French Fry, that's my brother, he don't mind the cold none, Mom say he's like her little Eskimo Pie, but with me—"

"Calbert," Brad interrupted, "we're playing."

"I figured we would, but my mom figured it'd be best to check with you to see for sure. She always says better safe than sorry and you should never count your eggs before—"

"I'll see you at the field at eight-thirty, like we said."

"Okay, Brad. *Hasta la vista.*"

Opening Day, and the Kikuyus had the mixed good fortune to have drawn a nine a.m. start against the Morgan Stanley Mau Maus. This did not promise an easy assignment, for the Kikuyus were short on coaches. Coach Bill had driven to Michigan for a wedding, Coach Kevin was still in Spain, and Coach Cort had to work.

This left most of the duties to Brad, who fortunately was more than well equipped by virtue of his experience as a counselor in a Maine summer camp. An easygoing Kansan, Brad could, however, flick a switch and transform himself into a take-no-guff drill sergeant who could utter phrases like "That's simply not acceptable" and make them sound genuinely threatening. The transformation came mostly through the stentorian resonance that Brad would put into his voice when he was laying down the law. It was incongruous coming from someone whose friendly brown eyes, jug ears, and mop of brown hair seemed designed to complement his nickname, Bucky, but it worked. "I'm not necessarily out here to be best friends with the kids," he said. "I really don't mind being the bad guy every once in a while, if it helps this team get organized."

It was still drizzling at eight-forty, when Brad's aging Honda Civic arrived at the field. Most of the Kikuyus were already there, loosening up their arms by tossing rocks at the El train. When they saw the car—the Hooptie, they called it, after a rattletrap in a Sir Mix-A-Lot music video— they flocked around it. Brad's tousled head emerged, followed shortly by a hand clutching a jumbo cup of coffee.

"All right." Brad squinted and blinked despite the cloudy conditions. "Get in line—in order of birthday."

He walked to the back of his car and ceremoniously unclicked the hatch. Sitting there, amid a scattering of soda cans, maps, and fast-food wrappers, was a plain brown box overflowing with yellows and greens. Eyes widened.

"Like the A's," said Maurice, reaching in.

The jerseys were bright yellow cotton with green and

white piping on the collar and sleeves. KIKUYU appeared across the chest in three-inch-high capital letters of an old-fashioned typeface. The hats were made of inexpensive green foam, with the sponsor name in yellow letters on the front and nylon mesh in the back. The pants were white, and a little dingy because most were recycled from the previous year. The green stirrup socks were crinkly and new. Following Maurice's lead, ten pairs of hands reached for the box.

"Just a second," said Brad, parrying the field of arms with his cup. "Order of birthday."

The line formed quickly, and after a brief argument over whether March came before April, Jalen was first. He chose number 3.

"Aren't you a little slender for that?" asked Brad. "That's Babe Ruth's number."

"Mine, you mean," said Jalen, glaring. He rummaged through the box. "Where my whatchacallit? I'm the *back*-catcher, and the backcatcher need a whatchacallit."

Brad dug around and located a jockstrap and protective cup. Jalen snatched it from him and put it to his nose. He made a sour face.

"This *musty*," he said. "I ain't wearing it."

"It's brand-new, Jalen," said Brad, shifting subtly into the Maine foghorn. "Wear it."

Louis, after much thought, settled on number 7. "Call me Lucky Seven," he said.

Harold tweezed a hat between his thumb and forefinger, then dropped it in disgust. "Why y'all so cheap, Brad?" he complained. "These hats has phony flycatcher stuff on the back—why can't you be a good coach and get us some Starter hats?"

"I don't want to hear it, Harold," boomed the foghorn. "Take it or leave it." Harold took number 10 and a cap.

David chose 11, extralarge size.

Rufus chose number 1, the smallest jersey. He didn't say anything, just hugged it to his chest and trotted away to show his mother.

Maurice picked number 8, same as his hero, Andre Dawson. The rest of the team moved quickly through, too excited by the prospect of uniforms to care which number they wore.

"Alonzo?" Brad looked around. "Your turn."

But Alonzo wasn't in line. He was standing in front of the Hooptie, holding his arm out with intense concentration.

"Quiet," he said in a stage whisper. *"Look."*

Brad walked closer. A large moth was perched on Alonzo's finger; its dusty gray legs hinged firmly around his nail. The insect seemed to have mistaken Alonzo for a tree. It sat solidly, twitching its antennae, unfolding and refolding its wings as if drying them. The wings were beautiful: velvety black with mustard-colored stripes.

"It's a butterfly," he said. "*Mon*arch."

A few players gathered around, one whispering fervent warnings that butterflies could bite. Alonzo, however, didn't listen. He waved his free hand and would not let them too near. After a short while, the moth took flight, moving uncertainly in the direction of the Oscar Mayer factory. Alonzo did not chase it.

"My butterfly stayed on my finger like two minutes, and that's good luck," Alonzo announced. "That means I ain't striking out but four . . . make that six times all year."

"What number?" asked Brad, escorting his budding entomologist to the box of uniforms.

"Fourteen—same as Ernie Banks," Alonzo said correctly.

As the players took turns suiting up in the Hooptie, Brad took a head count: twelve players, biggest turnout of the year. One uniform was left over. Brad took a mental roll call. Samuel. He tossed the uniform in his trunk. Number 13 would be his.

The Mau Maus were already on the field, looking sharp in their orange-and-black uniforms. They ran laps, took infield, reached their hands in a circle and shouted, "One, two, three, *Mau Maus*!" Their head coach, Dave McMahon, looked impassively at the scene. He worked as a broker for Morgan Stanley. He and his coaches ran a disciplined squad that had finished second in the league the previous year. His rules were simple: Miss practice, you sit a game. Talk back or throw equipment, you run laps. Anything more, and you're off the team. Word had it that McMahon already had booted his two best players off the team because they were too disruptive.

"Let's go," he shouted from the dugout. "Let's get *serious* out there, guys."

Until a week before, the Mau Maus had been avoiding the crowds at Carson by practicing at Seward Park, a block to the south. The first few practices had gone well, as they had the field entirely to themselves. But on the previous Thursday evening, someone in a highrise began tossing rocks and chunks of concrete onto the field. McMahon had called his team under the shelter of the backstop and waved down a passing squad car. He started to explain what was happening, but the officer didn't let him.

"What the hell are you doing here?" the officer had said. "You know you'll get killed for being here, for being white. They'll shoot you dead."

McMahon had said no, he hadn't known that, and told the officer about the assurances Al Carter had given him and the other coaches, that Seward Park was okay to practice in as long as you did it before nightfall.

"Listen," the officer had said. "It's your life. You want to gamble with it, fine." As he drove off, a group of youths appeared across the field, and one of the Mau Maus said that it looked as if they were carrying guns. The Mau Maus left in a hurry, and they had no plans to return.

The last Kikuyus emerged from the Hooptie just in time for the opening ceremony. Scrupulously careful not to sully their hightops with fresh chalk, they formed a ragged column along the baseline, tugging at the unfamiliar cotton and craning their necks to see the ciphers on their backs. The honored guest, Jesse White, state representative and founder of a nationally famous tumbling troupe, stood between Al Carter and Bob Muzikowski. Muzikowski wore a T-shirt that read "Jesus is my hero." Carter wore his umpire regalia. As league president, he had designated himself to handle the Kikuyus–Mau Maus game.

". . . And someday," White concluded his short speech, "maybe some of you will be playing in the major leagues. Who knows?"

Then he threw the first pitch, a one-hop fastball that skidded past the catcher. A crowd of maybe fifty people, made up mostly of the four teams that had early games, applauded.

Brad waved the Kikuyus together and called out the lineup. "Freddie, leading off, pitching. David, batting second, first base. Jalen, batting third and catching . . . uh, backcatching. Maurice, cleanup, centerfield. Harold, fifth, shortstop. Nathaniel, sixth, second base. Alonzo, you're seventh, third base. Rufus, double cleanup, right field, and Calbert, batting ninth, left field." He stopped. "Where's Calbert?"

"Here I am." Calbert was sitting on the bench, right in front. Brad had not noticed him because he had on a thick blue winter jacket, buttoned up to his chin, and black stonewashed jeans over his uniform pants.

"It's cold," he explained. Before Brad could say a word, Calbert reached into his pocket and handed him a small blue cylinder—his inhaler. "Brad, will you hold this in case I should have a fatal asthma attack?"

"Sure," said Brad, pocketing the item. He turned to Louis, Demetrius, and Otis, the three bench players. "Everybody plays today, guys."

"No, thanks," said Louis, pulling a hooded gray sweatshirt over his uniform. "I don't feel like playing today, anyway."

Brad nodded—no time to cater to Louis's moods. He walked down the dugout, trying to move the starting lineup on the field.

"Harry, how come your pants are falling down?"

Harold wore his uniform pants in the fashionable sag

style, the elastic waistband pushed a good four inches below the waist, exposing a pair of red briefs and forcing him to walk in a stiff-legged waddle.

"That's my look," Harold said. "You watch, Brad. Pretty soon everybody on the team be doin' this."

"Fine, Harry. Until then, pull your pants up so you can run."

"His name *Harold*!" yelled Jalen from behind the catcher's mask.

Harold pointed at Jalen. "He don't know 'Harry' is short for 'Harold.' " He patted his coach on the shoulder in a brotherly way. "You can call me Harry, Brad."

"Good." Brad turned toward the bench and spotted a vaguely familiar face—Feets, a Kikuyus coach from the previous year.

"Hey, hey, Opening Day," said Feets, sticking out his hand. "Whaddya say, Coach Brad?"

Feets, whose real name was Dave, had been a camp counselor with Bill, and now was known mostly for throwing fantastically large parties in his apartment above a bar in Lincoln Park. Feets hadn't shown up for any practices or meetings so far this year, but that wasn't unusual. Like some of the league's coaches, he had a reputation of being long on enthusiasm but shorter on follow-through. Bill could remember cooking and hauling canoes at camp while Feets and the kids played hide-and-seek.

"Hey, Coach Feets," Brad called. "Tell you what, why don't you—Calbert! Right field is that way!—why don't you warm up our pitcher."

"Yeah, no problem." Feets jogged into the dugout to grab a glove. A moment later he returned.

"Uh, Brad, who'd you say was the pitcher again?"

"Freddie."

"Yeah, right." Feets looked around. His voice dropped. "And he is . . ."

Brad pointed. Freddie sat on the bench, tugging at his pants, which were obviously too big for him. He had rolled the waistband several times, and they still hung like diapers.

Freddie looked up at his coaches. His brow was furrowed with the intense concern of a nine-year-old. "Do I look retarded?"

"You look . . ." Brad searched for the word. "You look the opposite of retarded. Now let's go."

When the Mau Maus saw the fat little boy in the too big pants take the mound, they laughed and said he looked like a buster. When the fat little boy struck out the first two batters, both looking, the laughter stopped. Freddie didn't smile after either strikeout. Freddie never smiled when he pitched.

"C'mon, guys," yelled the Mau Maus' coach, McMahon. "Let's get around on this guy."

Brad was happy that Freddie threw strikes. Defensive vigilance, it was apparent, was not among the Kikuyus' initial strong points.

"Calbert!" Brad shouted midway through the first inning. "Stand up!"

A moment later. "Harry! The game is over here!"

"His name Harold!" yelled Jalen.

"Rufus!" Brad pointed. "Take your glove off your head!"

Freddie ended the first by blowing a fastball past the third hitter and stalking off the mound, a cool hitch to his stride. Brad clapped him on the back, and the rest of the team filed in behind, businesslike and silent. Freddie had struck three batters out. That was expected. He did the same to everybody in practice.

"Way to go," said Brad, trying to drum up some enthusiasm. "Let's get a few runs now."

"Yeah, guys," shouted Feets, slapping hands. "Let's rip this guy."

The Mau Maus' pitcher, a tall, reedy boy named Lavar, who had replaced one of the boys kicked off the team, had a harder time than Freddie finding the strike zone. In warm-ups, he tossed one halfway up the screen, raising catcalls from the shorties clustered behind the backstop. They sensed weakness, and pounced.

"Man, Lavar a *buster*!"

"Old boy Lavar ain't got no heat. Man, they gonna whack his stuff."

One boy raised a chant, and others joined in: *Rally, rally, the pitcher's name is Sally. Rally, rally, the pitcher's name is Sally.*

"Man, look at him!" Alonzo chimed in. "He more of a buster than Louis!"

Louis, sitting at the end of the dugout with his gray hood over his head, pretended not to hear.

"He even more of a buster than *Cal*bert!" said Alonzo, on a roll.

"You the buster, Alonzo." Calbert shot his teammate an angry look.

Buster or not, Lavar made it through three innings allowing the Kikuyus only three runs, a two-run homer by David and a single and three stolen bases by Jalen. Alonzo, swinging from his heels, hit a double in the third, but Rufus, who had been on first, overran third base—he didn't know he couldn't—and was tagged out to end the inning. The rest of the team was swinging at balls well out of the strike zone and barely managing indignant looks as Al Carter called them out with his booming baritone.

The Mau Maus, in the meantime, had divined that their best offense was crouching as low as possible and hoping for a walk. In the top of the third, they scratched across two runs on three walks and a single that went under Harold's glove.

"Buster, buster," chanted the shorties.

"Maaaaan! Shut up!" yelled Harold.

As the Kikuyus went to bat in the bottom of the fourth, they were leading 3–2, with Rufus, Calbert, and Freddie due to bat. The mood in the dugout was dim. Jalen had announced already several times that they were going to lose because there were "too many busters on this team." Maurice, who so badly wanted to win, appeared on the verge of tears.

"Carter's *cheatin'*," he said, pointing to the umpire. "He call all the strikes on us and none on them." Other players nodded in agreement. At the end of the dugout, Feets was teaching Louis how to juggle.

"All right," said Brad, gathering the three batters around him, looking into their eyes. "I want you to do one thing," he said. "Watch the ball—just watch the ball."

Rufus walked on a three-and-two count, trotting so happily to first that he forgot to drop his bat. Calbert likewise walked. Freddie, swinging mightily, struck out, but then Harold cracked a three-run homer, Jalen walked, Maurice hit a fly ball that went for a two-run homer, and the rout was on. The Mau Maus threw their gloves in frustration and the chants of the shorties behind the backstop grew louder.

"Brad?" Louis waved his coach to the end of the bench for a private conference.

"If I changed my mind," he said carefully, "if I wanted to play, when would I get to?" His words carried a slight lilting sound, as if he were humoring his coach.

"Right now," said Brad, scanning the dugout. He knew the Little League rule: Every player must play at least two innings of each six-inning game and receive at least one at-bat. He did a quick inventory of who had missed the most practices. "Bat for Alonzo."

Alonzo, his helmet already on, looked up. He had singled the last time up, and hit a double, the farthest hit of his life, before that. His butterfly luck was working perfectly— and now he had to sit? So buster Louis could play? He ripped the helmet off and frisbeed it across the dugout, where it narrowly missed several heads.

"That's *it*, Alonzo." Brad grabbed his arm and shook him. "Sit down, *now*. You throw anything else, and you're out of here."

Alonzo shrugged out of Brad's grip and stalked to the far end of the dugout.

"Y'all gonna do me just like you did last year." He talked into the chain link, his voice thick and wet. "Tell me I'm gonna play and then pull me out and let a little buster play. Same as last year. Always *lyin'* to me."

He sat in the spot Louis had vacated, and would talk to no one, not even Maurice, who stopped by several times to inquire what was the matter. After a while, Alonzo surreptitiously sucked his thumb. "I got a cut on it," he announced when he saw Feets looking at him. "This keeps it from getting infected."

The rest of the game slid by quickly. David pitched a hitless final three innings, hit another homer and a triple, and proved himself an able coach on the field, repositioning the outfield for certain hitters. Lavar and his successors had little luck stopping the onslaught. The final score was 17–2. When the Kikuyus lined up for the customary postgame handshake, Alonzo started to walk away.

"Alonzo!"

It was Al Carter. Enlarged by the pads and covered in dust, he towered over the boy. Alonzo slouched, avoiding Al's gaze.

"I gotta get home," he said. "My mom said to go right home."

Al ignored his story. "What's *with* you today? You play a good game and then you pout like a little baby 'cause you get taken out? Get your *ass* over in line and shake hands."

Alonzo shook his head sadly, as if he knew how deeply Al had been deceived. He joined the line, but he wouldn't shake hands. He walked past the other players, his thumb in the corner of his mouth like a dollar cigar.

After observing the exchange, Brad walked over. He did not know Al well, but knew who he was.

"What's with him today?" Brad nodded toward Alonzo.

"Who knows?" Al washed his face with dusty hands. "You know about his father, right?"

"No." Brad stepped closer.

"He just got sent up for killing that white woman on Wells Street." Al's voice was flat, matter-of-fact. "He got ninety-eight years, I think."

Brad had indeed heard of it. Most everyone in Chicago had. In April 1991, after leaving her Old Town apartment building to walk her dog, a thirty-two-year-old woman was abducted, robbed, and then shot in the back of the head and left for dead in an alley on Wells Street, a few blocks from the Gold Coast. She remained in a coma for three days, then died. Within a few days of the shooting, a $50,000 reward had been offered for information leading to the killer's arrest, but there were no immediate breaks in the case. As time passed, pressure mounted for the police to find the Wells Street killer. "Every breath he takes," wrote one local newspaper columnist, "is an insult to the memory of his victim." Brad remembered the woman's image from the news: dark eyes, straight auburn hair, utterly beautiful.

It was with great fanfare that four months later police made an arrest—a thirty-four-year-old parolee with a record for petty crime and burglary. Less had been heard about the recent trial, in which the accused had been convicted on all counts, to the great relief of Gold Coast and Old Town residents.

"You're kidding," Brad said, looking at Alonzo, now with the team in the dugout.

"Cats get shot here every day, and there ain't nothing in the paper. One white girl get smoked, and it's all over the place. I guess that's just the way things is." Al shrugged. "I gotta go, gotta pick up my daughter from the library."

Brad nodded good-bye, and that he had to get going, too. He turned to the dugout, where most of the players were gathered, each creating his own highlight film. Bats and helmets were scattered everywhere. Feets had disappeared.

"Man!" said Maurice, pantomiming a swing. "I was *whacking* it to the gate!"

"Y'all check mine and see what a *real* homer looks like," said Harold, his eyes widening to saucers. "See old boy diving out the way so he don't get kilt."

"Just like my first game last year," said Alonzo. "Homer and a double to the gate."

"You did not," said Calbert suddenly. "You got a *single* and a *double*. Then you sat the bench and cried like my baby brother, and he only *two*."

Alonzo kept smiling, but his eyelids dropped. "Homer and a double to the gate," he said, and walked away.

Nine hours later, Maurice stood at home plate on the northeast diamond, waggling a blue bat and looking out to the mound. It was past eight o'clock now, and Opening Day had ended. The afternoon had turned hot and dry, burning away the clouds and loosening the fine dust of the infields, which now hung in the air like mist. The Acuras, Saabs, and Audis had driven off long before. Now there were only kids.

"Come on, Freddie, gimme your heat," Maurice yelled, corkscrewing his black XJ-9000s into the dust at the front of what should have been the batter's box, had any chalk remained to mark it. "I fittina whack it to the gate."

Freddie's attention, however, was occupied by a basketball game being played across the street. He stood quietly on the mound, his doe eyes squinting in concentration, his oversize red Chicago Bulls T-shirt blowing around his generous belly like a sari, his head canted to the side. The action on the courts was out of time with the sounds that floated across the outfield—the tiny popping of the dribbled basketball hitting pavement and the more audible clank of ball against rim. As he watched, Freddie's body moved in sync with the players, bobbing and weaving, and when a distant ballhandler faked a jump shot and drove the lane, so did Freddie, leaping up from the mound with the baseball cradled in his palm, then slamming it through an imaginary hoop. His work accomplished, he returned to earth and looked down at the ball and at the crater it had made in the dust. He kicked at it.

"Come *on,* man!" Maurice shouted.

"Maaaan!" Freddie used his all-purpose response, which in this case translated to: Hang on a second.

Maurice rubbed a dusty hand over the bat, clearing off its barrel. The battered aluminum thirty-incher, which he'd found under the El tracks the summer before, was his prize possession. Its handle was bare of tape and its surface had hundreds of tiny dents the size of teeth marks. Whenever he couldn't come up with a league ball or a tennis ball, Maurice hit rocks.

With slow, elaborate formality, Maurice steadied himself and went through the ritual: tapping the bat on the outside edge of home plate, pointing it toward the pitcher, then moving his hands in a practiced waggle, transforming himself into the gently rocking image of Andre Dawson.

Freddie settled himself on the mound and went into his glare. The few kids left in the field stopped to watch. Freddie's brow furrowed and his cheeks puffed out. He kicked and threw.

"Steeeeuuhhh-rike one!" shouted Demetrius, mimicking Al Carter's deep voice.

"Shut up, Demetrius," Maurice mumbled. He ran quickly through his ritual and took up his stance again. Freddie kicked and threw.

This time Maurice connected. The ball arced toward shallow left field, and he tracked it with words borrowed from Cubs announcer Harry Caray. "It might be . . . it could be . . . *it is!* Another home run for Maurice Dawson."

Even as the ball disappeared in a spray of dandelions, Maurice was well into his home-run trot, stomping in the spots where the bases should have been, carrying his bat with him, his fingers wound tightly around the barrel.

Freddie stood on the mound for a while, momentarily distraught that someone was able to hit his heat. But then he noticed some boys lobbing rocks at the passing El train and ran off to join them.

Maurice, his victory lap complete, decided to celebrate. He jogged over to his brother, who had been watching silently by the right-field fence.

"Rufie, you wanna go to Chester's and get some pizza?"

It was phrased gently enough, but to quiet, demure Rufus, the question held great portent. The two were standing on Sedgwick Avenue. To the north was home, where their mother, feeling ill, had gone several hours before; to the south was the alluring smell of Chester's Pizza. Over it all hovered their mother's three Nevers: Never run with a gang, never be caught out after dark, and if you see anything bad happen, never tell nobody but her about it—not even the police—because somebody might try to hurt you.

"Mama say we gotta get home right after the game." Rufus's voice rose to a whine. "We can't be gettin' no pizza—it gettin' dark."

"We go back soon," said Maurice, his hand automatically contracting into the gesture he made when persuading someone to do something: thumb and third finger touching, other fingers splayed; a thoughtful gesticulation resembling an "okay" signal. He nodded into his hand, affirming its authority. "Mama would want us to get some dinner anyway."

And he was gone across the glass-strewn sidewalk toward Division Street, swinging his bat like the cane of an English gentleman. Rufus hung back for a few seconds in silent protest, then ran to catch up, casting a backward glance toward home. They walked briskly, Rufus a half-step behind, Maurice tapping the head of his bat on the sidewalk and enjoying the sugary crunch of the glass beneath. They were a few steps from Division Street when they heard a voice.

"Hey, lil boy."

The two stiffened, but kept walking as if they hadn't heard. Maurice stopped tapping the bat and held it close to his leg, hoping whoever was talking to them wouldn't see it.

"Hey, lil boy," said the voice, "lemme use that bat for a second."

It was coming from the other side of the street. Maurice and Rufus picked up the pace. They were a few yards from Division Street, next to Carson Field's southwest backstop.

"Hey, lil boy!"

A girl was moving toward them in an urgent trot. She placed hands on passing cars as she crossed the street. Two other girls were with her, but they did not cross. Maurice and Rufus had never seen any of them before.

She was fourteen or fifteen years old but made up to look older. She wore red corduroy overalls and had her hair tied up fashionably with hundreds of red heart-shaped plastic beads. She stood more than a head taller than Maurice.

"Lil boy, you lemme borrow that bat and I'll give you some money," she said. Her voice was friendly, almost sisterly. "I give you a dolla."

"Come on," one of her companions yelled. "Ain't got much time."

A glance up the street told Maurice why the girls were in such a hurry. They were Forty-Ouncers, members of a girl gang from south of Division Street, and they were about to fight another girl gang, the BTPs, at the empty lot across the street from the baseball field. The Forty-Ouncers ("They have to drink a forty-ounce malt liquor bottle to join," Maurice explained) and the BTPs ("Big-Time Pu . . . you know what I'm gonna say," said Maurice) had formerly been Folks, but the Forty-Ouncers recently flipped, or switched alliances, providing the motive for this particular gathering. While not nearly as common as the boy gangs, girl gangs were becoming more so in Cabrini. Police didn't have much of an explanation, except to say that the girls were imitating the boys and they had the advantage of being able to haul guns and drugs without fear of being searched unless there was a female officer present, and there usually wasn't.

All at once, the girl in red was standing over Maurice

and reaching out her hand like a prim schoolmarm. She was utterly self-assured. "I don't want to have to take yo bat, lil boy, but I will if you make me."

"You can't have it." Maurice gave a weak smile and dropped his head, sending a message different from the words he spoke. The girl was bigger and heavier than Maurice, and she had friends with her. There was no sense in his protesting. She grabbed the barrel and with a quick twist wrenched it out of his hand.

"Thanks," she yelled as she ran away, the red hearts clicking in her hair. "I give it back, I promise." She laughed.

Maurice watched his bat go across the street, where the girl rejoined her friends at the front of the northward-moving group. He didn't say anything. The assemblage looked strangely pretty—tall, strong people in bright clothes, walking toward one another confidently, their shadows stretching across Sedgwick and onto the baseball diamond.

The two groups stopped a few feet from each other in front of a small brick-and-wood warehouse on the corner of Scott and Sedgwick. The building, flanked by empty lots, stood as a relic of the neighborhood's earlier days, its jaunty lines vaguely recalling an Old West storefront. The sign in front announced: "Ideal Provisions." After some posturing and shouting, two girls started a mild tussle on the building's doorstep. On the field, mitts and bats thunked to the ground as a handful of kids ran to the fence to watch. On Division Street, a police car passed. It did not stop.

Suddenly, one of the BTPs, a statuesque girl in stone-washed jeans, broke from the fight and ran west, behind the warehouse. Three Forty-Ouncers from the south, one of them the girl in red, put on the chase. The boys lost sight of them behind the bricks.

"Man!" Maurice grinned excitedly. "They gettin *into* it!"

The girls hadn't reappeared yet when the cry went up. "She gotta gun, she gotta gun!"

The girls now came into view, moving fast. The tall BTP,

the one in the lead, was running low to the ground, weaving purposely from side to side. She had put some distance between herself and her three pursuers, who were frustrated by her speed. Then one of the Forty-Ouncers, a chunky girl in black Bulls sweats, raised her arm and—*crack*—a puff of smoke came from her fist.

At the sound of the shot, everything stopped. Nobody ran, nobody screamed, nobody hit the dirt. Everybody just crouched a little, partly in self-defense but also in anticipation, waiting to see if someone fell.

No one did. The girl in the lead kept running, rounded a fence, and disappeared across the basketball courts. Everybody then shifted to face the girl in the Bulls sweats. She didn't look at anybody, but coolly tucked the gun in her pocket and walked slowly back to where her gang had gathered. There was no reason to run—no Slick Boys were around and everybody knew that none would be called.

Without taking their eyes off the girl with the gun, Maurice and Rufus backed slowly through the gate onto the southwest diamond, walked across the field, and stationed themselves with a few other kids behind the backstop under the El tracks.

"Man, you see that girl run?" said Maurice. "She be *jettin'.*"

"I think I heard the bullet," said Rufus, hopping gently over a crack on the sidewalk. "It go *fooooosh,* like right past my head!"

"What, you never seen nobody do no *shootin'* before?" asked Demetrius's high-pitched voice. "Man, I seen that mess every day."

"Same wid me, homey," said Tyrone, a bigger kid who played for the Ibos. "That girl ain't got nothin' but a lil old two-two."

"Yeah?" said Maurice, trying to sound knowledgeable. "I seen plenty shooting, just never saw a girl shoot another girl before."

"*Right,*" said Jalen, igniting a vigorous debate among the boys over who had seen the most shootings.

"Man, I seen like ten, twenty people get shot."

"I seen my cousin shoot this boy three times, and the boy lived."

"One time me and my friend, we shot this gun. It was under the El and we shot a bunch of times, but there weren't but one bullet inside."

As the group argued behind the backstop, Carson Field returned to normal. Freddie hopped on a borrowed white bicycle and wobbled gently across the dandelions, chasing something across the outfield. Along Scott Street, next to the field, a child in a pink jumper was learning to walk by holding on to the fence surrounding bare patches on the sidewalk where flower beds used to be. Three girls in dresses walked by, carrying red carnations in clear plastic containers, boutonnieres for prom night. A voice came from behind the ballplayers.

"Reese, what we gonna do?"

It was Rufus, and Maurice knew why he was scared. On Sedgwick, right between the boys and their home, the BTPs and the Forty-Ouncers were still milling about. The fighting had stopped, but neither gang wanted to leave lest it be perceived as the loser.

Maurice looked around. The shadows of the Oscar Mayer factory had enveloped them, and it was getting chilly. Rufus hugged a fencepost next to the backstop, his yellow windbreaker buttoned up around his doughy face, his eyes shining. Right now he seemed much more than three years younger than Maurice.

"We'll get home," said Maurice, giving his "okay" sign. "We'll figure something out."

Demetrius spoke up. "Climb the Oscar Mayer fence—you can outrun them fat-ass security guards."

"Nope," said Jalen, dismissing the idea with a contemptuous flick of his head. "Buster Rufus probably gonna trip and get caught." This looked like a distinct possibility. Jalen continued: "Go Scott to Wells, Wells up to whatchacallit North Avenue, then go back down Sedgwick. That get you home." He turned away, satisfied.

"That like a hundred *miles*, Jalen," said Maurice.

Tyrone, the big kid, said that they should just walk right past, that nobody would mess with them. "I stick out my chest and give them my crazy eyes."

Maurice finally settled on a route of his own devising: east on Scott to Wells, south to Division, and west to his grandma's apartment at 1150–1160 North Sedgwick. That was the Emp's building, and things were usually quiet there. They could hang out until their mother came to get them.

"Let's go," Maurice said, peeling his brother's fingers from the fencepost.

Just then, Freddie pedaled up, moving fast. He threw the bike into a skid and leaped off.

"I seen your *bat,* Reese—some girl be walkin' with it, *there.*"

Maurice followed Freddie's arm to the basketball court, where a tall figure in red walked slowly, swinging a bat.

"Come *on*, man!" Freddie stamped his foot impatiently. "Let's get it!"

Maurice looked at Freddie, at the girl, then at his brother. "Nah—I don't care about that bat, anyway," he lied softly. "I gots lots more of them at home."

JUNE

We come from the streets, raised in the projects,
Ghetto Land was the type of scene,
I lived, now I'll die, for Cabrini-Green.

From "CABRINI-GREEN," by the Slick Boys, a rap group made
up of Public Housing North police officers

ONE

By the second week of the season, the initial bloom of dandelions had blown away and been succeeded by cottonwood seeds. Few cottonwoods grew in Cabrini-Green, but many grew in Lincoln Park, a well-groomed strip of softball fields and jogging trails a half-mile to the northeast. The seeds rode over on a lake breeze, their unruly gossamer lining the gutters and encircling the damp rims of drinking fountains. In empty lots and alleys, other colors were showing: the white of Queen Anne's lace, the bright yellow stalks of goldenrod, and everywhere, the tiny blue flowers of chicory, which the native Indians once harvested and dried for tea. Beneath a sidewalk grating on the northwest corner of Carson Field, sharp young leaves of aspens and elms poked sunward.

One Monday practice, Coach Bill showed up uncharacteristically late. His face revealed nothing unusual, but, his silence made apparent, he was not in the best of moods. Business at North Pier had been slow. Though Bill's duties had recently expanded to selling retail space, prospects were so dim that the joke around the office was that he would be forced to change his title to "Retail Leasing Aspirant." He took some comfort in the fact that things were tough all over town, but he was going to have to scramble to make a decent commission this year.

His parents' divorce, too, was growing more complicated. Unable to divide family assets on their own, Bill's mother and father had turned the matter over to lawyers, who were now in the midst of a lengthy bartering session. The wait wouldn't hurt his father, who worked, but Bill's mother was anxious to settle and get on with her life. To help move things along, Bill decided to play a bit of emotional hardball. Whenever his father called to ask him to lunch or golf, Bill would ask coolly whether "this thing with the lawyers" was settled yet. As of early June, Bill and his father, never that close to begin with, hadn't seen each other in many weeks. "He gets the idea," Bill said.

At least the team was doing well. The Kikuyus were 2–0, having beaten the Linnco Futures Group Mandinkes 21–13 the previous Thursday. As the score indicated, it hadn't been a particularly pretty game. David had shown up late, so Freddie started on the mound. He fanned three in the first inning—it was becoming a custom for him— then proceeded to forget where home plate was, at one time walking five batters in a row. Led by Jalen and Harold, the other players grumbled, pointed fingers, threatened to quit. But helped by the good examples of David and Maurice, the coaches kept things under control long enough for the Kikuyus to score nine runs in the third inning. For his part, David hit two homers and closed out the game by pitching two hitless frames.

"Good old David," Coach Brad had said after the game. "Riding to the rescue again."

Now Bill stepped out of his car and pulled the equipment bag from the trunk. "Maurice," he said without looking. Maurice got out of the driver's seat and shut the door.

The Kikuyus had developed a loose routine in their last several weekly practices. First they played catch—or tried to—for fifteen minutes or so. Next, if there were enough coaches, they divided into two or three groups and worked on fly balls, grounders, pop-ups, bunting, baserunning, and whatever else was needed, players rotating between stations every few minutes for an hour or more. If, as happened today, there weren't enough coaches, they would play "situation ball," in which a full defensive lineup played "innings" against a coach who hit grounders and fly balls from home plate. Then, with a half-hour or so left, batting practice would begin—ten swings apiece—and continue until dark.

Within the team, a two-caste society had become fully operational, and the divisions were apparent as practice began. Along the first-base line, standing a few feet from each other, were the Busters: Rufus played catch with Nathaniel; Louis with Alonzo and Calbert. Scattered in the outfield, the Home-Run Hitters threw to one another: Freddie and Jalen; Maurice and David; Otis and Demetrius. The code of conduct was clear, as if it had been written down.

One: A Home-Run Hitter never warms up with a Buster, and vice versa. When an odd number of either group showed up, the affected parties had to enlist a coach or play three-way catch.

Two: Busters never play pitcher, first base, backcatcher, shortstop, or center field. These positions were strictly for Home-Run Hitters, who could be relied on to catch and throw the ball with some degree of reliability. Busters played second base, left field, occasionally third base, and always right field.

Three: Home-Run Hitters must actually hit home runs. It did not matter how a home run was achieved, only that it was achieved. Harold, for instance, had perfected a technique in which he simply never stopped running, no matter where he hit the ball. The excited opponents would invariably overthrow him at two or more bases, and he would coast home as if he had whacked one over the Sears Tower.

Four: A limited amount of mobility between the two groups is permitted. Many Home-Run Hitters reflected nostalgically to the year before, when they, too, occasionally struck out. ("It's all right, Rufie," Maurice told his brother during the game with the Mau Maus. "You know, I was a buster, too.") Conversely, a Buster could, through repeated success, improve his rank, but if he should ever meet with repeated failure, he would be returned speedily to his former lot.

Bill and the other coaches took measures to mix up the two groups, but the task was difficult. In soccer, football, and even basketball, coaches can camouflage shortcomings through numbers and judicious positioning. Little League baseball is different, undemocratic, unforgiving. Every child must stand at the plate alone and learn not to flinch as a ball is thrown near, and furthermore hit that ball so that it eludes the eight players arranged with the sole strategic goal of returning the child to the dugout heartbroken. Every child must learn to place himself in direct line with a skittering ground ball that could, at the touch of a pebble, undergo a painful change of course. In some ways, a Little League baseball diamond is nothing more than a cruelly public magnifying glass, beneath which normal differences in coordination and strength appear monstrous. "Cricket's easier," Alonzo observed. "The bat's flat, and you can hit it anywhere."

As Bill put the team into position for situation ball, Alonzo sought to improve his tenuous standing by pointing out the entire Buster clan taking the field.

"There Nathaniel Buster, there Rufus Buster, there Louis Buster and Calbert Buster," he said, his long finger aiming at each in turn. He looked at Bill accusingly. "Your team gonna lose, because you got too many busters."

"Every team has busters, Alonzo," Bill responded.

"Oh no, they don't," said the ever knowledgeable

Alonzo. "Some teams don't. *Pygmies* don't. *Bant*us don't. Ewes don't. *Everybody* want to play for the Ewes."

Bill didn't say anything, because Alonzo was right. Those three teams, at least this early in the season, looked like the class of the league. Bob Muzikowski's Pygmies and the Continental Bank Bantus had trounced their first opponents by several touchdowns, as had the defending champion J. P. Morgan Ewes. All three teams practiced three to five times a week. In their most intense week, the Kikuyus had practiced twice.

"Take third, Alonzo," Bill said, turning his attention to Coach Kevin, who was just walking onto the field. Bill reached into the equipment bag and tossed his roommate a bat. Kevin caught it by the barrel.

"Jet lag's not gonna keep you from hitting a little infield, is it?" Bill asked with a grin.

Kevin, who had returned from his three-week trip to Spain the night before, stepped quickly toward home plate. "Okay," he shouted, instantly all business. "First inning, nobody on, nobody out—where's the play?"

Like Bill, Kevin liked taking control of things. His job was teaching logic seminars to businessmen, most of whom were twice his age. Since his appearance hadn't changed much since his graduation from Yale a few years before—straight, unruly brown hair, off-center grin, clean-cut features that fit under the general category of all-American—he sometimes faced touchy situations at the outset of the $5,000-a-week seminars. "At first they look at me and I can tell they're thinking, 'I've got a son your age,'" he said once. "But when I get going with the message, they forget how old I am. The message is what's important."

On the baseball field, Kevin was the most vocal and active of the Kikuyus' coaches. Though his traveling made him regularly miss games and practices in his two seasons, he would always return from a trip as if he had never gone away, waving kids into position, shouting instructions with his sandpapery voice, and running a drill that in some ways symbolized his relationship to the team: With as many as three balls at once, Kevin would throw grounders and pop-ups to four or five players arranged in a semicircle around him, then catch from them, and toss again the instant the balls were returned to him, flicking them casually between his legs and behind his back, dazzling the players with what amounted to a skillful juggling act.

Now Kevin took his place in the batter's box, shoul-dered the bat, and hit a hard, skidding grounder toward first base. Freddie slid over, plucked it on the short hop, and jogged over to the bag with nonchalance.

"Okay, one out, nobody on." Kevin swung, and a slow roller made its way toward second base. Not moving his feet, Rufus bent his knees, lowered his body, and stuck out his left arm as if setting a trap. After a few long seconds, the ball rotated into his glove.

"*Charge* that ball, Rufus," said Kevin, pantomiming a run. "By the time it gets to you, it'll be a triple." Rufus smiled and shrugged, and rolled the ball back toward home plate.

"Man on first, one out." Kevin slapped a bouncer to David at shortstop. The big kid glided over, scooped, and in one smooth motion stepped on second and whipped the ball to first so hard that it almost took the glove off Freddie's hand.

"Great play," Kevin shouted. "New inning now. Nobody on, nobody out." The ball scooted toward third, where Alonzo had arranged himself in his distinctive ready posi-tion: back straight, legs like a wicket, knees bent, heels raised high enough to roll a golf ball beneath his Air Forces. As the grounder neared, he thrust his glove downward and tilted his chin upward simultaneously, somehow grabbed the ball, and lobbed it across the diamond to Freddie on three bounces.

"Nice scoop, but I think the runner beat it out."

"Thanks," said Alonzo, all confidence.

"Man on first, nobody out." Kevin skied the ball to left

field. Nathaniel, wobbling violently, stabbed and came up with the ball.

"Yeah . . . *yeah!*" he danced about, holding his prize aloft.

When Nathaniel was finished, Kevin shouldered the bat. "Okay, one out, man on first." He was about to hit when he noticed his right fielder facing the wrong way.

"Hey, Louis"—Kevin cupped his hand—"game's over here!" Louis didn't move, his hand on his hip. Kevin could tell that he had heard. *"Okay, one out, man on first. Who's ready?"*

Kevin swung and sent a line shot toward right field. Louis turned, located the ball, then tried to scramble out of the way. But he was too late. The ball bounced once and clipped his leg, and he fell heavily to the ground. He lay there, not moving.

"You okay there, chief?" Bill, who had been playing catch with Otis, walked to the outfield while Kevin continued to hit.

"If having a *broken leg* is okay, then I am," Louis said bitterly, readjusting his glasses. He stood up, and went into a greatly exaggerated limp. "I *told* him not to hit me any balls."

"This is practice, Louis," Bill said evenly. "You *have* to field some balls. How about if we put you in the infield?"

"Nope."

"Backcatcher?"

"Look at old buster baby limpin' around, man. Louis *gay.*" Demetrius, a late arrival, stood at shortstop, pointing. Bill gave him a look, and Demetrius turned away.

"How about first base?"

"Nope."

"Center field?"

"Nope."

"Louis, what would you like to do?" Bill never sounded exasperated, but this was close.

Louis cocked his head. A faint smile. He obviously enjoyed this.

"I think," he said in a singsong voice, "that I'll go home and eat some chicken."

The Sky Men were trailing the Brain Damagers by thirty-one points with only nine seconds left in the game. Eagle, the Sky Men's guard, inbounded it to his team's best player and namesake: Sky Man. They had one more chance.

The commentator's voice came on, hushed with excitement. "Sky Man brings it up the court, guarded by Hammers. Hammers is on him, tries to foul, but Sky Man is too quick—he jumps over him and crosses the time line. Three seconds left. He head-fakes, then takes off! He's . . . he's . . . he's gonna try the thirty-two-pointer! This is the whole ballgame!"

Sky Man leaped and, without looking, tossed the ball against the wall, did a 360, and bounced it off his head. The ball went into the basket, almost popped out, and fell back in.

"Yessss!" the commentator crowed. "Sky Man drains the thirty-two-pointer, and the crowd is going crazy! Our final score today: Sky Men ninety-nine, Brain Damagers ninety-eight, and the Sky Men stay undefeated in the LBL!"

Louis extracted the Nerf ball from the laundry basket and smoothed the dent in his hair. That would be the last game of the day for the Louis Basketball League, and he was grateful. Playing Sky Men games always tired him out. They always came from behind at the last second, and sometimes he had to shoot the thirty-two-pointer six or seven times—getting fouled on each attempt, of course—before it fell.

"Louis." It was his mother's voice. "Please keep it down in there. Your father's trying to sleep."

"Okay." Louis was used to that. His father often napped between his job and night school. In sock feet, Louis padded out of his room and into the living room, to his computer. His feet slid easily on the blond hardwood. There weren't many walk-ups on Hudson Street nice enough to have smooth hardwood floors, and Louis was glad his family lived in one. It was like living on a basketball court.

He pulled his swivel chair over, removed the plastic dust cover, and booted up the Commodore SP-9000. It whirred and clicked, and soon the stats were on the screen: point totals, signature shots, even hometowns and salary information for every player on the twenty-six LBL teams. The Sky Men held first place with twenty-one wins and no losses, followed by the Champs, the Lasers, the Zooms, the Dark Nights, the Brain Damagers, the Blastomatics, the Extinguishers, and eighteen others. Green numbers glowed as Louis tapped in the point totals for this last game and updated the standings.

He had received the Commodore for Christmas a couple years back. Occasionally he used it for book reports, but its main function was to monitor the activities of Louis's two leagues: LBL and FSB—Football, Soccer, and Baseball, a combination sport played with a sock and an orange plastic bat. For both the LBL and FSB, Louis was the players, referees, TV announcers, spectators, team owners, and commissioners. He needed the computer. There was a lot to keep track of.

"The teams are always changing, because the coaches play dirty," he explained. "If they want a player, they just pay him more zaphers—that's equal to a thousand dollars—so a team might steal players from another team for a big game. It's just like real life."

Louis was also a budding musician. Four years before, his mother had bought a used forty-nine-key Casio electric piano down at the Maxwell Street market for thirty-five dollars. She had intended to learn how to play herself, but Louis soon was spending whole days in his room, headphones on lest he disturb anyone, noodling around and puzzling out songs. Music came easily to him. By the time he was ten and a half, he could hear a song on the radio and fifteen minutes later resurrect it in full, including harmonies. When he turned eleven, his mother, over his strenuous objections, had signed him up to play in the church combo on Sundays, and the organist had been so impressed with the boy's abilities that she gave Louis free lessons. "You keep at it," she told him. "You got some good spirit in them hands."

In the past year or so, Louis had become a small sensation in his neighborhood church. He played two services every Sunday, resplendent in a white tuxedo with robin's-egg-blue trim, soaring through "I'm on the Battlefield for My Lord" and "Blessed Assurance." Lately, his mother had taken him to play at other churches. The response was always the same—they loved him. After he played at one political rally, his picture appeared in the pages of the *Chicago Defender,* a black-owned newspaper. In the photograph, he was seated at the organ, atop the small pillow his mother always brought for him, his glasses reflecting the flash bulb's light. Louis sealed the clipping in plastic and kept it in a small vinyl folder on his desk. He didn't show it to anyone.

Since his church, like most area churches, was attended mainly by women and elderly men, Louis's musical abilities remained hidden from neighborhood kids. He preferred it that way. On Sundays, he would leave for church early, carrying his tuxedo in a brown paper bag. He flinched when old women stopped to pat his cheeks on the street. As Louis became more involved with music, his mother noticed him drifting from his friends and beginning to take an almost perverse pleasure in not fitting in. He still didn't mention his music to anyone, but he was far less shy about other matters: he bragged about his computer and his video games, showed off his fashionable clothes, openly eschewed street sports in favor of his imaginary leagues. Louis spent more time alone in his room, playing music into his headphones. Some days he never left the house.

In 1991 his mother had bought him a glove and signed him up for the new baseball league. She thought it would help him make new friends. But things hadn't worked out as well as she'd hoped: Louis struck out most of the time and the kids called him a buster. He was so embarrassed that halfway through the season he informed his parents that they weren't allowed to come to the games.

Coach Cort once asked Louis who his best friends were.

"I don't have any. My best friend is my piano." Louis didn't say it as if feeling sorry for himself. He was just stating the facts.

On this day, as Louis typed the updated LBL statistics, then waited for a printout, his concerns lay with the Sky Men's next game, and more specifically with one of their new players. His name was John, and he was only twelve years old. John was short and couldn't jump as high as the rest of the players, so most teams figured him for a buster. But he was fast and smart, and had a special move, the flash, where he ran from the kitchen fast as lightning and shot the ball real low, so no other player—not even Sky Man himself—could touch it. Nobody in the league took him seriously yet, but Louis decided that young John might surprise them all.

TWO

 Greg White was pissed. Not only had Al Carter faxed a memo announcing the league's trip to Operation PUSH headquarters directly to the coaches, but he hadn't consulted a soul before doing it. To Al, arranging league events was his inalienable right as president. But to Greg, the commissioner, Al's fax was a breach of protocol, through which the person in charge of all activities and communication—namely, Greg—was reduced to gleaning information secondhand from puzzled individuals who had the indicator light on his voice mail winking like a strobe.

What's going on? the coaches wanted to know. What's this People United to Save Humanity thing on Saturday? Why wasn't it on the schedule you sent us? Are we really going to have to forfeit games if we don't attend? What's Al Carter doing?

Greg returned the calls promptly, as he always did, and did his best to put a good face on the matter. "We got our wires a little bit crossed there," he told each coach with a

chuckle. "The PUSH event is totally optional, so don't
worry about forfeiting any games. And don't worry about
pushing back Saturday's games—no pun intended—they'll
all go on as scheduled. Carter? Don't you worry about Al
Carter. We'll get things squared away."

Bob Muzikowski was in New York on business, but his
wife had received similar calls from coaches. She phoned
Greg, and they agreed that something had to be done. They
would hold a meeting, and tell Al face to face that he
couldn't go outside the league's organizational machinery
and order people around as if he still were running this out
of the back of his car.

"This is an organization," Greg told Tina passionately.
"People have got to follow the rules if this thing is going to
work."

The night after the faxes had been sent, Greg phoned Al
and told him that the league's six-member board would
meet to discuss the PUSH event at eight on Thursday
morning, after Bob had returned from New York. Greg
didn't want to cause a stir, so he didn't let Al know how
upset everyone was. Al said he'd be there, and that was the
end of the conversation.

If there was anything Greg White abhorred, it was disor-
ganization. Each element of his life was carefully planned
to minimize inefficiency and maximize productivity. He
worked as a real estate lender partly because it was strictly
eight-thirty to five, no weekends, no surprises, nothing that
might have interfered with his teaching at Keller Graduate
School of Management, his meetings of the Harvard Business School Club of Chicago, his work with the Lakefront
Single Room Occupancy Corporation, a not-for-profit bet-
ter-housing agency, and his mornings with the Saturday
Enrichment Program, in which he accompanied underprivileged kids to various cultural events. Greg did not
watch television. His mother had given him a set two
Christmases back, but it remained in its box in a closet in

his apartment. To quote Habit 3 from his well-thumbed copy of *The 7 Habits of Highly Effective People:* Put first things first.

Greg had joined the Little League during its first year, and had ascended gradually from volunteer coach to Bob Muzikowski's right-hand man. With his starched shirts, clear voice, and karate-chop gestures, Greg assumed control of league operations, playing air-cooled administrative machine to Bob's inspirational fire. Two months after the first season ended, Greg already had put the final touches on a two-page document that outlined the league's goals for its second year, and constructed a "critical path," a month-by-month list of objectives that took the league from November ("Collect roster of coaches and sponsors; plan Christmas party") to September ("Closing ceremony; send thank-you letters to sponsors").

"Were the pyramids built by disorganized people?" Greg once asked at a meeting, smoothing his crisp tie with his left hand and karate-chopping with his right. "If you're gonna do something, you got to do your homework"—chop—"you build a plan"—chop—"and you stick to the plan"—chop, chop. "The rest is easy."

Before the start of this season, Bob had been on the lookout for a new league president. Al Carter, in the opinion of Bob, Greg, and others, had proved to be a less than ideal manager of coaches, and might serve the league better in another capacity. Bob could have done the job himself, but as he put it, "having a white guy out in front might not play too well in the neighborhood." He finally had arrived at a candidate: Greg White, the twenty-eight-year-old success story, the kid who had used the gospel of organization to pull himself out of working-class Baltimore to Brown University and Harvard Business School. Though some in the league thought him longer on ideas than on follow-through ("He'll draw up ten flow charts, and then, when things go wrong, he'll draw up ten more," said one coach), Bob wasn't concerned. He had big plans—a near doubling of the league's size, the purchase of a van, team outings to an Iowa camp, a parent-run refreshment stand, portable toilets—and plenty of volunteer muscle with which to accomplish them. Flow charts, he could use. Earlier in the season, Bob had met with the league's five-member board, and everybody, including Al Carter, had agreed that Greg should be president. A few days later, however, everything had changed. Al telephoned Greg and told him he had reconsidered: He would remain president.

Nobody had known what to do, and when Bob tried to change Al's mind, things turned nasty. "He told me he wasn't going to turn over the league to some Harvard-educated Oreo from downtown," Bob related. Angry, but unwilling to alienate his founding partner, Bob hit on a compromise. Al would continue as president, but his duties would be altered. He would oversee all board meetings, run the weekly self-awareness educational program, and in a more informal way, employ his neighborhood expertise to make sure that Carson Field remained insulated from gang violence. Greg would occupy the new office of commissioner and run the day-to-day operations of the league. In addition, Bob helped raise several thousand dollars to arrange for a church-employed community organizer named Bill Seitz to serve as Carson Field's groundskeeper and organize the league's nascent tutoring program. According to this scheme, Al was still running the league in the big sense, but the key resources—the volunteer coaches and the sponsors—would be in Greg's hands. "The bottom line on Al," Greg explained, "is that he would make a much worse enemy than he would a pissed-off ally."

Aside from May's fracas over the African-American Liberation Day parade and the Christian baseball clinic, the new framework had functioned reasonably well. Al seemed secure in his new role, adopting even more of a hands-off policy than Bob had anticipated. Al missed most of the meetings—the Department of Human Services had reassigned him to a four-to-midnight shift—but he assured

Bob and Greg that whatever they did was fine by him. "We're getting along fine," Greg had said in early June. "Al's laying back, and it seems good for us and good for him."

Now, as far as Greg and the Muzikowskis were concerned, the Al problem had resurfaced. In his fax and his announcement at a sparsely attended coaches' meeting he called a few days before, Al had communicated a few details about the Operation PUSH trip, describing it only as a "youth day" and a "cross between a rally and a prayer meeting." In their haste to react, neither Greg nor Bob had made any effort to find out more about the event. All they knew was that Al was making demands.

"A few of the coaches—and some of them are black coaches—don't necessarily agree with Operation PUSH's politics," Greg said the night before the board's emergency meeting with Al. "The rest of the coaches probably don't give a damn—but that isn't really the point. The point is that you've got to have respect for people's time and you've got to have things organized, you've got to interface and motivate and inspire, not demand at the last minute. If Al had come before the board two weeks ago and told us exactly what this event was about and why the league should be there, then maybe we'd tell the coaches to support it. But you can't keep calling a fire and hoping people jump. This time the league isn't jumping."

Tina Muzikowski, waiting at home for Bob to return from New York, felt the same, but for different reasons. "These people volunteered to be baseball coaches, not to be part of somebody's agenda. We can't let Al just trot this league out on a stage and take credit for it all."

Bill Seitz also was angry with Al. The previous week had seen several gang-related scuffles at Carson Field that Bill attributed partly to Al, or more precisely, to his absence. "Where was he?" he had said after the latest incident, waving his arms. "I thought this stuff was his department. It's been weeks since he's been out here—somebody better remind Al that he's the president of this league."

The Muzikowskis had been receiving calls from a

handful of coaches who urged them to stand up to Al, to stop letting him ruin a good baseball league. These coaches, mostly friends of theirs, listed slights large and small: Al's criticism of the volunteer coaches in a *Tribune* article; his attempt to commander for his foundation the leftover chicken from a year-end banquet; his calling a coach a racist; his claiming sole credit for the league in a speech at the previous year's banquet. One coach, the Ibos' Keith Melanson, told Tina that he was considering pulling his team from the league if these "distractions" kept up. Few of the callers had gone so far as to confront Al directly, but to their thinking, it wasn't necessary. They had been in the league for more than a year now. They had seen the way things worked, and the solution to the present problem was clear: Stop dancing around Al, and acknowledge what everybody already knew, that the league would be better off with Bob calling the shots. A wave of indignation and anger was building. "These are successful people who didn't get where they are by screwing up," Bob said. "They're not going to stand around and let somebody call them racist and not do anything about it."

Of course, not every coach felt that way. Some, including the Kikuyus' Bill, felt the disputes were overblown, and worried that personality clashes were getting in the way of the league's true objectives. "A visit to Operation PUSH? What's the big deal?" Bill said. "If Al says it looks good, I'm willing to believe that he knows more about these things than I do. Put the kids on the bus and have them back in time to play the games, that's all."

Other coaches, particularly the black coaches, were more tolerant of Al because they recognized something in him. "Al's been working in the neighborhood for a long time," said Charles Hudson, coach of the Ewes. "He's seen a lot of racism, and it's made him into a fireball. It's a generational thing that a lot of black men my father's age have. They've been fucked over, they're being fucked over, and they don't want to take it no more."

But on the night before the meeting, no one on the

league board was interested in discussing character. "Tomorrow we'll have an honest talk," said Greg. "Al appreciates honesty, and that's what we'll give him. He can get all his accolades and take all the credit he wants. But when it comes to running the league, he's got to lead, follow, or get the fuck out of the way."

Bob and Tina Muzikowski, running five minutes late as usual, hustled toward Bob's highrise office on the morning of the meeting. As they entered Northwestern Mutual Life's eighth-floor suite, they ran into Al Carter walking out. Greg White stood behind him, exasperated.

"I do not *need* this aggravation," Al said loudly, heading for the lobby.

"*Whoooa,*" said Bob, setting down his briefcase and putting his hand on the shoulder of Al's black sweatsuit. He spoke softly. "Whatever it is, Al, we can figure it out. Let's make this thing work, okay? Are we going to make this thing work?"

Al looked straight ahead and didn't say anything. He and Greg had been arguing since they rode up in the elevator together. Greg had begun by telling Al that he couldn't order the coaches around without giving them the necessary information. Al had told Greg that he was the president of this damn league, and he wasn't going to buy his corporate bullshit. Things had gone downhill from there.

"Bob, I'm glad you're here." Greg smoothed his tie and forced his voice into a friendly tone. "We were just having a discussion about what the procedure should be to have the league attend an event."

"Procedure, my ass," spat Al. "The procedure is that I'm the president of the league, and I've lived in this neighborhood my entire life, and this is a good event for the children to attend, and the coaches should support that. And if they don't, those cats can go back downtown or to Kenilworth or wherever the hell they belong."

"You can't just *do* that," Greg said. "You can't just snap

your fingers and have everybody put everything on hold. This is about respect—respect for people's time."

"I don't have time for this," said Al. "Are we done? I got to go pick up my daughter."

Now Tina spoke, raising some of Bill Seitz's concerns about violence. "What about the Maasai, Al? They're afraid to come to their games because they're being threatened. What will you do about them?"

Al dismissed it with a wave. "The Maasai aren't committed. Their coach has to show them the way."

"Their coach is Mike Martin, a neighborhood guy." Bob's voice was low, insistent. "The kids are scared out of their fucking minds. This is what we talked about at the beginning of the year. This is where you have to step in and take charge. Like you said, you're the president. Right?"

"I got to go pick up my daughter. I'll look into it."

"All right, man." Bob offered his hand, and Al took it. Bob said later that he saw tears in Al's eyes. He couldn't tell whether they were from frustration or some other emotion. Al did not wipe them away, and he walked out.

Greg, Bob, Tina, and Bill Seitz stayed behind and talked. Among other things, they affirmed that the Operation PUSH trip was strictly voluntary, and that the day's games would go on as scheduled. If Al didn't like it, Greg said, he was free to scream and yell all he wanted, because it wouldn't make any difference.

THREE

On the Saturday of the game against the Ibos, Coach Cort arrived at Carson Field at two-fifteen. He usually didn't show up forty-five minutes before game time, but today was different. With Kevin out of town, Bill squeezing in a nine-forty-five tee time at Skokie Country Club, Cort was the only coach available for warm-ups. "Why don't you get there early, so you're not fooling around with all the equipment when the kids show up," was how Bill had put it. It hadn't been a question.

Cort pulled the equipment bag from the trunk of his car and tossed it over his shoulder. He was accustomed to the weight. Though a divinity student nine months of the year, Cort worked summers at a wealthy suburban golf course, playing counter jockey and pursuing his ultimate goal: the Professional Golfers Association teaching certification, which would entitle him to give lessons. He had some work to do: the requirement for certification included two consecutive tournament rounds under 150. Cort's best two rounds totaled 156. "I always choke," he explained with characteristic self-deprecation. "I get close and then I don't know what happens—I just fall apart."

Walking onto the field with the equipment bag slung easily on his shoulder, Cort didn't look quite like a golf pro. He wore black Chuck Taylor hightops, oversize khaki shorts, and a raggedy white T-shirt with a picture of a man stomping on a fish. His longish blond hair was pushed into his eyes by a white baseball cap, and his face bore the usual sleepy-eyed expression that once inspired Alonzo to compare Cort to Huckleberry Hound. On an unused corner of the diamond, Cort dumped out the bag. The few early arrivals, Maurice, Rufus, Nathaniel, Demetrius, dug out balls and gloves.

"Awright, guys," Cort said with his flat Kansas drawl. "Let's get this thing going."

As the kids scattered, Cort saw Coach Brad's Hooptie pull up on Scott Street. Having another coach was a big relief. Cort had never been any good at ordering people around. During practice he would let Bill, Brad, and Kevin do the yelling and run the drills. He preferred to float, act as unofficial Buster Coach. He would shamble up to a distraught player, draw him into conversation, and escort him to the outfield for a private lesson. There he would lob balls and ask questions. Is it better to keep your glove wide open while you catch, or close it some? Is it better to step toward the pitcher when you swing, or better to step away? "I know the right way to do it," he said, "but I want them to figure it out, so it means something."

Some friends thought it odd that a low-key guy like Cort would live with Bill and Kevin. Indeed, there were times when Cort felt overshadowed by the other two, with their high-power jobs, their Ivy League connections, their hypercompetence at everything they tried. But Cort didn't want to compete. He went the other direction, losing himself in his books—Sartre, Vonnegut, Heller; once, after reading *The Sun Also Rises,* he drank nothing but Spanish red wine for a week. He liked big questions, and these were what drew him to divinity school; sometimes the same questions were a source of mild friction around the apartment. "You say you like something, and Cort always wants to know why," Kevin commented. " 'Why this, why that . . .' I don't know—I just *like* it!"

As Cort turned to greet Brad, a loud yell came from home plate. Demetrius stood there, his bat frozen in follow-through, a line drive headed directly for a group of Busters playing catch.

"Nath—"

Nathaniel turned but saw the ball too late, and it hit his upper arm with a sick thud. He dropped instantly and writhed in pain, his eyes squeezing out tears, grass sticking to his yellow jersey as he rolled. With the clinical detachment known only to children, the team gathered around him to reenact the scene.

"Man," said Harold. "He walk right *into* it." He performed a Chaplinesque waddle across the infield, eyes cartoonishly skyward. *"Bam!"* Harold fell and wriggled.

"Yop," said Jalen. "He a buster, walkin' all over like that."

"My fault, Nathaniel," said Demetrius. That was as close as anybody on the team ever got to an "I'm sorry." Then he leaned over, excited. "Hey, you think your arm busted?"

Brad waded into the group.

"Freddie, Harry, Jalen! Demetrius!" honked the Maine foghorn. "Everybody take a step back and give your teammate a little room, please!"

Cort didn't say anything. He knelt next to Nathaniel and rolled him on his back. He unwound the boy's fingers from his injured arm, felt where the ball had hit, and ever so gently moved the arm back and forth. In a voice not much louder than a whisper, Cort assured Nathaniel that he would have just a little bump, nothing more. As Brad forcefully ushered the rest of the team back to their games of catch, Cort put his hands under Nathaniel's arms and lifted him up, and they went for a walk down to the water fountain so no one would be able to tell that he'd been crying.

* * *

The Griffin, Kubik, Stephens & Thompson Ibos had a 2–0 record, sharp red-and-white uniforms, and the league's finest repertoire of dugout chants ("Who's gonna win? *Eebows.* How do you spell it? I-B-O"; then their variation on an L.L. Cool J tune: "Who's gonna knock you out? Ibos gonna knock you out"). They were coached by Keith Melanson, a handsome bond salesman who had large pectorals, a six-foot-tall blonde fiancée, and a well-deserved reputation as one of the league's more competitive coaches. On David's third warm-up pitch before the game, Melanson was already nearing the Kikuyus' dugout, jaw firmly set, clipboard in hand.

"All right, gentlemen," he said knowingly. "Let's see the birth certificate. That guy looks old enough to drive the team bus."

Bill, who had expected as much, pulled out an insurance form David had brought to the game. Melanson took a close look, smirked, and flicked it back at Bill.

"If he's going to fake it, he should at least try to do a good job. Birthdate's penciled over. He can't play."

Bill looked. Melanson, damn him, was right. The month had been changed clumsily from a 7 to a 10. Bill didn't say anything for a moment. Then he waved David, who had been intently watching the exchange, to the bench and brought Freddie in to pitch. Bill and David talked awhile, looking at the insurance paper, and David began to cry. Bill patted him on the shoulder and returned to the other coaches.

"He did it," said Bill, sighing through his nose. "He says he only missed the deadline by a few weeks, and didn't want to move up to the older league. But he's got nothing to worry about. He's good enough to more than hold his own with the big kids."

"He will," said Cort, "but what about us?"

"Maaaan!" yelled Jalen, having sussed out the situation

from his backcatcher's position. "We gonna lose now for *sure.*"

As illegal players were a leaguewide problem and there was no system in place for documenting players' ages, the Kikuyus weren't at risk of forfeiting the wins over the Mau Maus or the Mandinkes. But the Ibos game was another matter. Freddie, discombobulated by the switch, walked eight batters in the first inning and gave up two doubles as well. By the time the Kikuyus returned to the dugout, they were looking at a score of 8–0 and their best player was sitting at the end of the bench in shame, his wet cheeks slowly drying in the sun.

"Why they *do* that?" asked Maurice. "How come they take David away?"

"Who's gonna knock you out? Ibos gonna knock you out," came the chant from the other dugout.

"Why they *do* that?" repeated Rufus, nearly in tears himself. "They *cheatin'.*"

"Don't let 'em do that, Bill," said Harold. "Half they team thirteen anyway—make them prove how old they is."

"Ibos gonna knock you out."

"Maaaan!" yelled Jalen. "We *definitely* gonna lose!" Jalen's wrath was directed not at David, but out toward the street, where a small figure in a Miami Hurricanes jacket pedaled a white bike toward the Kikuyus' dugout.

Jalen turned to Bill, finger aimed accusingly at the newcomer. "Y'all *better* not let him be playin' in this game."

"Samuel is on the team," Bill said evenly. "Everybody who is on the team gets to play."

"Then this team *phony!*" Jalen stomped off, the catcher's chest pad swinging on his narrow frame. Bill could hear him mumble.

"Big-nose, Big Bird, pigeon-neck . . ."

"Don't forget 'Baldy,' " Bill called cheerfully, pushing back his hair to show his scalp. Jalen had come up with that nickname the previous practice.

"Baby!" Jalen shouted.

Samuel braked next to the dugout and hung his fingers

on the fence. He carried a ragged left-hander's mitt whose webbing was held together with a shoestring. His bike was an ancient Huffy. Its broken spokes twanged lightly against the chain link as he rocked back and forth, waiting.

"Hey there, chief, how you doing?" Bill grasped the fingers and gave them a friendly shake.

"Fine," said Samuel, looking at the ground.

"Hey, guys, why don't you say hello to your teammate, Samuel," said Bill.

"Hey, Samuel," greeted Maurice.

"My name's Calbert, but you can call me Ice T., because my middle name is Tyrone," said Calbert.

The other players didn't turn around.

"Samuel, where you been?" Bill's voice was light and easy-going, as if Samuel had been missing only a few minutes, not the first six weeks of the season. "You've been getting our calls, right?"

Samuel looked at his thumb. A small, ragged cut, pink and oozy, ran along his knuckle. He picked at it with his teeth, nibbling off a thin fringe of whitened skin, and his brow creased with three deep lines. Samuel's face hadn't yet lost the attractive geometry of an infant, with its high forehead, big cheeks, small mouth, and fawnlike, velvet-lashed eyes. He would have been extraordinarily cute, except that he never smiled; his expression tended more toward blankness. As he gnawed his cut, he did not narrow his eyes in concentration, but kept them wide open.

"Well," Bill said. "It's good that you're here now. Since you missed practice, you won't be able to play the whole game today, but don't worry, we'll get you in there."

Brad dug uniform number 13 out of the Hooptie's trunk and Samuel wheeled his bike to the end of the bench, where Alonzo was explaining to Cort why he preferred menthol to regular cigarettes.

"It's more *smoother*," said Alonzo. "It goes better with my coffee."

"How many packs a day do you smoke, Alonzo?" Cort asked with a smile.

"Two . . . make that three," said Alonzo. "They don't let us smoke in school, so I usually have a few before I go to bed."

"Oh." Cort never could really tell when Alonzo was exaggerating, and he had stopped trying to figure it out. "What do you think, Samuel?"

Again Samuel said nothing.

"All right, guys," Brad announced. "Freddie leading off, Jalen on deck, Maurice in the hole."

"We gonna looo-oose," said Louis in his singsong.

"Yop," said Rufus. "They *cheatin'*."

"I think I gotta go home," said Nathaniel. "There's a show I gotta watch, and it starts—"

"Coach Brad, I have a question," Bill interrupted with concern. "Isn't it still the first inning?"

"Why, yes, Coach Bill, it is the first inning," said Brad, slipping into vaudeville delivery.

"That's good, because I couldn't figure out what these guys"—Bill gestured broadly toward Louis, Rufus, and Nathaniel—"are talking about. According to the rules, we do get six at-bats in this game, right, Coach Brad?"

"That's right, Coach Bill," said Brad. "Eighteen outs."

"Well, I'd say that anybody who thinks we should give up now is a little bit mistaken, wouldn't you?"

Louis, Rufus, and Nathaniel were quiet.

"We *still* gonna lose," yelled Jalen. "You want to bet me a slice of pizza?"

Bill's answer was obliterated by the boom of a passing El train.

Freddie and Jalen started the bottom of the first with infield singles. Maurice slapped a hard grounder that rolled past the right fielder for a three-run homer. Harold followed with one of his patented never-stop-running, three-overthrow specialties, and suddenly it was 8–4, nobody out, and everybody was yelling.

"Yeah, boy!" Freddie danced in the dugout, teeth and eyes flashing. "Gonna whack, whack, whack their stuff."

"Let's go now." Bill stood up on the bench to get a better view.

Louis, who had struck out or walked in every at-bat for the first two games, approached the plate gingerly. He shifted his weight from one foot to the other as if the dirt in the batter's box were heated.

"Coach?" It was Samuel, tugging at the hem of Bill's shorts.

"Just a sec, Samuel." Louis swung and missed the ball by a foot. "Hang in there, Louis," Bill called. "Hit it if it's there."

The pitcher wound and threw.

"Coach? My daddy die."

Louis swung and, perhaps for the first time in his life, made contact. The ball trickled toward shortstop, and the dugout erupted.

Bill didn't see. He had stepped down from the bench and was looking at Samuel. He put a hand on the boy's shoulder.

"Run!" the Kikuyus screamed at Louis, who was frozen in the batter's box. Having never hit the ball before, he did not know what to do next.

Bill took Samuel to the end of the bench and they sat down. A moment later, Louis returned to the dugout trying hard to feign anger. He had been thrown out at first, and now he slammed his helmet down and dramatically refused the coaches' congratulations.

"My daddy die," Samuel told Bill softly. "That's how come I don't come to practice."

"When did it happen?"

"A while ago." Samuel's big eyes looked straight ahead. "Mama say he got the HID, like Magic Johnson."

"Oh." Bill nodded. "You doing okay?"

"Yop," Samuel said, looking down.

"Your mother doing okay?"

"Yop."

There was a long silence.

"If you, uh, need anything, you got my number, right? It's on that list we gave you."

Samuel nodded.

"Okay, chief. You hang in there, okay?"

Bill walked to the other end of the bench and quietly motioned for the coaches to gather. He gave them the news. Brad and Cort glanced at the far end of the bench, then tried not to. A few minutes went by. The inning ended without the Kikuyus' scoring any more runs. The team returned to the field.

"Hey, Samuel." The big eyes looked up. It was Cort, hat askew, Chuck Taylors untied, popping a ball into a glove.

"If you're gonna play, you better get that arm of yours warmed up," he said, smiling. He reached to the bench and tossed Samuel his glove.

The game ended with the score 17–11 in favor of the Ibos, and the mood in the Kikuyus' dugout was sour. A group of Home-Run Hitters gathered around Bill.

"*Man,* Bill," said Harold, his saggy pants, long torso, and tiny legs recalling a funhouse-mirror image. "You *know* that I should be the one pitching. I whacked the most homers of anybody on this team, and that means I'm the *best.*"

"We two-and-one, and without David we ain't *never* gonna make the playoffs," said Jalen. He pointed at the end of the bench. "How come I can't pitch when you let buster Samuel play and he don't even be comin' to *practice*?"

At the mention of his name, Samuel looked up. He had substituted for Calbert halfway through the game, and when he had gone to hit, the umpire had to show him how to hold the bat. He struck out once and walked once, and had shown no expression either time. But he had smiled a little when he had played catch with Cort, and when he had thumb-wrestled with Brad's girlfriend, Dianna.

"Hold on a second, guys," said Bill. "This is a team game. The best player out there doesn't mean anything unless he's got eight other guys ready to back him up. It takes everybody to win."

From his usual spot at the end of the bench, Louis listened approvingly. Besides his first-ever contact, he had played a nice game in right field, hustling after balls with a speed that made the coaches forget his old heel-toe, Tin Man running style.

"When's next practice, everybody?" Bill cupped a hand by his ear.

"Monday, six-thirty," several voices chanted.

"Monday, six-thirty," Bill repeated, making sure that Samuel heard.

"Six . . . six-thirty," he said, getting on his bike and pedaling slowly away.

The Monday after the game against the Ibos, Samuel got up early and went to buy honey buns. It was always better to go early, when there was less chance of shooting. Samuel hauled his bike down the dark stairs, pointed it toward Elm Street, and pedaled fast.

He was a good pedaler. When he was little, he said, he thought he could pedal faster than bullets. He knew that wasn't true now, not after the past summer. He had been sitting in his beanbag chair, watching *Fresh Prince,* and the bullets had come through the window, missing him by a few inches and ricocheting off his door. He had told everybody at school about it, mimicking the sounds. *"Placka-placka-placka—ping ping ping!"* He liked making the *ping* sounds.

For almost as long as Samuel could remember, he had lived in the Castle. When he and his mother and sister, Gloria, had first moved in, five or six years back, there had been a lot more kids to play with. Now there were only ten families left in the whole building, and the shooting was nearly constant. Sometimes, at night, Samuel would get out of bed and sleep against the wall, turning up the volume on his TV to block out the noise. When things got bad, his mother sometimes talked about moving to the South Side, where she had relatives. But they never did. Her chronic asthma, which kept her housebound for days at a time, would have made a move too much trouble and expense. Besides, as Samuel's mother was quick to point out, things in the Castle weren't that bad. They were only a block from school. Samuel and Gloria each had their own room, their own TV, and though they couldn't play much outside, they could go on the ramp anytime they wanted, except at night. Gloria had a boyfriend who lived in the building, a sixteen-year-old who bought her clothes and who sometimes would buy Samuel "suits"—shirt, shorts, hat, and jacket for each of the various teams. Samuel had the Miami Hurricanes, the Georgetown Hoyas, and the Michigan Wolverines. Sometimes Gloria's boyfriend would call him Little Brother. Samuel liked that.

Samuel didn't like going to school. Just getting there was a little scary. Edward Jenner Elementary School was on Oak Street, a boundary between Folks and People turf. To compensate, the school was careful to keep its students' comings and goings arranged by gang affiliation, using separate entrances and allowing teachers to divide their classes during fire drills: People out one door, Folks out another. Many of its teachers were talented and committed professionals, and theirs was not an easy job. When shooting started, classes were held in the hallways. Substitutes occasionally abandoned their classes in mid-morning, overwhelmed by the task of keeping order. Two veteran eighth-grade teachers had had a running bet that none of their students would get shot or pregnant, but they recently had stopped betting after neither had won in a decade.

A year before, when Samuel was in third grade, his teacher had discovered that this quiet, big-eyed child could neither read nor write, and had placed him in a special class. Samuel liked the class, but it lasted only one or two hours a day. The rest of the time, he sat in his regular classroom. He rarely did any work, and he didn't have to: school district policy did not permit learning-disabled students to be failed. So he spent his days doodling and pretending to do work. He especially liked drawing the number eight with two circles around it, so that it resembled an eight-ball. Eight was the best number, Samuel decided, because you could never confuse it with another. Even if you turned it upside down, it was always the same.

Feet circling furiously on the pedals, Samuel spun down Elm to Orleans, made a right, and headed for Hipp's and the honey buns. When he got there, however, something felt wrong. He dismounted and approached the entrance warily.

"What happen to the sto'?" Samuel asked.

The Arab shopkeeper was sitting on the steps with his head in his hands. Beneath him lay a brightly colored carpet of Twix, Butterfinger, Twinkie, and Now and Later wrappers, all attached seamlessly to the concrete, as if heat-pressed on. Behind him, the heavy accordion security door had been pulled from its moorings, and the doorknob had been wrenched off, so only a small disk of jagged metal was left. Inside, behind Plexiglas-and-wire security partitions, shelves stood bare except for broken glass, crushed boxes, and garbage.

"What happen to the sto'?" Samuel asked again.

"They came in, they smashed everything, they cleaned me out," said the shopkeeper, not looking up. "Total loss."

A white van was idling at the curb. "WBBM, Channel 2," read the side panel. A handsome, slightly pudgy reporter stood near it, tapping a cordless microphone and glancing occasionally at his watch. Samuel could see red and black wires emerging from the reporter's navy sport coat and running to a circuit board on the side of the van. Atop the van was a retractable antenna encircled by an orange cable as thick as a python. With a light hum, the antenna came to life, rose up several feet above the van and pulled the orange cable with it. Now everything hummed and thumped, and the red and black wires vibrated and sent tiny ripples up the all-weather polyester of the reporter's sport coat. Samuel's eyes widened. It seemed the man might explode.

Just then a group of girls from five to ten years old arrived. They stepped past the reporter with seasoned disdain and poked their heads inside the store.

"Yop—they got him, too," said the lead girl, who wore pink flowered shorts and orange plastic sandals. "Man, they got all the sto's."

"Yop," said a chubby girl with glittery silver fingernails. "They got the sto' on Chicago Avenue, they busted the window at Chester's, they got all them sto's on Larrabee. I heard they even got the Jewel's."

"They din't get Sammy's," said the girl in orange jellies, referring to the hot-dog stand and liquor store on Division. "Sammy got him an Uzi behind the counter."

"Who done this?" Samuel asked the girls. He had heard a lot of shooting and yelling the night before, but not much more than usual for a Sunday.

"Boy, you don't know nothing, do you?" said the chubby girl, waggling a finger at Samuel. "Bulls won the championship last night, beat the Blazers. People be celebratin' and trashin' things."

Samuel frowned. The riot after the Bulls' victory—a citywide affair causing $10 million in damage—was bad news. He wanted his honey buns. He would buy four or five at a time and hide them in his clothes drawer, beneath his underwear. A couple of weeks before, he had eaten four honey buns. His mother had yelled at him when he tried to bring one to his Aunt Patricia's funeral. She had died of kidney failure, but Samuel told his friends that she had been shot in the back of the head by robbers. He liked that story better. It seemed as if everybody he knew was sick.

An elderly bearded man walked up to the entrance of the store. He wore a green T-shirt and black nylon sweatpants. Samuel had seen him around before, usually with a bottle in a paper bag. But today his eyes were clear.

"Mornin', ladies," he said, doffing a blue baseball cap. "Shouldn't you be at school this time of day?"

"We *outta* school, old man!" shouted the chubby girl. The others laughed, egging her on. "Where you supposed to be, you nappy-haired gray-headed fool?"

A little taken aback, the man dropped down on one knee, removing his cap and running his fingers through his silvery hair. He put his face squarely into the face of the girl.

"I suppose what you say is true, my hair is nappy and a little gray. But you got to learn one thing, girl. You got to learn respect. If you was mine, I'd . . ."

"I'm not yours, so you best shut your mouth," shouted the girl, the words bubbling out as she and her friends ran away, laughing wildly, jellies slapping on the pavement.

The old man replaced his cap and turned to enter the store. He looked at the wreckage, then at the shopkeeper, and shook his head.

"Man, they shouldn'ta done that." He patted the shopkeeper on the arm. "I don't like to see that, no, not at all. You run a good store, and they shouldn'ta done that."

The shopkeeper, his head still down, nodded.

"Yep, there's no way they shoulda done that," the old man said. "I don't like to see such a thing."

The newsman motioned to his cameraman, who was inside the van, to get a shot of the exchange.

Then the shopkeeper got up, saying something softly. Samuel couldn't hear what he said, but it made the elderly man start up suddenly.

"No, no, *no,* that ain't right," he shouted. "I ain't *looking* for no handout."

"All right, all right." The shopkeeper made a pacifying wave, but the other man would have none of it.

"That's the *problem* with you people—you don't ever listen."

"All right, okay." The shopkeeper kept waving. He wanted the man to be quiet and leave him with his ruined shop.

"No, it *ain't* all right, and it ain't never gonna *be* all right until you start *listening* and we get *along*." The cameraman scrambled out of the van, shouldering his machine and pressing buttons.

"All right, all right." The shopkeeper's voice was soothing, agreeable, tired.

The old man threw up his hands and stalked down the street. The camera clicked on and followed him until he disappeared.

"Shit!" said the newsman. "We didn't get the good stuff."

Samuel stayed for a while longer. Sammy's would have honey buns, he knew; they were kept out on the counter, next to the cash register. He couldn't go straight there, of course—he would have to ride around to Wells, then double back along Division. He looked up at the sun. It was getting to be a hot day, and he knew that by the time he got them, the honey buns would be melty and he would have to lick the plastic to taste all the sugar.

FOUR

As coach Bill drove to Carson Field on Saturday morning, he was thankful that the Ambrosi & Associates Hausas were next on the Kikuyus' schedule. After losing David, it would have been risky to face the Pygmies, Bantus, Ewes, or another of the league's juggernauts. The Hausas were a different matter. They wore friendly orange uniforms and had managed to come through all of their first season without winning a game. But their head coach did not give up easily. After each of their five losses so far this year, Mike Wychocki had lodged vigorous protests with the league, claiming that the opposing teams had overage players.

"This guy makes Keith Melanson look easygoing," Bill told another coach. "What's he thinking—that he can win the championship by protesting every game?"

Still, this game wasn't a sure thing, not the way Jalen and Harold were behaving. If the Hausas jumped out in front, it was entirely possible that the Kikuyus could fall into a violent finger-pointing session and lose any chance for victory. Today's prospects weren't improved by the fact that because of an unfortunate alignment of work, golf, and travel schedules, Bill would be coaching the team solo.

As Bill parked his car under the El, he noticed Freddie playing catch with a young man on the field. Bill strolled closer, and recognized the man as Freddie's cousin. They had met before, toward the end of the past season. Bill remembered the scene clearly: the two leaning comfortably against a stoop at sunset, sharing a Little Hug and some chips. The cousin's name was Michael, and it immediately had been obvious to Bill that despite the difference in age—Michael was in his late twenties—he and Freddie were close.

"Who taught you to play ball, Freddie?" Michael had asked, gently nudging his cousin's leg.

Freddie had smiled, his fat cheeks dimpling. "You did, Michael."

"Who taught you to pitch hard, and to hit homers?"

"You did, Michael."

Michael had smiled proudly and run a hand over his cousin's close-shaven head. "That's right, man, I did."

Now Bill walked up behind him. "How's that fastball working?"

Michael turned around, his eyes flashing suspicion.

"Michael, right?" Bill extended a hand. "I'm Bill, Freddie's coach. We met last year."

"Yeah." Michael smiled, and they shook hands. "How you doin'?"

"Little hung over from last night." Bill stretched casually. "But not bad." Michael laughed and nodded sympathetically—same with him. They talked a few minutes, about the weather, the Cubs, Michael and Freddie's family, and then Bill made his move.

"Hey"—his voice went light and casual—"if you're not doing anything in half an hour, why don't you come over to the field? We're short a couple of coaches. . . ."

"Uh, I dunno, man. I got some things I got to do. . . ."

"No sweat," Bill said. Now he would have to play his

trump card. "Hey, Freddie," he called, "whaddya think about Michael coming down and helping us coach today?"

"*Yeah?*" Freddie smiled. "Mike gonna *coach?*"

When game time rolled around, Michael was standing next to Bill in the dugout. Even before the game was under way, he made his presence felt. When Jalen began bellyaching about one of Alonzo's throws, Michael silenced him with a look. When Nathaniel and Rufus kicked dirt at each other, Michael grabbed their jerseys and broke it up. Though Bill later had to point out to Michael that it wasn't sportsmanlike to shout that the opposing backcatcher was "fat and lazy," and thereby encourage the Kikuyus to steal, Michael was a fine coach—and as the kids actually did what he said, potentially invaluable.

The game went well. Maurice, finding his control, pitched a four-hitter, Louis made two plays in the outfield, and Demetrius whacked one to the gate. At Michael's urging, Freddie played backcatcher, and though there was a sticky moment when Mike Wychocki pointed out that official Little League Regulation 1.12 stipulated that the catcher be equipped with a catcher's mitt and not, as Freddie was using, a first baseman's, Bill, after rolling his eyes, had Freddie make the switch.

The game's high point came in the first inning. Up 1–0, the Hausas had runners on first and third with one out.

"Be ready," the Hausas' coaches yelled. They had taught the team the conventional Little League strategy for such a situation: The runner on first steals, attempting to entice a throw; if the catcher takes the bait, the runner on third goes home.

"Reese!" Freddie shouted from behind the plate. "Let's do that thing."

Maurice nodded knowingly. In the dugout, Bill observed the exchange with interest, unaware of their plans.

Maurice wound and threw, and the runner on first broke. Freddie caught the pitch, threw toward second, and the runner on third started home—then froze, realizing he'd been tricked. Freddie's throw had gone not to second, but to Maurice, who was now bearing down on the runner with a huge smile on his face. The Hausa tried for home, Maurice applied the tag, and the celebration began. The Kikuyus scored ten runs in the next inning and coasted on, 14–2. They were 3–1, back on the winning track.

"This is great," Michael told Bill. "I could do this every day."

"What do you think about coaching for the rest of the year?"

"I wish I could." Michael shook his head. "But I can't, man, I can't."

"Is there some other team that's giving you a better offer?" Bill smiled.

"Nah." Michael's sneaker scuffed the ground. "I got some things I got to take care of, some traveling. I ain't gonna be around much."

"Tell you what." Bill dug into his manila folder and pulled out a schedule. "Here's the rest of the games. Make whatever ones you can."

"All right."

The two shook hands, and as Bill put the equipment into his car, he could hear Freddie shouting up the street to an unseen friend. "Man, Michael, he gonna *coach*!"

In Cabrini-Green, as in many other inner-city areas, police and drug dealers alike keep track of the academic calendar. The reason is simple: When school ends, things change. Crime goes up. Gangs start recruiting. Grudges built up over the school year finally have a chance to be acted out. Heat forces everyone outdoors. Shooting increases. To those interested in maintaining some semblance of order, namely the Slick Boys and Rat, the last day of school marks the start of the most difficult, dangerous season.

School had been out only a few weeks, and already the body count was rising. On Saturday, June 27, a fifteen-year-old girl named Bonita Hemphill, by some accounts a member of the Gangster Disciples, was shot in the face after a sidewalk argument with a group of Vice Lords. The doctors saved her unborn baby, but she died. On the day of the funeral, police pulled over a carload of VLs brandishing shotguns; word at the station had it that they were headed to the funeral home to shoot the body. Shortly after the funeral, an ornate R.I.P. BONITA appeared in five-foot-tall spray-painted letters next to the entrance of her building.

Though three other people were shot the same day, Bonita Hemphill's killing did not ignite an all-out war, at least not right away. Everyone viewed this as fortunate, especially Rat, who was facing enough difficulty these days. The Illinois Department of Public Aid recently had announced that as of July 1, employable single adults and married adults without children would be ineligible for the $154 monthly General Assistance check. This essentially cut off the main source of income for most of the men in Cabrini and the junkies who were Rat's best customers. Not that the junkies had money to spare; many were usually on a hundred dollars of credit with Rat by the time the check arrived. Some had started using broken-off car antennas for crack pipes, stuffing the usual bit of Brillo pad into one end to recycle the vapors and provide an extra hit. Others dabbled in prostitution: a dime bag for a date. With no GA, things would be tight.

To compensate for the future losses, Rat was focusing more attention on the rowhouses and looking for occupied apartments that his lieutenants could use as bases for their sales. The arrangement with tenants was usually $200 a month, plus a few dime bags if they were users; the advantages were that selling in the rowhouses was safer and more lucrative than selling amid the highrises, where you always had to watch your back for Slick Boys and snipers. Already, Rat had one apartment set up on Cambridge Street, and it was clearing more than $1,000 on aid days. If the shooting was going to keep up in the highrises, the rowhouses were the place to be.

Relocation wasn't a simple matter. The rowhouses were partly the domain of T-Bop and B.O., free-lance GD dealers who ran small, private operations sanctioned by the gang leadership. The previous winter, just after being released from prison, Rat had gotten into a click with T-Bop over turf, and it had cost them both money. Now, on the eve of the General Assistance cutoff, they had learned their lesson. Rat moved in, and the free-lancers offered no resistance.

But in late June, Rat encountered a minor problem. He was pulled over on the South Side for a moving violation, and the police discovered six ounces of rock in his van. Bond was set at $75,000.

Then, within a few hours, Rat was back on the street. Police at Public Housing North figured that he had posted bond or, more likely, that he had worked the usual angle: giving up guns in exchange for the dropping of lesser narcotics charges, a trade made possible at least partially by the Chicago Police Department's rating system (which was not used by Public Housing North or any other Special Functions divisions). At the time of Rat's arrest, a single narcotics felony arrest was worth 5 points to the arresting officer; assault rated 10; sexual assault or armed robbery, 15. Recovering a gun from a building, on the other hand, scored the officer 20 points; from a vehicle, 25. Two days after Rat's arrest, police "recovered" four handguns from a rowhouse apartment; some fortunate officers received the point equivalent of sixteen narcotics felony arrests. While distasteful, the system embodied a powerful logic. If police didn't drop the charges, Rat would post bail anyway, and when the long and expensive trial was finished, he probably wouldn't serve any time. In this way, they could get some guns off the street and might save some lives. And though they didn't admit it, the police in Cabrini were somewhat relieved when they heard Rat was back. The neighborhood was perhaps safer with him in charge, rather than with a bunch of young gunslingers squabbling to be new top dog.

FIVE

"Sssshhhhh!"

Alonzo treaded stealthily toward the chicory plant, placing the reinforced rubber soles of his Air Forces on the larger chunks of broken concrete. Grasshopper Field held just enough concrete and rocks that you could walk without making a sound.

"How big is he?" J-Nice shifted sideways to see.

"*Quiet.*" A look of parental irritation creased Alonzo's face.

"*Maaaan!*" said J-Nice, bouncing up and down.

Alonzo shot him another look. J-Nice grew quiet. He had not been out to Grasshopper Field very often, but Alonzo didn't have time to explain everything.

Alonzo turned toward the spray of blue flowers that hid his quarry. This was the biggest grasshopper they'd seen, a full two inches long by Alonzo's estimation. He had spotted it near Oak Street and chased it over here into the center of the field, flushing it again and again from its hideaways. That was the good thing about this place: plenty of things to chase, and nothing that could chase you. What Alonzo called Grasshopper Field, a long strip of unsightly rubble and grass along Wells between Oak and Hill, was part of Cabrini's no-man's-land: too close to the project to be desirable and too close to the Gold Coast to be inexpensive. Alonzo and J-Nice came here whenever they could.

Alonzo raised his leg for the crucial final lunge, hanging his foot above a small chunk of rock, tilting it this way and that until he settled on the best angle. He could just make out the speckled cigar-shaped body amid the green stems.

J-Nice was unable to contain himself any longer.

"Get him!"

At the sound, the grasshopper bounced up, hovered briefly, and landed with a papery thwack beneath a big fern ten feet away. Alonzo turned around in disgust.

"Maaan!" he kicked at the ground. "You don't know *nothin'* about catchin' no grasshoppers."

"I do *so*. I kilt me sixty of them yesterday." J-Nice shook his butt in defiance.

Alonzo didn't argue. It was no use. The two had been together all day yesterday, and they hadn't come to Grasshopper Field. But Alonzo said, "J-Nice just don't listen sometimes.

"You got to learn to be quiet and fast, like me," Alonzo instructed. "Once I get out here in the forest, there's not a gangbanger who can catch me. I'm too *fast*. I'm too slippery."

J-Nice wiped his nose and looked concerned. "Is them gang-gangers fast?"

"Nope," Alonzo said confidently. "You just got to learn to dodge the bullets like I do." He crouched low to the ground and shifted back and forth quickly. "Like that."

J-Nice tried it, jumping wildly from side to side.

"Nope." Alonzo shook his head. "More *slip*perier, so they don't know you're dodging them."

J-Nice tried again, but his teacher wasn't watching. Alonzo was staring at the fern.

"Hey!" he whispered. "I see him!"

Crouching in a Groucho Marx–like hunting posture, Alonzo moved slowly forward, each footfall sending forth a shower of smaller grasshoppers. He drew close and leaned over, gesturing for J-Nice to stay behind him so that their shadows didn't fall on the quarry. The grasshopper was hanging on a wheatlike plant, its wiry legs wrapped around the fluffy tip, its weight making the stalk bend like a fishing pole.

In a sudden, smooth motion, Alonzo cupped his hands around the grasshopper, plant and all, and pulled up. He gave his catch a stern shake, pulled the broken stem out with his teeth, and deftly reached inside his cupped palms as if he were doing a hidden-coin trick. He held his prize aloft, grasping its back legs between his index finger and thumb.

"This the *Gran*daddy Grasshopper," he said, lowering it so J-Nice could see.

The insect's green-and-yellow armor shone in the sun, its hind legs dotted with rows of short black barbs that raked lightly across Alonzo's fingernail as it kicked and clawed. Thin, almost transparent wings were folded neatly against its body. A brown jewelet of sputum hung from its jaws.

Carefully, Alonzo put a drop of the liquid on his finger and held it under J-Nice's nose.

"To*bac*co," he said as J-Nice sniffed. "You can tell because it smell sweet. Grasshoppers always be chewing tobacco, like ballplayers."

Alonzo liked explaining things. His mother, a tall, stern woman, always warned him not to talk about things he didn't know anything about. She even bought a wooden sign and placed it atop the family's television—CAUTION: MAKE SURE BRAIN IS ENGAGED BEFORE SETTING MOUTH INTO MOTION—and whenever she thought Alonzo was talking too much, she would point at the sign. "You're just like your father," she would say, and Alonzo would smile. He liked being just like his father. At least, he had before all the bad things happened.

Alonzo had been close to his father. They did a lot together: fished for catfish out in McHenry County, went to the Rosemont Horizon for Wrestlemania, scalped tickets to Cubs and Sox games. To Alonzo, it seemed that no matter what situation they found themselves in, his father already knew all about it. He knew how to put a worm on a hook, which wrestler was going to win, how to grip a baseball for a curveball and a slider. He knew about old movies—*The Tramp* was his favorite—and decorated the apartment with posters of Chaplin and Bogart. He once talked his way into the luxury boxes of old Comiskey Park, where he then actually shook hands with Oakland A's manager Tony La Russa. Alonzo could not remember asking his father a question he couldn't answer.

Though Alonzo was only dimly aware of it, answering questions was also what brought about his father's arrest and conviction for the Wells Street murder. Several days after the April 1991 crime, with the story still in the headlines, police proceeded with a massive investigation in and around Cabrini-Green. When Officer Jim Ward spotted Alonzo's father outside a building on Hudson Street, he waved him over for a chat.

"He was always a good person to talk to," Ward said later. "Usually good for a tip here and there. But when I asked him if he knew anything about the white woman who got shot, he just started sweating. It wasn't real hot, and he was *sweating*. Then he told me he had seen somebody running out of an alley on Wells, but he couldn't tell who it was."

When word got out that Alonzo's father had been questioned about the crime, people in Cabrini weren't surprised. Alonzo's father was well known in the neighborhood as a canny operator who had made a career out of working both sides of the law. He washed windows, ran a janitorial service, sold a cocaine simulant called baso to unsuspecting whites, occasionally gave tips to police—anything to make a buck. His ability to sell himself was legendary. He once walked into the office of 42nd Ward alderman Burton Natarus, and walked out with a window-washing contract. "He had this way of talking to people where he could get right at their level," said an old acquaintance. "Didn't matter who they were, but he could talk to them and make them like him." When Officer Ward questioned him, Alonzo's father had just completed an eighteen-month sentence for burglary, and reportedly he had been smoking a lot of rock—a habit that brought Alonzo's mother to kick him out of their apartment. Still, no one, not even most police, seriously believed he might have committed murder, particularly one as brutal as this. "He was a con man," said one policeman. "Killing wasn't his m.o."

Ward made a point of running into Alonzo's father again, and this time he had something to add. He knew more about the crime, he said, but he couldn't say anything because he was frightened for his wife and son. If he spoke too much, someone might try to kill him. Playing it cool, Ward did not push.

"It was obvious that he really knew something," Ward said. "He wasn't the run-of-the-mill criminal. If he didn't pull the trigger, he'd be smart enough to get himself out."

Over the next few months, Alonzo's father revealed more, occasionally phoning Ward and area detectives to talk. Finally, in August, he admitted that he had participated in the abduction of the woman, but that another man, Charles "Chuck A Luck" Guyton, had pulled the trigger. By placing himself at the scene, however, Alonzo's father made himself culpable of murder. He was arrested, and his photograph made the front page of the *Tribune*: a bearded man with a loose white T-shirt and an alarmed expression.

"He cried—that's why this got solved," said Ward. "He had a conscience, and he was bothered by the shit and he couldn't live with himself. That's what I think, anyway."

Alonzo's father went on trial, and at the end the prosecution characterized its case as "difficult and complex." There was no gun, no forensic evidence linking the accused to the crime, and only one witness, a woman who said she had passed the victim walking with three black men that night; she testified that she was nearly certain, but not absolutely, that one of those men was the defendant. Chuck A Luck Guyton, the man who Alonzo's father said had pulled the trigger, claimed he had been elsewhere that night, and several people vouched for him. Ultimately, the only evidence used to convict Alonzo's father and send him to prison for ninety years was the evidence that he, for whatever reason, had given them.

"Watch me," Alonzo commanded J-Nice, tweezing one of the grasshopper's back legs between his fingers. Squinting in concentration, he carefully torqued the insect's hip joint until the exoskeleton made an audible pop. Bright green fluid showed.

"Maaaan!" J-Nice's eyes were wide.

"That's the blood—it's green." Alonzo gestured professorially with the disembodied leg. "This a Vulcan grasshopper, it belong to Spock."

"Serious?"

"Yop." Alonzo looked serious. "And it have two hearts, one in front and one in back."

"Maaan!" J-Nice smiled.

Alonzo dropped the insect and the leg to the ground and walked off. His friend hesitated. "It gonna die?" he asked.

Alonzo didn't slow down. "It'll grow back. Grasshoppers can do that."

On the last Saturday of June, the temperature crested to ninety degrees. To mark the event, somebody unscrewed the cap on a fire hydrant on Scott Street, and all morning dusty Lincolns and El Caminos cruised past for a free rinse, assisted by the troupe of small boys staging a water fight with Little Hug containers. The old men drinking wine on Sedgwick Street scooted their paint-bucket thrones a step closer to the scrawny shade trees. Nearby, three girls jumped double dutch, the white cords whirring like an electric fan, ruby-colored beads clicking in their hair.

On Carson Field, the Kikuyus were preparing for a three-o'clock game. Spirits were high. The team had spent the morning at Operation PUSH headquarters with Al Carter and a few dozen players from other teams. They had sung songs, heard inspirational speeches, and generally had a good time, especially when players got to go up to the microphone and say what the league meant to them. Now, after a break for hot dogs, they were to face the Nilotes, losers of their first four games and, reputation had it, even bigger busters than the Hausas. As Alonzo had pointed out, if you rearranged the letters of their name, you could almost spell "toilets."

"We gonna win today, maybe a hundred three to zero," predicted an emboldened Rufus, dried catsup on his upper lip.

"You sound pretty sure of yourself there, chief," said Coach Bill, giving Rufus's lip an ineffective swipe with his shirttail. "Looks like we'd better bat you leadoff."

"Nuh-*uuhhh*!" said Rufus, his eyes widening.

"Why not?"

"You know." Rufus toed at the dirt and shrugged.

"Okay," said Bill. "You'll bat fifth. Power spot. Ribbie City, you're the mayor."

Rufus laughed uncertainly, and toddled off.

Bill took out the scorecard and penciled in Rufus at the fifth spot. He was starting to inject a certain randomness to the batting order. By keeping the players a little off-guard, Bill figured, they might be less apt to criticize one another. This didn't mean that Nathaniel would be headed for the pitcher's mound anytime soon, but some of the team's louder complainers would be gaining an appreciation for new and difficult positions.

Bill had tried it for the first time two days earlier, against the Fantes. After several practices in which Jalen berated his teammates incessantly for their poor play, Bill informed him he would be starting as pitcher. At first his ploy seemed to backfire.

"I'm *pitch*ing, I'm *pitch*ing," Jalen teased Freddie, who responded with his best scowl. But after the Fantes scored seven runs in the first inning, Jalen wanted out.

"I wanna backcatch," he said, his head down. Bill pretended to give the matter a great deal of thought, then called Freddie in to pitch. For the next few innings, Jalen had been a new player: quiet, focused, even supportive.

The game had turned out almost equally well. Freddie, his cheeks puffing fiercely, held the Fantes scoreless the rest of the way. Meanwhile, the Kikuyus got around on the Fantes' pitcher: Freddie and Jalen homered, Harold tripled Demetrius in and hit a two-run, three-overthrow homer, and by the bottom of the sixth it was 7–6, two outs, full count, Freddie and Rude Dude at the plate. The Kikuyus' dugout was on its feet, pleading with Freddie to get ahold of one. But he didn't. The pitcher blazed it past him for strike three, and the Fantes celebrated.

"I *told* you we weren't gonna win," Jalen yelled, reverting to his old self. "We ain't *never* gonna make the playoffs now."

Now Bill checked his watch: ten minutes to three. The one-o'clock game was still in the fourth inning; it would be a while before the Kikuyus and Nilotes could take the field. He filled out the rest of the lineup.

Freddie would lead off and backcatch. Louis, who was becoming a decent outfielder, would bat second and play center field, followed by Jalen at first base, Maurice at pitcher, Rufus at second, Alonzo at third, Harold at short, Nathaniel in right, and Calbert in left. On the bench would be Demetrius, who had missed the two previous practices, and Otis, the quiet, smiley kid from the Whites who had missed much of the early season. Bill thought he might bring Otis in for Nathaniel, or maybe Harold. He checked the street for Samuel—if he showed up, he could go in for Nathaniel. Then he felt a hand on his shoulder.

"I'm not gonna play the whole game, am I?"

It was Alonzo. His arms were folded around his Kirby Puckett glove. He looked accusingly at the names on the sheet, then at Bill.

"I don't know about that, Alonzo," Bill said slowly. "If I were a betting man, I would say that you probably will play the whole game at third base."

"Nope," said Alonzo with finality, his face dropping into a slack-eyed mask. "There's extra players. You watch. I'm not gonna play."

Bill took a deep breath. "So are you saying that you don't *want* to play the game?" His voice was equanimous, curious. He hadn't witnessed Alonzo's helmet-throwing outburst on Opening Day.

"I'm *saying* you gonna take me out. Watch."

Bill rarely lost patience, but sometimes his voice took on a quality that might pass for sarcasm. "Okay, Alonzo. You let me know if you want to play. Whatever you want to do is fine."

"*Told* you!" Alonzo stalked away.

By the top of the third inning, the Nilotes were acting as if they had won the World Series. They had scored what for them was an unheard-of six runs in two innings, four of those runs on a grand slam, and they trailed by a mere three runs. The Kikuyus' dugout, on the other hand, was silent, partly because of the close score and partly because of the diversion now being created by one player. Alonzo sat in the newly installed bleachers, having removed his jersey and announced loudly that he had quit the team and was now playing for the "Wildcats." Bill had dispatched Maurice and the assistant coaches to talk Alonzo into returning, but he would have none of it. "Bill be *lyin'* to me," he told each emissary. "If I play, he just gonna take me out anyway." Covertly, he began to suck his thumb.

Back in the dugout, Coach Brad was looking for a lead-off hitter. "Where's Calbert?"

"There." Bill pointed to the snack table behind the backstop. Mary Robinson, the Seward Park supervisor, was selling cookies, candy, hot dogs, and pickles to benefit the park.

"I *know, I know,*" Calbert shouted, shoving a pickle in his pocket and grabbing a short blue bat.

"Go, Nilotes. Beat the buster Kikuyus!" Alonzo yelled from the bleachers. "Fastball or curve, don't matter, 'cause Fat Boy can't hit."

Calbert glared. "Least I can play."

"Go, Nilotes!" Alonzo shouted.

"Why he *doin'* that?" Rufus asked in the dugout, his brow crinkling.

"I don't know," said Brad. "Let's just play the game."

"Go, Niyotay," Alonzo yelled around his thumb. "Bee the buther Kikoos."

A boy maybe five years old walked up to Alonzo. He carried a can of Grape Crush opened in the neighborhood fashion. He had cracked the pull tab slightly to create a slit from which he sucked the soda; it was, in effect, an aluminum baby bottle.

"Ain't you a Kikuyu?"

"Nope," said Alonzo loudly, turning his head so his words carried to his former team's dugout. "I used to be, they kicked me off. Now I'm on the Wildcats."

The boy kept squinting at Alonzo, sucking noisily on his Grape Crush. Then he pointed.

"How come you still got they hat?"

It was true. Alonzo pulled it off and, with a flick of his wrist, spun it on the pavement, where it settled next to a broken malt liquor bottle. Two girls started playing with it, pretending they were baseball players. Alonzo watched out of the corner of his eye, but made no move.

On the field, meanwhile, the mood appeared to be intensifying.

"Come on, fellas, let's go get 'em!" A blond, blue-eyed man with a jutting jaw and a Yale T-shirt stood on the

Nilotes' bench, slapping his clipboard against his blue jeans in a nervous rhythm. "We can win this thing!"

"What's with him?" Brad asked.

"I dunno," Cort drawled. "Maybe one of us should go give him a back massage."

The man with the clipboard was Laird Koldyke, son of Martin "Mike" Koldyke, prominent Chicago businessman, philanthropist, and chairman of the Chicago School Finance Authority. Laird was a partner in his father's $300 million venture-capital firm and, at Bob Muzikowski's behest, had employed his considerable clout to secure the donation of the league's uniforms from a former Wilson Sporting Goods executive. He also had become somewhat notorious for his almost daily calls to Bob complaining about lack of players, lack of quality fields, and lack of overall organization. Bob and Greg gave prompt attention to his entreaties, but privately they chuckled.

"Laird's having a bit of a culture shock," Greg once explained with a smile. "He's discovering he's not in Wilmette anymore."

But Koldyke had stuck with it, filling his roster with cast-offs and kids he met on the field, rearranging business meetings so he could attend practices, and purchasing genuine cloth Northwestern University baseball hats that made the Nilotes the sartorial envy of the league. And now he wanted desperately to win a game.

"Atta-*baby,* Marshan, keep throwin' strikes now, hum babe," he called as his pitcher fanned Calbert. "Rock and fire, big man, rock and fire."

"He certainly gives excellent chatter," deadpanned Brad from across the diamond.

Freddie was up next, his big eyes narrowing as he assumed his threatening stance. As usual, he swung at the first pitch and, as usual, he made contact, grounding sharply off Marshan's glove for an infield single.

"No problem, big man, no problem," Koldyke said clapping. "Get this one now, get this one. No-hitter now."

Louis watched three pitches; the fourth plunked him in the shoulder and sent him hopping in pain down the first-base line. Bill called for time and rubbed the shoulder until Louis decided, with a suitably dramatic nod, that he could continue.

Then the hitting started. Jalen cantilevered Rude Dude to produce a single, sending Freddie home. Maurice, waggling a new black bat, doubled to left field, scoring Louis and Jalen. Rufus walked, Demetrius, who had taken Alonzo's spot at third, whacked a two-run double to left center, and Harold hit a genuine homer. The dugout resounded with dusty jubilation.

"I am the best player on this team," Harold yelled as he strode across the plate. "*Tell* me I ain't."

"Bill, make me be up again," pleaded Rufus.

"Gonna whack it to the gate, bay-bee!" Freddie sang.

"This is a team game, Harold," said Brad over the ruckus. "I don't want to hear this 'I' stuff."

"*Tell* me I ain't, Brad, *tell* me I ain't."

"You aren't, Harold."

Nobody saw Alonzo at first. He edged into the dugout, head down, and slid in next to Bill. His face was impassive.

Bill waited a few moments before speaking. "Hey, Alonzo."

Silence.

"So how's everything going with the Wildcats?"

Alonzo toed the dirt.

Bill leaned over and spoke low, so the other players would not hear. "Do you want to play?"

Alonzo looked straight ahead, out to the field, where Nathaniel was in the process of striking out. "I don't care."

Bill sat back. He didn't want to give in too easily. Like everyone else, he had heard many coaches sing the praises of strict discipline, and tell how their team's play and morale benefited from frequent benchings and suspensions. But Bill, at heart, saw things differently. To him, it didn't make any sense to play drill sergeant when he could achieve the same ends by doing what he did best; that is, talking to the kids. Why manage by fear when you could treat the players like adults, give them responsibility, and create good relationships?

"Well," Bill said, still casual, "I guess I don't care too much, either."

Long pause.

"What do you think about going in for Demetrius next inning?"

Alonzo's head dipped almost imperceptibly.

Brad, who had been watching this exchange, walked around the dugout to retrieve Alonzo's cap from the girls. He put it on Alonzo's head and rubbed his head affectionately.

"Let's go beat them Ni-toilets."

By the time the Nilotes came to bat in the bottom of the sixth, they were trailing 18–7. But with Coach Koldyke instructing his hitters not to swing until they took a strike, they worked Maurice for four straight walks. With their number-three hitter coming up and only one out, Koldyke sensed a chance for a morale-building rally.

"Let's go!" he called to his bench, most of which was engrossed in a six-person rock-paper-scissors game around the lemonade cooler. "Let's hear some *chatter*."

"All fastballs, Maurice," Bill said, as if the boy knew any other pitch. "Fastballs."

Maurice nodded and straightened his cap.

"Come on, babe, wait for your pitch now," said Koldyke. He turned to the baserunners, extending his index finger. "Only one out—run if it's on the ground, hold up if it's in the air."

Maurice reared and threw, and the batter, swinging mightily, lofted a pop-up toward second base. "Damn," Koldyke exhaled, gazing up.

Rufus moved toward it tentatively, hopeful that someone else might swoop in and catch it. But Harold was playing too close to third, and the ball wasn't deep enough in the outfield for Louis. Rufus was the only one. Three stories up, the ball reached its apex and began to fall. Rufus gingerly set his feet and offered up his mitt with a straight arm, as if reaching to put something on a shelf. The ball neared, and he turned his head away.

"Get back!" Koldyke shouted, realizing that his baserunners had disregarded his instructions and were now wheeling around the bases, heads down, trying to score. "Get baaaack!" He hopped and waved furiously. "Backback-backbackback!"

It was a full second before Rufus realized that the ball was in his mitt, and that everybody was yelling for him to touch second base. So he did, jogged over to double off the runner, end the game, and send the Kikuyus out of June with a respectable 4–2 record, good for third place in Conference B behind the Bakongos and Ibos.

"The Velcro glove!" shouted Brad, heading out to the field, where the team was celebrating. Unlike some Little League teams, whose players pile on each other after every victory, most Cabrini teams celebrated as individuals. Freddie shook his butt, Louis threw his glove, Harold spread his arms and proclaimed that he had won the game single-handedly, Maurice punched the air, and Nathaniel, who didn't realize the game was over, put on a batting helmet.

Rufus stood on second base, holding the ball and smiling. He looked surprised when the ebullient coaches converged on him, patting him on the back and touching his glove, telling him what a great play he had made.

"Coaches in this league have to do more of that, because the players don't," Bill said later. "It's sad. He made the play, and nobody said anything. But if he had dropped the ball, he'd have been a buster."

The Kikuyus gathered to shake hands with the dispirited Nilotes and their frazzled coach. As they formed a ragged line across the pitcher's mound, a dusty hand reached out and patted Rufus on the head.

"Nice play," Alonzo said. "Just like I woulda done it."

*   *   *

Two weeks later, Freddie's mother baked a cherry chocolate cake for his cousin's good-bye party. Michael was going to Stateville Prison in Joliet for six years, after being convicted for robbery and burglary. His recent record was varied; it included battery, sexual abuse, property damage, disorderly conduct.

"Yeah, I know Michael," one police officer said. "He was a real good kid for a long time, went to college, got into a frat, did the whole thing. Then he came back here, got a girl pregnant, and started getting into the shit. He was hanging on Cambridge Street, doing a little heroin, and that's what got him screwed up. Sad to see, you know, because he was a pretty good kid."

JULY

When the elephants fight, it is the grass that suffers.

—Kikuyu Proverb

ONE

By the time the first Kikuyus arrived at Carson Field, the Chapman and Cutler Bakongos were in the midst of their drills. The Bakongos made for an impressive sight, arrayed along the left-field foul line in two evenly spaced rows, resplendent in their freshly washed blue-and-white uniforms, arcing pop-ups to one another like so many automatons. Already they had completed their ten minutes of catch, their ten minutes of grounders, and when the coach signaled, they would gather into small groups and play ten minutes of the toss-and-hit game called pepper. Then, as they always did, they would kneel around the head coach, blunt-nosed blond attorney Kevin Kalinich, and listen to the Questions. The Questions were asked before every Bakongos practice and before every game, and they never varied. As a University of Michigan law student, Kalinich had coached football under the ferocious and legendary Bo Schembechler. Bo Schembechler, by proxy, now coached the Bakongos.

"What do you do if a grounder is hit to you?" Kalinich would ask loudly.

"Put your glove on the ground," a dozen tiny voices would chant.

"What do you do if a ball is hit to you in the air?"

"Use both hands."

"If you're an outfielder and a ball is hit to you, what do you do with it?"

"Don't hold it—throw it to the nearest infielder."

The Bakongos had built a reputation as the league's Horatio Alger story. After a horrendous 1–12 record in 1991, Kalinich had marshaled his troops to 5–0–1 so far this season; they had tied the powerful Ibos. Several of their victories were the come-from-behind variety—a phenomenon partially attributable to the fact that the Bakongos never knew how far behind they were. Kalinich instructed his coaches never to let on the correct score, lest the team get too excited or too depressed.

"Would you take a look at that?" said Coach Bill, gazing enviously at the parallel lines of white jerseys in left field, then at the random scattering of yellow in right. "I think we need to import a little bit of that, at least for the next few games."

Indeed, the first three weeks of July appeared merciless: first the Bakongos, then Bob Muzikowski's undefeated Northwestern Mutual Life Pygmies, then the tough Merrill Lynch Watusi, then the Continental Bank Bantus, which had just thumped the defending champion Ewes 8–4. The month ended with, Bill hoped, easier contests against the Yoruba and Xhosa, but neither of those promised a sure win. To make things worse, Harold would miss today's game for an aunt's birthday party, and Jalen had announced that he was going to visit relatives in Kentucky and would miss the Pygmies game. To the Kikuyus' coaches, who were vaguely familiar with the other teams, it looked like a rough stretch, particularly without David. To the players, who knew firsthand how talented some of the other teams were, it looked impossible.

"Y'all gonna lose *every* game without me," Jalen yelled during warm-ups, and his teammates had nodded. Yes, they agreed, they were definitely going to lose.

"The Bantus they is *good*." Rufus ran his words together excitedly. "They got this boy his name Jermaine and he throw *hard*."

"I seen some boy on the Pygmies whack it all the way *over* the gate," said Maurice, trying as always to top his teammates. "And they had this other boy who could whack it even farther!"

While prospects appeared dim, they were balanced somewhat by the recent addition of an actual baseball player to the coaching staff. Coach Steve was a quiet, amiable friend of Kevin's who had played shortstop at Yale and who had scored instant cachet by driving a Blazer, the same vehicle as Michael Jordan drove, and by wearing real baseball clothes, including pants, turf spikes, and a wet-shiny Mizuno sweat-top, the same kind major-leaguers wore under their jerseys in spring training. When Steve came to his first practice, heads had turned. "What pro team do you play for?" Harold wanted to know. "Do you mind if I drive your Blazer?" asked Maurice.

As the Kikuyus warmed up for the Bakongos game, some sense of order took over the proceedings. Steve crouched behind a makeshift plate along the foul line, teaching Freddie to shorten his pitching stride. Kevin was hitting infield with his usual gravelly authority, Cort was tossing fly balls quietly to the outfield, and Bill was filling out one of his calculatedly random lineup cards—Demetrius at first base, Louis in center field, Freddie on the hill—when a skinny hand draped over his shoulder.

"Bill," Demetrius said, "lemme pitch."

Bill let out a long sigh. The last few practices, Demetrius had been a one-boy crime wave, teasing, making fun of coaches, picking fights at every opportunity. Even by his lofty standards, he was breaking new ground. The previous week a policeman had spotted him smashing the outdoor lights at the old Church's Fried Chicken, across from the field. Demetrius had been let off with a warning, but his brief visit to the police station had enhanced his bad-ass credibility. But now something was up. He was being serious. He wanted to pitch.

"I been *practicin'*, Bill." He reached into the pocket of his shorts and pulled out a small leather case. "And I got me some glasses, so I'm fittin' to throw strikes for *sure*."

Bill didn't reply right away, but took the glasses out of their case and put them on Demetrius. "Pretty sharp there, chief," he said admiringly. "Kind of an intellectual look for you."

Demetrius didn't buy the diversion. "*C'mon,* man, I wanna *pitch*."

"We'll see." Bill snapped the glasses back into their case. "You get a little more positive attitude on the field, and maybe you'll get on the hill some time."

"I'll be *good,*" Demetrius told Bill, lowering his voice and checking over his shoulder to make sure no teammates were witnessing his prostration. "I *promise* I'll be good."

"We'll see." Bill turned toward the dugout. "Let's go. Game's about to start."

Demetrius looked at Bill. "But can I *pitch*?"

"We'll see."

To start the game, Freddie and Demetrius struck out, prompting a chorus of "We gonna lose" from Nathaniel and Louis. But then Maurice grounded a single to left, Jalen followed suit, and both of them scored when Otis bounced another single up the middle and the center fielder threw the ball away. The Kikuyus perked up and started to cheer when, after giving up a solo homer, Freddie struck out the side in the bottom of the first. Even Jalen looked happier.

"Yeah, bay-bee." He skip-hopped off the field after the third out, caught himself as he neared the dugout, and quickly slipped back into his usual persona. "Maaan! Y'all *better* get some runs."

Keyed by Rufus's looping double to right field, the

Kikuyus scored four more times in the top of the second, and Freddie held the Bakongos scoreless in the same inning. After two it was 6–1: something was up. Against a good team, the Kikuyus were playing their best ball of the year. Players weren't yelling at one another. Several were even dropping into their ready position, though the way Freddie was pitching, it was hardly necessary.

Demetrius, however, was behaving strangely. One moment he would be the picture of control, leaning over in his ready position. The next, he would be racing to stomp Rufus's cap or exchange taunts with the Bakongo dugout or tease someone with his high-pitched hyena laugh. When the team returned to the dugout for the top of the third, Brad took him aside in a friendly way.

"What's up with you today, Demetrius?"

"Whatchutalkinbout?" Demetrius's eyes flickered suspiciously.

"Nothing," Brad said quickly. "I just thought you seemed kinda . . . energetic."

"Nah," said Demetrius. A moment passed. Demetrius hunched forward, serious, his eyes going to slits.

"Straight up, Brad—how much you ever done with a girl—ever?"

Brad shifted his shoulders uncomfortably and laughed.

"I might've, um, kissed a girl once or twice," he said finally.

Demetrius didn't get irony. "That's all?" he said. "That's *it*?"

Brad looked at Demetrius, unsure of whether to ask the question. Curiosity won.

"Welllll . . ." He hesitated. "How much have *you* ever done with a girl?"

Demetrius smiled, a handsome, sharp-toothed smile.

"More'n *you*."

Her name was Treesie. She had light skin and slender legs and tall, blondish hair that she wore straight up off her forehead like a miniature field of corn. With the hair, she was taller than Demetrius. She was thirteen.

He first saw her while he was riding his bike along Sedgwick. She caught his eye right away because she was pretty and light-complected. "I always like light-complected girls," he explained. "Some people even think that she be *white.*"

Demetrius, true to the dictates of sixth-grade decorum, sent a friend over to this corn-haired vision to see if she wanted to meet him. Treesie refused, and won his heart.

"She say, 'If he's got something to say to me, then he can walk his ass over here and say it,' " Demetrius recalled with pride. "So I went over."

Their second time together, they kissed. Demetrius had kissed girls before, but none who was thirteen. The third time together, they tried French kissing, but neither of them liked it much. Too many germs, they decided. The fifth or sixth time together, they had sex. It was Demetrius's first time; an uncle who was eighteen gave him some jimmies to use and a key to his apartment. Don't never have sex without a jimmie, his uncle told him, not even if the girl says she's on the pill. He said that a lot of girls got pregnant on purpose, so they could get their own apartment, that getting pregnant gave them power, control over a man. Demetrius didn't need much convincing. He had seen boys not much older than he being teased for carrying diapers. Demetrius used a jimmie every time. He didn't want any family, not yet.

By the time of the Bakongos game, Demetrius and Treesie had done it on quite a few occasions. It was easy enough, though sometimes his auntie, whom he lived with, would ask him where he had been. During the school year he told her that he had to stay late; now that school had ended, his excuse was baseball. Either way, she could not check, busy as she was with five children in the house.

Treesie's birthday was in a few weeks, and Demetrius was planning to take the bus to the Maxwell Street market to buy her a gold ring. They weren't going to get married, at least not now. But he thought that she'd like a ring. And making her feel good was all he wanted to do. Even when she wasn't around, he wanted to show off for her. And when she was around, he wanted to do more. That was why he was acting so funny during the game. That was why he had asked to pitch.

He thought about her all the time.

In the bottom of the fourth inning, with the Kikuyus leading the Bakongos 7–2, Freddie began to lose it. He walked several batters, gave up two runs, and pouted, saying that he was tired of pitching and wanted to play backcatcher. Bill knew that Freddie was ineffective when angry, and decided to cut a deal. Strike out these next two guys, he said, and you can backcatch.

"*Yeah*, boy!" Freddie raced to the mound with new enthusiasm.

Bill scanned the field, and spotted Demetrius doing pelvic thrusts off first base. He called a meeting with Kevin, Brad, and Cort.

"What do you guys think . . . ?" he asked, pointing to the young troublemaker. They talked and came to an agreement: Demetrius would pitch if, as Kevin put it, "We're far enough ahead that it won't matter."

Freddie struck out the last two batters, and the Kikuyus scored five runs in the top of the sixth. So in the bottom of the sixth, with a 12–4 lead, Demetrius placed his new spectacles on his nose and marched solemnly to the mound. He started well, getting two strikeouts while allowing a single and a walk.

"Attaway," came the shouts from the dugout.

"Looks like we got ourselves a pitcher," said Cort.

But the next batter drew a walk. The Bakongos began to cheer.

"No sweat, Demetrius," the Kikuyus' coaches yelled. "Get this one now."

The next batter walked as well, forcing in a run. As did

the next. And the next. And the next. With each base-on-
balls and consequent run, the sound level in the Bakongos'
dugout ratcheted upward. They didn't know the score, but
they knew they were getting close. Demetrius had lost all
semblance of form and was stiff-arming the ball as if shot-
putting. The shorties behind the backstop were paying attention now, and they rode him unmercifully. His coaches
shouted the usual advice—shorten your stride, look to the
glove, step to the plate, just put it over and let your defense
do the job—but nothing took hold. Demetrius kept missing, and began sneaking desperate looks toward the dugout.

"Don't worry about it, Demetrius," the coaches shouted,
and clapped for the thousandth time. "Get this guy and
we're out of here."

He finally threw a strike, but the hitter smacked it for a
two-run single. Now it was 12–10, winning run at the
plate.

"Rally, rally, the pitcher's name is Sally!" The shorties
danced.

"Maaaan, Demetrius!" Puffs of dust appeared where the
Kikuyus stomped. "Why you *do* that?"

Demetrius, however, wouldn't look at anyone. He
wiped the sweat off his nose and pulled the brim of his cap
lower, as if it might serve as a blinder.

"Oh, boy," Kevin said quietly. "You think we should put
Freddie back in?"

"Nah," said Bill, doing his best to sound unworried.
"Let's see what happens."

The next batter hit a sharp, skidding grounder to Jalen
at shortstop. He scooped it, and stomped on second to get
the force out and end the game. As he did, it was difficult to
tell that the Kikuyus had won.

"Maaaaaan!" Jalen yelled.

"Yop," Rufus chimed in. "He can't throw no heat."

"He walkin' *everybody*!" Freddie threw his mitt, trying to
match the other players' anger. "Y'all *better* not let him
pitch again."

Bill turned to his pitcher, and for perhaps the first time this season, Demetrius had nothing to say. He sat on the bench, his jersey untucked, his new glasses opaque with sweat, totally spent. In the days and weeks that followed, Bill would recount with satisfaction how he had left Demetrius in the game while the Bakongos circled the bases, and he would point to this managerial gambit as a turning point, temporary though it was, in Demetrius's behavior.

"Nice job out there," Bill said, patting the boy on the shoulder.

But Demetrius wasn't paying attention. He was looking toward the bleachers, toward a tall light-haired girl who was waving at him. He waved back.

Bill nudged Cort. "Looks like our pitcher's got himself a sweetie."

After the game, as he sometimes did, Bill perused the scoresheet. His finger moved quickly across the bottom third of the page, which for the previous six games was filled with K's, signifying strikeouts. Today, though, it was covered with diamonds, numerals, slash marks, and the more complicated scratch of productive hitting. Louis had had a walk and two singles. Alonzo, two walks and two runs scored. Rufus's big day included a double, a single, three RBIs, and two runs scored. For the first time, the Busters had contributed to the team's success, scoring or knocking in seven of the twelve runs.

But the most important statistic was one that Bill kept in his head: the number of players who quit equaled a perfect zero. In fact, the team had behaved well, at least until the walk-a-thon in the final inning. It wasn't easy to figure out why. Maybe it was the example set by the Bakongos. Maybe it was the absence of the increasingly mouthy Harold. Maybe it was something more: perhaps the loss of David had helped the team grow together.

If the team was coming together, the player most de-

serving of credit was undoubtedly Maurice. Good old
Maurice, with his goofy Arthur Ashe hair and his grown-up
manner. Always cheerful. Always eager to please. Though
he was second to none when it came to exaggerating his
feats on the baseball field, his older-brother presence was
having an impact. When Freddie had returned to the dugout in tears after striking out in his last at-bat against the
Bakongos, Bill did not hurry over to comfort him as he
might have a few weeks earlier. Rather, he tapped Maurice,
wise Maurice, and told him to go have a word with his
pitcher. Soon Freddie was smiling. One night later in the
season, the coaches each picked a player they identified
with the most, someone they could imagine being if they
had been born in Cabrini. Predictably, most of the coaches
picked Louis—the Kikuyus' nearest version of a nerdy
white kid. No one picked Maurice.

"He's . . . he's too *good*," said Cort, and his colleagues
nodded in agreement. "The way he handles himself out
there, he's like a little adult. I could never be that strong."

"We've got to let the solid kids like Maurice step up and
take responsibility, take leadership of the team," Bill said. "I
wish we had ten more just like him."

TWO

Maurice and Rufus were halfway up the stairs when the shots came. Automatics, nine-millimeters, smaller pistols—Maurice could pick out a few as he ran. Some of his friends could imitate the reports of different guns like birdcalls, but Maurice and Rufus weren't so skilled. Their windows faced the back alley, and besides, there wasn't as much shooting on Sedgwick Street as in the highrises.

"Come on now, *go!*"

The boys' mother didn't really have any reason to yell. Once on the long stairway, they were shielded from the street and from the shots, fired presumably in yet another leadership rift among the Stones, the gang who ran their street. Still, Mary hurried them, and they bounded two and three steps at a time. With a practiced motion she unlocked the deadbolt, swept the two boys inside, pulled the steel security gate in front of the door, and fisted the padlock closed with a smack.

"First!" Rufus yelled, but Maurice was too quick. He

raced to the refrigerator and pulled the game cartridge from
the butter keeper—cold made it last longer—and dived
over the couch toward the twenty-seven-inch solid-state
Zenith Chromacolor II with real oak paneling that Mary
had bought for fifty dollars from her uncle. It took a few
minutes to warm up, and the picture was so fuzzy you had
to watch it with all the lights out, but it worked. Soon, the
microchip organ-grinder commenced its endless tinny
whirl, and the glimmering figure of Bam-Bam Bigelow was
body-slamming the Honky-Tonk Man, and the shots in the
street could hardly be heard over the boys' excited commentary.

"Boom!"

"Buster ain't got nothing. . . ."

"Whoooa, helicopter slam . . ."

"Pin, baby, pin!"

The apartment, dimly lit by the flickering screen, wasn't
much to look at. The walls leaned against each other
precariously, the foamboard squares of the suspended ceiling lay at various angles, and the fake-marble linoleum
floor was so worn that walkways between rooms dipped in
the center like steps to a medieval cathedral. Bedsheets
served as drapes over dirt-clouded windows; furnishings
consisted of a table and three Eisenhower-era metal chairs,
two stained twin mattresses—one for Mary and one for the
boys—a velvety three-piece couch that had cost forty dollars. The living room walls were blank except for a framed
print of Gustav Klimt's *The Kiss* and a two-by-four with the
wood-burned instruction PARTY HARDY. Clothes and dishes
were scattered liberally on the floor, and the apartment
emanated a dank, acrid smell. Mary usually kept a nicer
house, but lately she had been sick, and it was all she could
do to keep up the energy to accompany the boys to the
baseball field. Though walking caused her pain, she rarely
let the boys go outside alone. That was her rule.

"I was *born* with this gray hair," she would say, touching
her head and turning her considerable voice up to full volume. "I don't *need* no more from you."

They had lived in this apartment for nine months now, ever since they had moved from a Cabrini highrise. Maurice hadn't wanted to move, but his mother said that it was becoming too dangerous; she wanted to get out before her children were too old. They had packed everything in plastic bags and hauled them three blocks north to Cabrini's "suburbs": Sedgwick Street, the motley stretch of walk-ups, bungalows, bars, and barbershops that was home to so many unpredictable characters that the police referred to it as "Sesame Street." Life wasn't great here, but it was better than in the highrises. There were working families, less gunfire, and up near North Avenue on Hudson and Cleveland streets, attractive frame houses with well-kept yards. Though rents were many times what they would have been in Cabrini, and though residents complained about the recent wave of white urban pioneers moving into the area, Maurice and his family felt fortunate to live on Sedgwick. Like everyone in the suburbs, they made a point of always referring to Cabrini as "the projects."

Maurice often reminded his friends that he hadn't always lived around here. When he was eight, they had taken a bus to Tennessee and lived with relatives for six months. He had liked it better than any place he had ever been to. They had lived in a small blue duplex with a yard, Mary had gotten a job at a local child-care center, and he and Rufus had been able to go out by themselves and walk just about anywhere they wanted. "They had lots of dogs and animals down there, and nobody ever did no shooting," Maurice recalled. "We was, like, in the *country*." Mary was making plans to stay, but when her mother fell ill she had to return to Cabrini to care for her. She sometimes talked about returning to Tennessee, but even Rufus knew they probably didn't have the money for it.

On a paint-peeled wall between the kitchen and the dining room hung remembrances of what had happened since they'd returned from Tennessee: two small framed funeral announcements, calligraphied words encircling dim photocopied portraits, with flowers pressed behind the cracked glass. On the left, the announcement for the boys' cousin Eddie, a sweet-faced twenty-year-old whose body was found under some garbage on the West Side; he had been shot in the temple, his insides kicked in. They never knew for sure why he had been killed, but people said he had refused to carry out a hit, and his gang had V'ed him as punishment. On the right, the announcement for cousin Lonzo, who had been shot and killed the previous summer, and about whom Maurice had the recurring dream. Lonzo had been playing lookout for a Cobra dealer in the lobby of 1159 North Larrabee when some Slick Boys ran up, trying for a bust. The dealer had run, but for some reason Lonzo had turned and shot twice. An officer fired back and dropped him with two shots to the head.

"Lonzo was real hard when he was on the street," Mary remembered. "*Real* hard. But sometimes he seemed like just a little child. He'd always yell, 'I love you,' whenever he saw me, and he weren't embarrassed about it or anything. He would be real sweet to the boys, too, and would put them on his knee and tell them not to get involved in gangs. But then he'd walk outside, and he was a different person."

Maurice didn't like looking at the announcements. If he looked at his cousins' faces too much, he figured, he might end up as they did. To Maurice, this was no idle fear, for lately he had happened onto a small but important secret: Many things in his life were mysteriously linked, and he was able to figure out the connections. "It's like I can know what's gonna happen before it do happen," he tried to explain once. "It's like telling fortunes."

It had started in the summer of 1991, with Nintendo. Maurice noticed that on the days he scored well in Bases Loaded 2, he played well in Kikuyus games. He tested to see whether this cause-and-effect worked elsewhere, and sure enough, it did. If he wore his Charlotte Hornets T-shirt, it usually meant that he would pitch well. If he didn't cut his hair, he played better in everything. At times, it was as if he were drawing lines on some partially finished map.

"I knew Andre was going to hit it out," he said while watching a Cubs game. "He always tap the plate twice when he's fittina whack a homer." He thought further. "I knew it, 'cause I do the same thing."

"I knew that car was going to pass us," he said while driving with Brad. "It was red, like Bill's car that I drove that one time, and so I knew it had to be fast."

"That painting should be in a museum," he remarked of a poster in one coach's apartment. "You probably bought it at a museum, then hung it up here so it gets more valuable, and then later you'll sell it for more money. Yep." He turned away, not interested in any explanation.

But some areas couldn't be delineated on Maurice's map quite so easily, things that he found better to ignore or deny. One day a friend of his saw a large roach crawling across the floor of Maurice's apartment and commented on its size.

"A *roach*?" said Maurice incredulously, tilting his head to get a better look. "I ain't never seen those around here before."

Maurice knew about his father. His mother had told him too many times to forget—how she had dropped out of college to have Maurice, how on the day Maurice was born his father was arrested for robbery, how he was around for a while a few years later but then got into cocaine. Yet Maurice never fully understood the story, not even when he saw him on the street, the sad, stooped man with papery skin and a white plastic rosary around his neck. Maurice sometimes imagined that his father was not a skinny junkie, but someone else, a famous athlete maybe, someone who would, when Maurice was a famous athlete himself, come forward and reveal the truth.

The day of the Bakongos game, Maurice's mother had given him a piece of important but disturbing news: His father wanted to see him. She had run into him on Sedgwick, and he had said that he was moving to Los Angeles in a few weeks. He had some friends who could set him up with a janitorial job, he said. Real good work, high-paying, with benefits and everything. He would send for Maurice to visit after a few months, definitely. Mary had nodded and smiled and told him that she'd bring their son over to say good-bye on the morning of his departure. She didn't tell him that she had heard a different story—that late one night in a Sedgwick bar, he and a buddy of his, Lavarus, had gotten into it with a Stone named Frog, and Lavarus had shot Frog, and the Stones had put out a hit on Maurice's father and Lavarus in retaliation.

"He ain't much of a father, but he deserve to see his son before he go," she told Maurice. "Maybe something out there in California will straighten him up."

At night, when the Zenith was no longer buzzing and his mother and brother were asleep, Maurice sometimes heard a strange, high-pitched noise, similar to giggling. It had scared him at first, but eventually he had figured out its source—horses, which lived at the stable next door and spent their days pulling glossy carriages of tourists and honeymooners around the Gold Coast for thirty dollars a half-hour. Maurice liked watching the horses, though he felt sorry for them, penned up in the small yard chewing hay. Some of the old men who sat drinking wine on the sidewalk outside the stable felt sorry for them, too, and would sometimes slip a piece of candy into their wet, lippy mouths and talk to them like old friends. For a nickel and a bottle of Wild Irish, they said, they'd trade places. Three squares a day, afternoons hauling folks around the Gold Coast, Hispanic boys combing your back. It wouldn't be half bad.

THREE

Fifteen minutes before the big game against the Pygmies, Coach Bill counted yellow jerseys. Five. He counted blue jerseys. Fourteen.

"Say, Bob"—Bill approached the opposing dugout—"how about a player-coach game today?"

Bill was joking, but underneath he was peeved. He had looked forward to this game for a long time, not just because Bob Muzikowski's Pygmies were a league powerhouse, but also because Bob loved to tell how undersize and untalented his team was, just before they thumped you by fifteen runs and prayed afterward as if it had been some sort of miracle. Bill liked Bob well enough, but the David-and-Goliath routine was by now irritating. Fact was, the Pygmies were the class of the league, featuring a lineup of wiry line-drive hitters and perhaps the league's best pitcher, a kid named Shondrae. In two years they had never been defeated in a regular-season game. It would require saintly intervention for the Kikuyus, especially without Jalen, to stay up with them.

Bill shaded his eyes and looked for more players. The evening had turned muggy, and steam puffing out of the Oscar Mayer smokestacks carried the faint smell of olive loaf. Bill didn't understand why more kids weren't showing up. Practice on Monday had gone well, morale had been reasonably high. As they put the equipment away, Bill had reminded the team of the previous year's game against the Pygmies, in which the Kikuyus had played far above their heads and come within a hairbreadth of winning. The Pygmies had scored two late runs to win 3–1.

"Let's see if we can't beat them this year," Bill had concluded. "And if you're not going to make it to the game on Thursday, call one of us coaches and let us know."

"Yeah, Bill," Harold had piped up. "I won't make it."

"What's your excuse?"

"My excuse is that y'all are busters and you definitely can't win without Jalen and me." The big kid bugged out his eyes and propped his elbow on his friend's skinny shoulder. "I bet anybody here five dollars that y'all lose. That goes for you too, Bill, unless you too poor."

Bill had ignored the remark.

"You *scared*!" Harold crowed. "You scared 'cause you *know* I be takin' your money!"

"Sit down and shut up, Harold," Brad had said finally.

While the Pygmies raced through their warm-ups, five more Kikuyus materialized on the field—Harold not among them—and Bill was able to fill out the scorecard: Freddie pitching, Maurice replacing Jalen at backcatcher, Otis replacing Harold at shortstop, Demetrius at first, Rufus at second, Alonzo at third. Bill took a calculated risk by playing Nathaniel, Louis, and Calbert in the outfield, hoping that Freddie could keep the Pygmies from hitting the ball there and that, if he couldn't, Louis would step up his play another notch. If he did, and if the infield did as well as it had against the Bakongos, maybe . . .

Bill looked out to the field, where Shondrae was throwing laser beams and the Pygmy infielders were completing their warm-ups with a tidy 5–4–3 double play. Rainclouds hovered north of the field, but it didn't look as if they'd arrive in time.

By the bottom of the fifth, the Pygmies were leading 24–6. Freddie had given up only a handful of legitimate hits, but he had walked a dozen batters, and everything they touched seemed to roll for a home run. Louis, weary of chasing the ball, already had sat down in centerfield, and Alonzo had announced that he was considering rejoining the mythical Wildcats. The only players not at least mildly depressed were Demetrius, who showed off for his girl-friend almost unceasingly, and Rufus, who had heard a rumor—false, however—that Shondrae was thirteen years old and who thus concluded that the Kikuyus were victorious, no matter the score. "We won," he would happily inform each of the Pygmies during the postgame handshake. "You cheatin'."

But something was going on with Bob Muzikowski and Al Carter. They stood a hundred yards apart, Al in right field being interviewed by a local television journalist for a story on the league, Bob umpiring behind home plate and trying to control a rapidly building fury. His jaw was tight, his hair electrified, his fists clenching and unclenching. He cast glances into the nearby dugouts, trying to catch some-one's eye. He found Bill's.

"Can you *believe* this shit?" Bob pointed toward Al. "Can you be-fucking-lieve this?"

Bill was confused. Like everyone else, he was well at-tuned to the friction between the league's two dominant personalities. Not a meeting went by that the tension didn't show in some way—Al railing against the league's being too corporate, Bob challenging him to bring more black men from the community to coach; Al pushing for an African-American focus, Bob pushing more subtly for Christianity. And yet even in the most heated arguments,

Bob and even Al expended some effort to preserve their partnership, to cast their disagreements in the light of healthy family debate.

"I'm not angry with the Bob Muzikowskis and the Greg Whites, all of you who show up and do a good job," Al would often say after one of his tirades. "I'm angry with the ones who aren't out here."

"Al's basically a good guy," Bob would say. "We fight sometimes, but we always work it out. Our strength is in our difference. How boring would this thing be if we never challenged one another, never learned what somebody else had to say?"

But on this evening, with Al and Bob at opposite corners of Carson Field, the niceties vanished. For the first time it was evident that their partnership, already under considerable strain, was falling apart.

This latest trouble began back in the days after the Los Angeles riots, when a speedily formed coalition of local civic groups and businesses raised $2.5 million to defuse tensions among Chicago's youth. In June the organization, The Chicago Initiative, announced that it was seeking grant proposals from qualified organizations in four main areas: arts and culture, gang intervention, jobs, and sports and recreation.

Like dozens of other community organizations around Cabrini, Demicco Youth Services, an educational and social agency of which Al Carter was a board member, submitted an application. The Chicago Initiative ruled favorably, and in early July awarded the agency $35,000. The purpose of the grant, according to TCI's summary, was to provide a "youth baseball and basketball program in conjunction with the African-American Youth League and the Al Carter Youth Foundation."

A few days after Demicco received the grant, Al Carter was hired by Demicco to put together a ten-week three-on-three basketball tournament. He placed a number of youths on hourly wages as referees and commissioners; purchased jerseys, scorecards, nets, and basketballs; and enlisted three men from the neighborhood to umpire the Near North Little League games for a few dollars an hour. He also resigned temporarily from the Demicco board, in accordance with that group's bylaws prohibiting board members from engaging in activities that might create a conflict of interests.

The trouble began when Bill Seitz, the man Bob had brought in to help in the league, caught wind of the grant and Al's resignation. As it turned out, Bill and Bob Muzikowski also had applied for a TCI grant in the name of the Near North Little League, and had been rejected. Losing out on the potential windfall was bad enough, but when Bill told Bob that the money they had wanted to put toward a refreshment stand and a van was somehow in the hands of the league president, who apparently had no intention of funding either, Bob hit the roof.

Characteristically, it took Bob all of five seconds to arrive at a conclusion: Al had used the league's success and credentials to obtain the money, and never had intended any of it for the baseball program. Not that the league needed money; as Greg White had pointed out earlier when he urged Bob not to apply for the grant, there was about $10,000 in the coffers, and they could always go back to the corporations for more. But that didn't lessen Bob's anger. As he reflected, his fury rose. All the favors he had done for Al, all the abuse he had taken in response, all the tongue-biting he had endured for the last two years, all the hours he had spent on the field while Al sat back and criticized—it finally had a righteous outlet. The indig-fucking-nation! Here was this guy, barely involved in the league, suckering city philanthropists, and getting away with it by hiring a few umpires? Umpires who, in their first few games, had shown up with beers in hand? By the afternoon of the Kikuyus–Pygmies game, Bob had reached the boiling point.

"He gets thirty-five grand by taking credit for our work, then uses the money to hire some umpire who's too crocked to show up, so I'm back there sucking dust behind home plate umping my own team's game while Al is out in center field slamming us on TV like he always does, criticizing the white folks who come in for their halos," Bob said. "We're supposed to believe that he's spending the money on some three-on-three basketball tournament? What's that gonna run you, a few hundred bucks? A thousand? Come on."

Bob didn't go so far as to ask Demicco or Al about the details of the grant, which Bob understood only sketchily and, in some aspects, incorrectly. For instance, he and Bill Seitz believed that Al, not Demicco, had written the grant proposal; further, they did not view Al as Demicco's employee, seeing him instead as the grant's controlling interest.

One day on the field, Bill Seitz asked Al point-blank about the $35,000. Al exploded, telling him that he was being paid as a private volunteer to run a basketball league, not as president of the goddamn corporate baseball league, which had enough money, anyway. And he had worked in this neighborhood a long time, and he didn't have to ask anybody's permission before he helped its young people, thank you very much.

Bill relayed Al's message to his boss. Bob, more convinced than ever that something was amiss, told Bill to dig around, to see if he could find an application or anything that would prove beyond a shadow of a doubt that Al had received the money under false pretenses. In the meantime, Bob and Tina weren't shy about expressing their suspicions about the grant to other coaches. Within days the rumor was rampant around the league. For the next month neither Bob nor Tina nor anyone else said anything to Al about the matter, and by then the damage had been done.

Cold rain fell for most of the third week in July, wiping out the Kikuyus' game against the Merrill Lynch Watusi. Volcano weather, people called it, and the Kikuyus' coaches were grateful. Discipline and morale at weekly practices had hit a new low. The loss to the Pygmies had made it painfully evident that, while the Kikuyus could beat up on weaklings such as the Nilotes and Hausas, they were not yet within hailing distance of the league's better teams. Players, frustrated by their lack of success, had turned prickly and self-protective, acting tough to prop up bruised egos. Initially, most of the wrath had been directed at team-mates and Busters. Yet more and more, it was targeted at the coaches.

"I ain't your *slave*," Jalen shouted when Coach Brad asked him to help put away the equipment. "Do it your-self."

"You ain't my daddy," Freddie said when Coach Kevin told him to sit down during a team meeting.

Unlike Kevin and Brad, who yelled themselves hoarse over such conflicts, Bill appeared immune to frustration. He counteracted mutinous remarks with quiet good humor, broadsiding offenders with smiles, as if to say, "Come on now, I'm in on your little joke. We both know you don't really mean what you're saying." This discipli-nary sleight-of-hand seemed to work; by implying that players and coaches shared some common ground, it was almost as if that ground existed. And when smiles failed, Bill had another tactic. He would take the player aside and engage him in man-to-man conversation that combined ego-stroking with an implicit challenge. "You're a leader on this team," he would say in a tone at once matter-of-fact and confidential. "If you have a good attitude, other people will follow your lead. If you decide to be a crybaby about everything, then so will everybody else." Pause. "If every-body's complaining and busting on one another, how are we supposed to play as a team? How are we supposed to win?" Longer pause. "Which kind of player do you want to be?"

Sitting on the bench, leg against leg with their grave and impressive head coach, Jalen, Demetrius, Harold, and the rest invariably tilted their heads and shuffled their feet and whispered yes, they wanted to have a good attitude, and no, they didn't want to be crybabies. But once out of the coach's shadow, good intentions evaporated. The first booted grounder or ugly strikeout would ignite the catcalling, which would demand a response, and the cycle would begin again.

When the team gathered at Carson Field on Saturday afternoon for the game against the Continental Bank Bantus, the players seemed antsy. They sprayed one another at the water fountain and played "open chest thump," a bruising game whose object is to slug unsuspecting bystanders in the sternum. Squadrons of newly hatched dragonflies made strafing runs at eye level, and inspired gate-mouthed yells of fear from Freddie and Demetrius, who like many Cabrini children believed them to be poisonous. Behind the backstop, the man in the blue "Boss" hat instructed Rufus on how to charge grounders.

"Come on now," the man said, hunching down on creaky knees. "Can't field it if you don't move your feet, now."

Rufus shook his head obstinately.

After five minutes, the man gave up and lit a Tareyton. "All you boys today, why you got to be so *hard*headed all the time?" he rasped. "Can't do nothin' without making a big fuss."

In the dugout, Brad was having an animated discussion with Harold, who had decided that a new Starter shirt with "Bulls" in raised, slightly furry script across the chest suited him better than his jersey. After a few minutes of cajoling and several volleys of "Yes you will," "No I won't," Brad cranked up the Maine foghorn to full volume and told Harold that he either wore the team jersey or rode the bench.

"Coach Bill, Coach Bill," Harold called out mockingly. "Brad just kicked me off the team."

Bill set down his folder and walked down the dugout, serious. Though Jalen had returned from Kentucky, just eight Kikuyus had shown up, and now it looked as if that might have shrunk to seven. Bill stood over Harold, smiling and shaking his head in a combination of amusement and disappointment, waiting for his presence to sink in. It didn't work.

"Maaaan." Harold folded his arms and tipped his head in his best defiant pose. "Brad pushing me around."

"Coach Brad's pushing you around?" Bill repeated it slowly, with a note of incredulity.

"He trying to kick me off the team just 'cause my jersey too small."

Bill picked up Harold's jersey and put it against his shoulders. "That would be this jersey? The one you've worn for the last eight games, right?"

"It *shrunk.*"

"It shrunk," Bill repeated, smiling.

While the two talked, Brad busied himself by helping Kevin with the infield warm-up. Ten minutes later, when the Kikuyus took the field, Harold ran out to shortstop. He was wearing the Bulls jersey. He waved at Brad.

"I told him he could wear it for this game and no other." Bill shrugged. "Hey . . . we got eight players."

Brad nodded blankly. He felt his authority had been undermined by Bill, but he didn't say anything.

"We talked about a few things," Bill continued. He didn't say he was sorry, but he stretched the conversation to convey that he was aware of the situation—which was as close as Bill ever came to an apology. "I think he might be coming around," he concluded.

"Uh-huh," said Brad, looking straight ahead.

The game started out well. Freddie held the Bantus scoreless in the first inning, and began the second with a strikeout. But then the Bantus, who practiced four days a week, started to time Freddie's pitches. They scored six runs in the second inning and five in the third, and Freddie's composure, always tenuous, fell apart. His head drooped, his motion became lackadaisical, his angelic face closed up like a fist. "Mother*fucker!*" he yelled after the umpire made a call he disagreed with, but luckily, the umpire didn't hear. Bill visited the mound several times to talk to him, but Freddie folded his arms and wouldn't listen.

"What's wrong, man?" asked Coach Feets, who had appeared for the second time since Opening Day.

Meanwhile, the Bantus' star pitcher, Jermaine, mowed through the Kikuyus' lineup, giving up only a triple to Harold and a hard groundout to Demetrius, who fell down on his way to first and stayed there, shouting a line from a senior citizen's medical-alert commercial: "I've fallen and I can't get up!" His humor was the only bright spot: of the first eight Kikuyus at the plate, seven struck out.

"*Tell* me I'm not the best player on this team." Harold strode up and down the silent dugout with his saggy gangster pants and his bug-eyed Cheshire grin, challenging everyone in his street honk. "Brad try to kick me off, but if it wasn't for me, y'all wouldn't have nobody who could hit the high gas. Y'all might not never even win another game."

"Hey, Harold, what did we talk about before?" Bill said in a low voice, trying to position his body between Harold and the rest of the team. "I thought great athletes let their bats do the talking for them, remember?"

Harold reflected on this, then gave a broad smile. "I guess that makes me greater than great, because I talk with my bat *and* my mouth."

In the top of the fifth, with the Bantus leading 11–3, everything fell apart. Calbert, playing third base out of necessity, was hit in the knee by a line drive and retired to the bench to eat a pickle. By way of response, Harold, at shortstop, engaged in a solo sit-down strike, proclaiming that he could no longer waste his talent on so many busters. In a desperate attempt to prove that they weren't busters, half of the team sat down as well, shouting and pointing fingers at the others. The Kikuyus coaches were all forced onto the field, where they pulled the players to their feet so that the game could be completed. When it finally ended, the Kikuyus' record had dropped to 5–4, and the team's mood covered the spectrum between rage and depression.

"I *told* you we was gonna lose."

"Man, this team got too many busters on it."

"Y'all a bunch of faggedy-ass, nappy-headed babies, y'all can't never hit like me."

"Shut up, man."

"*You* shut up."

"Hey, guys, cut it out!" Feets tried to get through. No one listened.

"I'm *telling* you, shut up, man."

"We ain't *never* going to the 'ship," Jalen barked. "We ain't even gonna make the playoffs! I quit!"

Bill's hat tipped up. "What was that?" he asked with a dangerous mildness.

The dugout fell hushed as Bill and Jalen squared off. Harold may have been the loudest on the team, and Demetrius the cleverest, but skinny Jalen carried the most weight. If he mutinied, the ripples would be felt by the lowliest buster.

They eyed one another for an instant, the coach and the player, each unsure of himself but unwilling to back down. Then, as Jalen felt the gaze of his teammates on him, he acted. He had to. Bill could stand there forever, but Jalen, he had people *watching*. He tore off his jersey, threw his cap to the ground, and walked away stiff-legged.

"Uh, Jalen."

The boy turned. He tried hard to keep his scowl, but the tiny gleam of a triumphant smile played on his lips. Was he being asked back? Had he won? But Bill was pointing at his feet.

"Socks."

Jalen kicked out of his Scottie Pippens, shook off the stirrups, and flipped them into Bill's palm. They curled up like little green snakes.

"Thanks. See you later, Jalen."

"*Right.*"

*   *   *

In later July, things in the Reds were heating up. The reason, as usual, was petty. At a Folks party in 923 North Hudson one Saturday night, some Black Gangster Disciples from the Whites harassed some Gangster Disciple girls, asking them for sex. There was a scuffle, and as a result, the always uncertain BGD-GD alliance was broken. The following Wednesday afternoon, the BGDs did a drive-by past the basketball courts at Durso Park, one of the sites for Al Carter's tournament. Though nobody was killed, one boy was shot in the leg.

The next night, just after midnight, fifteen-year-old Laquanda Edwards was shot and killed as she crossed Larrabee Street in front of a GD building. Two conflicting stories hit the street. One had her involved in a fight between GDs and BGDs, and a boy on the street shooting her with a pistol. The other, picked up by most of the papers and the police, had her being shot at random by a sniper from 1117–1119 North Cleveland, the People-controlled Castle. As usual, it didn't really matter which story was true.

"This is the start," a Chicago Housing Authority security guard told a reporter. "We thought we were lucky, that we could get away with a quiet summer. But now that's over, and we can start the count from here."

The shooting came every night, and often during the day, peaking around the time of police shift-changes, at ten a.m., six p.m., and two a.m. In accordance with the loose war protocol that governed Cabrini, the Cobras spray-painted their snake insignia on two BGD highrises and thus served notice that they were about to take those buildings; the Vice Lords at 500–502 West Oak painted an upside-down Cobra next to the building entrance, to signify that the VL-Cobra alliance was broken. In the highrises, the snipering took its toll: A GD enforcer was shot in the lobby of 862 North Sedgwick. A seventy-five-year-old woman was shot in the hip as she walked through the lobby of 939 North Sedgwick at seven-thirty one evening. A sixty-nine-year-old woman in the Castle was injured by shrapnel when bullets came through her door. Rat, never one for violence, turned his attention elsewhere until things settled down.

The Slick Boys weren't so lucky. CHA security officers, several 18th District cars and officers, and occasionally a gang-crimes tactical team worked the area, but the majority of law enforcement duties in Cabrini-Green fell to the thirty or so on-duty officers of the Public Housing North Special Functions Division. From their makeshift station at 365 West Oak, in the Reds, they were assigned to police the 50,000 residents of the six CHA projects north of Ogden Avenue. Most of their time, however, was spent in Cabrini. And when the shooting came down as it did during those long days and nights of late July, they did what everybody else did. They ducked.

"You think they give a fuck who they shoot?" said Officer Eric Davis. "You got babies with guns, and they just get up there and start poppin', poppin', poppin'."

Though many of the upper floors of highrises were sealed and locked, gangs could gain access to them by replacing locks with their own or simply by battering doors down. Once on an open floor, they sledgehammered holes in the cinder-block walls to create passages for the shooters, who could then move around without being detected on the ramps. In the upper floors of 500–502 West Oak, the network of passages was said to be so complete that the VLs could run from one end of the building to the other without ever opening a door.

Hiding guns was more difficult. Elevator emergency-phone boxes and stairwell light fixtures were convenient, nonincriminating spots for handguns, but apartments were more secure. Yet they, too, could be risky, as the CHA now and then ran unannounced security sweeps, in which police officers checked each apartment for contraband. There were ways to beat the system, despite the bare concrete ceilings, cinder-block walls, and concrete floors. Enterprising gun owners could always unscrew the electrical-outlet panel in the bathroom and hang a weapon by fishing line inside the wall, or tuck it into a slit-open mattress. Getting past a lockdown—by which a building would be staffed with a security guard and all visitors had to be signed in by a resident—was sometimes tricky. Still, guns could be passed through first-floor windows, and security guards could be intimidated; many buildings, the Castle among them, were not locked down. The police gradually caught on to some ploys, and would check for chipped paint on the heads of the tiny screws that electrical-outlet panels held in place, for instance; but as soon as they discovered one technique, the gangs would come up with another.

The shooting continued through the last week of July. A ten-year-old girl in the Reds was shot in the ear. The next evening, outside Schiller Elementary School near the Whites, a girl jumping rope was hit in the arm. At about this time, the Chicago Police Department made an announcement: As part of a general realignment designed to make better use of existing personnel, it would close the Public Housing North station in Cabrini on October 1. The officers of Public Housing North greeted the announcement with disbelieving laughter. A month before, the city had suspended a program by which off-duty officers were paid overtime for working in CHA property; this cost the unit twenty police per day. Now they were going to disband the entire unit and leave Cabrini to the regular 18th District police. "If they were proposing cutting patrols on the Gold Coast, there'd be screaming and hollering," said one officer. "But here, hell, we can let them die. They ain't but shooting at each other, anyway."

The rumor in the projects was that the VLs were sending reinforcements from the West Side to help hold the Castle in the wake of relentless Disciple fire. These new boys were tough, people said, able to shoot with both hands. They had quality guns, nines and better, and they weren't shy about using them. People paid the newcomers the same respect they paid to any hard, serious person in Cabrini.

"These boys don't play," said one sixteen-year-old from the Castle, shaking his head. "They don't play."

*   *   *

In the dugout before a game, Rufus, Nathaniel, and Louis were playing rock-paper-scissors.

"One . . . two . . . *three*," they chanted, and revealed their choices. Louis's hand was clenched into a fist; Nathaniel's was held flat. Rufus's index finger and thumb were extended, trigger style.

"Paper cover rock," said Nathaniel.

"Rock crush scissors," said Louis.

"Unnhh-*uhhhh*," corrected Rufus with a satisfied grin. "This a gun. Gun beat everything."

FOUR

The Monday after the Bantus game, Bill arrived early at his North Pier office. He didn't usually come early; as he said, his job wasn't brain surgery. But today he had a few things to mull over, and he preferred the quiet clutter of his office to home.

He settled in at his desk, paging absentmindedly through the *Tribune* and sipping his coffee. Things around the office weren't good. His mock title of Retail Leasing Aspirant was ringing a little too accurately. It had been several weeks since Bill or any of his colleagues had reeled in a new client—bad timing in light of a $42 million construction loan coming due in October, which his company now lacked the funds to repay. The company's shareholders were said to be uneasy with the direction things were going in, and there was an increasing possibility that the management would be ousted.

"It's tough to tell what all that could mean," Bill said. "But if they clean house, I could be on the street."

Things on the home front weren't much better. The old Audi had finally expired; Bill had replaced it with a used red Saab. His yearlong relationship with Molly, while still good, had become awkward as the question of marriage began to loom. And Bill's parents' divorce was dragging into its final throes. In the latest negotiation Bill was aware of, his mother had been awarded the dinette set and his father had bartered for the oil painting that hung in the living room. His father phoned occasionally to see when they could get together, but Bill continued to give him the cold shoulder. "When this gets done, I could see doing something with him," he said. "Not before then."

This morning, however, Bill's thoughts were on the Kikuyus, and more specifically on the Bantus debacle. He opened up the battered manila folder and looked over the roster. Several alterations had been made since Bill first assembled it—Rickey and T.J. deleted, Otis added, David added and then deleted—and now it looked complete. Twelve names, ages, dates of birth, addresses, and phone numbers, arranged neatly, even the names of parents and guardians in the far-right column. It looked so orderly. Why wasn't it?

Bill was not new at the trials and tribulations of dealing with adolescents. He had worked as a summer camp counselor during his high school years, then as a lacrosse coach during college, and most recently as a ski instructor in Copper Mountain, Colorado, the year after his graduation. Growing up as he had in the flatlands, Bill was hardly the best skier who tried out for the job. But he was hired because his employers noticed his unique talent with children, especially the way he treated them like adults. He asked questions, listened carefully to their answers, and always worked from a distance, managing situations rather than trying to control his pupils with stern pep talks or false praise. Early in his stint at Copper Mountain, Bill had hit on a trick that would become his signature. At the end-of-class time trial, he sent the slowest skier last, and had him or her start outside the timing gate. When the skier was partway down the course and still out of sight of the others, Bill would trip the mechanism with his ski pole, assuring the slow skier of a fast time. "The skier would get to the bottom, and everybody would be floored," Bill recalled with pride. "By the time I pulled in, the whole class would be patting the person on the back, saying, 'Wow, I didn't realize you were so good,' and I could just stand there, not say a thing. It was great."

With the Kikuyus, though, things weren't so great. He was treating them like adults, and the team was in near chaos. Was it the environment? Were the kids different? Was he different?

Bill pulled out a red pen and worked his way down the roster, checking and circling names of troublemakers like a teacher grading papers. As he did, faint cries filtered through the drywall from the pediatrician's office next door, suitable accompaniment to such accounting work.

The pen moved first at Harold's name. Ah, Harold. The bully. The mouth. The braggart. Of course, Bill had dealt with bullies and braggarts before. When he was eleven, while pedaling home from a Little League game he had been waylaid by Big J.J., the unrivaled scourge of the neighborhood, who threatened to put his glove in a maildrop.

"You can't do that," a righteous Bill had yelled through tears. "That's a *federal offense!*"

"Oh, yeah?" said Big J.J.

"Yeah," said Bill. "You'll go to *jail!*"

Bill's threat, however weepily delivered, had worked. Big J.J. redirected his aim at some nearby train tracks, leaving young Bill to scramble breathlessly to retrieve his precious mitt. Big J.J. eventually lost his fear of federal regulations; the last Bill had heard, he was doing time for illegal arms sales.

But Harold was tougher than Big J.J. Rules didn't scare him; neither did authority, not anymore. He defied coaches, he picked fights, he showed up late. Most of all, he had an uncanny ability to provoke, a native radar that sought out weak points in others and hammered at them mercilessly with insult after insult. His monologues, cajoling, teasing, demanding a response, and usually delivered at a nose-to-nose distance of about six inches, had become the background rhythm at practice.

"Why don't you give me some money, Bill? You got lots of money, you drive a nice big car, wear some good threads. Can't you lend your best player no seventy-five cents for a little old piece of pizza? Or does you got something real important to spend that on?"

"How come your hair so nappy, Maurice? I ain't never seen anybody whose hair as raggedy as yours. I got a nickel if you want to go get it cut, or maybe you could just go rub your raggedy-butt hair on the ground like a Rasta boy. Course, you so kiss-ass with Coach Bill, maybe one of them rub it on the ground for you."

Bill shook his head in wonder. "I have never met a kid," he said, "who, no matter what he said, made it sound like an accusation. He could say, 'Happy Mother's Day,' and it would come across like 'Go to hell.' "

As Harold's impact on the team increased, Bill and the other coaches began relating to him not as a twelve-year-old boy, but as a peer, a personal rival for the team's attention, whose influence, if it couldn't be stopped, had to be negated in other ways. Before long, coaches found themselves employing sarcasm, bodily force, or psychological games such as pointedly ignoring him when he hit a home run—anything to keep him quiet. Fuses shortened.

"Hey, Brad," Harold would say during a team meeting, "tell me I'm not the best. . . ."

"Sit down and shut up, Harold," three coaches would say simultaneously.

But as good as that sometimes felt, Bill and the other coaches knew that the solution was not in bullying Harold or, on the other extreme, lying back and allowing him to manipulate coaches against one another as he had in the jersey episode at the Bantus game. If they could not make him fall in line, there had to be something else, perhaps something outside the team that could. After all, Bill had to remind himself, this was the same boy who had acted so courteous for a while at his first practice.

"It's like Jekyll and Hyde," Bill said. "He was this nice, polite kid, and then his identical twin took over and turned him into a loudmouth jerk. We've got to figure out a way to keep the good side out and the bad side hidden."

Bill knew a little about Harold's home life. He lived north of Cabrini, in a brick apartment building not that different from the Lincoln Park walk-ups where the coaches lived. Brad theorized that Harold's behavior stemmed from his living outside Cabrini; that he felt a constant need to prove himself. As far as Bill could tell, this seemed the case. Alone, Harold was a quiet, intelligent kid; it was only on the baseball diamond that he transformed himself into the saggy-pants intimidator. It was as if he were play-acting, rehearsing his tough gangster strut in the relatively safe confines of the team.

Occasionally, flashes of the good Harold appeared. A few nights earlier, he had called Bill, wanting to know when the next game was. They talked awhile, and then Harold had cut Bill off in midsentence.

"Hey," he had said in a tone of genuine excitement, "tell my dad how good I can hit."

Harold's father got on the line, and he and Bill chatted for ten minutes. They talked about Harold, the team, the league. Harold's father said he had been working a lot of overtime, and he would try to make it to more games in the future. Bill, low-key as usual, said that would be a good idea. He didn't want to burn any bridges, so he resisted mentioning Harold's bad behavior. He thought he might do so later. "He sounded like a nice guy," Bill decided. "Maybe he's the solution."

Demetrius's name was next to be circled. Bill was familiar with the saying in Cabrini that every child in the project was ten years older than his chronological age. Demetrius, however, seemed the exception—he was more like twenty years older. Nothing slipped past his bright, narrow eyes.

When Bill tried to give a pep talk, Demetrius was sure to parody him in a faultless white accent. When coaches tried to shake his hand in the neighborhood three-grip fashion, he would look up and roll his eyes as if to say, Who do you think you're kidding? When any of the coaches spouted typical Little League platitudes—"Hey, let's hear some chatter out there, guys," and so on—it was always Demetrius, his thin lips set in a permanent wry smile, who managed to convey a group sense of deep and utter skepticism. While Harold was an active mutineer, Demetrius represented a built-in resistance to the rule of law, a passive cynicism that was highly contagious among the rest of the team.

"You hit me, I'm gonna sue you and take your car," he said during one early practice, and the refrain soon was adopted by Rufus, Nathaniel, and others.

But Bill had seen another side to Demetrius as well, a serious side that he revealed only in some of their man-to-man talks. "Straight up," he'd say, then embark with a coach on a long conversation about the team, school, or girls. Once in his thoughtful mode, he would pry for information, trying to get Bill to tell him whether he planned on marrying Molly, or quitting his job, or which players he liked most, or which was better, automatic or manual transmission. But on the field, in front of an audience, Demetrius's serious side fell away. He became skeptic, show-off, wise-ass.

Demetrius never talked much about home. Bill knew that he lived in a crowded apartment ruled by his elderly Great-aunt Carol. From his limited contact with her, Bill judged her a solid person, grave and reliable, and overworked as family lifeboat. Demetrius's mother was another matter. She lived a few blocks away, and for some unclear reason had been declared an unfit mother by the courts. She had come to a game once, a tall, imposing woman in black tights and a zebra-striped fez, and had caused a scene by teasing the other team in a manner not unlike her son's.

When a coach had asked Demetrius if the young-looking woman was his older sister, he drew close and whispered quietly, "That's my *mother*."

Jalen's name was next, but Bill moved the pen halfheartedly. Bill always had a special place for Jalen. The other coaches saw him only as a pain, a complainer, a grouchy old man; Brad had nicknamed him "Skinny Angry." But there was something about the boy that Bill liked. Harold and Demetrius were actors, misbehaving in order to impress others or reassure themselves; Jalen wanted to succeed, and he yelled at anything that got in the way. He yelled at simple things: The game was unfair, the team wasn't very good, other coaches bought their teams more pizza. To Bill, the predictability of Jalen's wrath became almost comforting; the boy was like a bell that could be relied on to sound off at any perceived injustice, no matter how slight.

But as Bill knew, his feelings didn't lessen Jalen's effect on the team. The younger kids were afraid of him; and even the older players such as Harold and Demetrius usually followed his lead. Jalen's relationship to the team was reflected in his walk—sticklike arms down at his sides, head lowered slightly, torso steely and straight, body not bobbing and weaving in a streetwise hop, but moving directly and efficiently. It was the walk of someone who expected everyone to get out of the way, and for the most part, everyone did.

Like the other troublemakers, Jalen had a soft side, a shyness that showed only on occasion. When he showed up late to a game once, he explained it was because his mother had punished him. When Bill asked why, Jalen wouldn't say. "Boy," Bill said, "whatever you did, it must've been bad, to have you miss part of a game." "It *was*," said Jalen.

"He didn't put away his Nintendo!" shouted his six-year-old sister, who had been tagging along. Jalen blushed deeply, and told her to shut up. It was good to see him blush.

Parents, of course, represented a possible cure for disciplinary ills. It was no coincidence that the two best-behaved players on the team were Maurice and Rufus, whose mother accompanied them to almost every game and practice. Bill had made several efforts at the beginning of the season to draw parents to the games. He had told them about the parents' committee Greg White had set up, and how the parents on it had organized several meetings and were planning a banquet. He told them about the possibility of a parents' softball game, which some other teams had held.

Still, practice after practice and game after game, Maurice and Rufus's mother stood alone. Some parents, Bill knew, had good reasons why they couldn't attend: Louis's parents and Jalen's mother worked odd hours; Harold's father had a job far away; Calbert's mother was having a hard time getting around since her car had been stolen; Demetrius's great-aunt was seventy-seven. Others, while eager to turn the supervision of their children over to coaches whom they had never met, simply never made the effort. *Well, sure he can make it to the game, but I'm fittina have some things going on, so I can't make it. What time will you be bringing him home?*

But even if parents attended more games, would that be enough? Didn't discipline, in the end, need to come from the top? Perhaps, as Brad sometimes urged, Bill needed to be more strict, to put people on the bench, to make them sit out games when they mouthed off. Though Bill had agreed in principle, he had never really acted on it. When Brad pressed, Bill demurred by saying there weren't enough players for him to bench anyone. This was true, yet it wasn't a full explanation. When other coaches benched and suspended players, it usually resulted in better discipline as well as increased attendance; the threat of not being allowed to play baseball was the greatest motivator. Bill, however, would rather "just sit and talk with the kids," Brad said. "He's great at it, but at some point talk isn't enough."

In the end, though, Bill was reassured by the fact that every team, no matter how disciplined, had seen its share of disasters. He had heard about the Hausa who urinated on first base, the Big Yoruba players who threw their gloves over the El track, the highly disciplined Mau Mau squad who, after a loss, sent hats and gloves flying around the field like popping corn. Some teams had even folded, most recently the Little Yoruba, whose coach had been overwhelmed by the task of simply fielding a team, and who had forfeited to the Kikuyus the previous week. ("These guys don't even have *phones,*" he said. "Maybe the league will work in four or five years, when the kinks get ironed out, but right now, it's a zoo.") Each incident highlighted the basic tension of the enterprise: You couldn't just pull a dozen kids from one of the worst housing projects in America, put them on a field with a bunch of suburban-bred businessmen, have them play a difficult and frustrating sport, and expect it to come off with complete decorum. Of *course* things were disorderly. Perhaps they were supposed to be that way.

Picking his way down the roster, flecks of new silver showing in his hair, Bill was like a kindly but ambivalent grandfather, well aware of the faults of his grandchildren, yet unable or unwilling to work up any real anger toward them. Yes, some of them were headaches. Yes, they sometimes misbehaved. But ultimately, he'd rather think about the better times.

Like the time when Maurice had put his hand on Bill's shoulder and told him to relax, that it was only a game. Or the time when, a half-hour after Bill mentioned that it was his mother's birthday, Otis departed saying, "Wish your mother a happy birthday from me." Or the time when, after the riots following the Bulls' victory, Alonzo wrote a letter to Michael Jordan, advising him that he should tell people not to tear up their own neighborhoods. "Call it *Jordan Rules Two,*" he said with a satisfied smile, invoking the title of a popular book. Or the time when, during the team outing to Wrigley Field, Bill had to break it to Freddie that no, they weren't actually going to be *playing* against the Cubs, they were going only to watch. "Okay," said Freddie, nodding thoughtfully. "That sound good, too."

Dozens of stories like these were carefully stored in Bill's considerable memory, and he took great pleasure in recounting them to colleagues and friends. On the walls of his office, there were only three items on display: a photo of him and his fellow ski instructors atop a Colorado mountain, a 1930 postcard of the Chicago railroad yards, and the Kikuyus' team picture. When Bill took down the picture and told his stories, there was the distinct impression that he was talking about family. While his parents' lawyers argued over dinette sets and oil paintings, Bill sat in his office and told stories about "the kids."

Just before the game against the Bantus, Maurice and Rufus's mother had approached Bill as he unloaded the team's equipment from his car. Smiling, Mary had held out a piece of paper to him.

"Here," she said shyly. "The boys wanted to give this to their coaches."

On the piece of paper, a generic certificate decorated with calligraphy, the blank lines had been filled in with painstaking cursive. Bill held it up.

CERTIFICATE OF APPRECIATION

To, all My Coaches
is awarded this certificate in appreciation of
notable contributions to
Kikuyu L.L. Baseball
Our sincere gratitude and thanks
This *18* day of *July*, 1992
Signed *Rufus, Maurice*

"Thanks!" Bill had to shout to be heard over the roar of the passing El train. "This is great!"

*   *   *

On the last Monday of July, the league board gathered at
the Seward Park fieldhouse for its first official meeting
since June's early-morning Operation PUSH rhubarb. The
board members trickled in: Greg White, who arrived ten
minutes early, attired in Lycra running shorts; real estate
executive and league secretary Jonathan Strain, who pulled
up in his Audi; Bob and Tina, now seven months pregnant
with their third child; and Bill Seitz, who walked over from
Carson Field. The local YMCA director, John Stevens, who
held the title of Player Representative, arrived at five, the
designated hour for the meeting.

The group waited at the fieldhouse entrance, making
small talk. It was a beautiful afternoon. Skies were clear for
the first time in a week, though small horsetails of cirrus
streamed west of the field; sea gulls from Lake Michigan
wheeled overhead in their never-ending patrol for open
Dumpsters. But none of the board members seemed to notice. Their conversation was hurried; their laughter rang
too loudly. Greg looked at his watch. Ten minutes past five,
and no Al Carter.

"We can't wait forever," he said. "Let's get going."

"Give him five more minutes." Bob showed his palm.
"He guaranteed me he'd be here."

"A guarantee?" Greg's eyebrows went up. "I wonder
how much that's worth."

"I guess that's the thirty-five-thousand-dollar question."
Bill Seitz's voice was heavy with sarcasm, but he kept it low
so John Stevens wouldn't hear. John and Al Carter went
back a long time; Al had once worked for John at the
YMCA. The two frequently were allies at board meetings.

Ostensibly, this meeting had been called to discuss the
playoff format and the end-of-season banquet. But for Bob,
the agenda was Al Carter and the mysterious grant. Bill
Seitz's detective work had not produced the grant proposal, but he had obtained The Chicago Initiative's sum-
mary describing the purpose of the grant as a "youth

baseball and basketball program in conjunction with the African-American Youth League and the Al Carter Youth Foundation." Bill Seitz had also discovered that Carter's organization, though registered with the federal government as a 501(c)(3) nonprofit, was not state-certified to solicit or hold grants, charitable contributions, or any funds whatsoever. It was a long way from proof—particularly if you considered Bob's incomplete knowledge of the role of Demicco Youth Services—but it was something, and it fueled his indignation. For her part, Tina made several telephone calls to The Chicago Initiative, claiming that one of its grants had been misappropriated and insisting vehemently that something be done.

Since the discovery of the grant, Bob had taken to reflecting on the many favors he had done for Al since they had met almost two years before: paying for his weekend at the Downtown Athletic Club in New York, covering for him at league meetings, directing the press to Al when Bob knew the action wouldn't be reciprocated, helping Al's friends—in one case an ex-con with a murder record—get jobs.

Bob's ire had intensified at Al's recent sudden suspension of the league's weekly African-American educational classes he was supposed to oversee. In a sternly worded fax announcing the move, Al wrote that the suspension was due to nonparticipation. That, however, was only partly true. Many players and coaches had attended, and more often than not it was the teachers who had not shown. When Al canceled the program, Bob hardly could contain his anger.

"The more I see this, the more I see Al as a guy who can't let anything good happen in the neighborhood unless he can control it," Bob said. "He's a poverty pimp. He's like Jesse Jackson and all those people, directing all the anger at prejudice and racism, always saying that it's them, them, them, when *they're* the real problem in the community."

At fifteen minutes after five, Al strode in the door in his black sweatsuit. He shook hands with Bob in the three-grip style and, giving no explanation for his lateness, led the group up the stairs and into a room that looked out on Carson Field to the north.

The board members pulled ancient metal folding chairs noisily from a rack and arranged them in a loose circle, each chair separated from the next by several feet of blond hardwood. Greg White sat immediately to Al's left; Bob and Tina chose seats across from them. After a few niceties, Bill Seitz stood up nervously, adjusted his baggy pants, and faced Al. A small colony of pigeons flapped and purred in the rafters outside.

Bill's voice bubbled up, nervous and quick. "I gotta go soon, so I just want to know one thing. What are you doing with the money?" His eyes were on the floor, but his index finger was pointed squarely at Al. "That's all I want to know—where the money is. You know the money I'm talking about, and you should tell us what you're doing with it." He gave a martyrlike shrug. "Then I have to go, because *somebody* has to make sure the field gets lined for tomorrow's games."

No one said anything. A big, twisty vein on the left side of Al's forehead began to pulse.

"I do not like rumors," Al said, the vein in his temple lengthening. "I do not like that bullshit."

"Al," Tina interrupted, her voice cracking, "do you *have* to use that type of language?"

Al turned to her, ramrod straight. "If you've got a problem with my language, I suggest that you spend this meeting in another room."

Tina rolled her eyes and looked to Bob for support. She got none.

"I will say this only one time," Al continued. "This grant is for *sports* and *recreation* in the community. It was given to Demicco Youth Services, who gave it to the Al Carter Youth Foundation, and that is who will spend the money supporting *sports* and *recreation* in the community. I am paying twenty-one gang members by the hour to run the basketball tournament. We bought balls, nets, scorecards, jerseys, everything. We get umpires for the Little League—and I decide who those umpires will be. No one else."

"Come *on*, Al." Through clenched teeth, Bob's voice was quiet, almost conspiratorial. "The Chicago Initiative says the grant is for basketball and baseball. You're telling me that a few umps and a three-on-three basketball tournament is running you thirty-five grand?" Bob repeated the figure slowly, dramatically: "Thurr . . . tee . . . fye . . . ev . . . guh . . . rand?"

"And you're paying umpires who show up half crocked most of the time?" Tina said, tears brimming in her eyes. "What do we tell all the volunteers who work fifty-hour weeks and still find time to come out to the field? That we can't pay them, but we can pay these other guys to drink?"

Al paused and leaned toward Bob, his tone suddenly diplomatic. "You got some umpires that should be getting paid? Give me their names and I'll get them on the list, no problem."

"That isn't what we want," Tina said, as Bob and Greg exchanged knowing looks. "This is a volunteer league. Nobody should be getting paid."

Al checked Bob's face, having quickly realized that his offer had been rejected. "I don't give a shit *what* you think," he said, his words coming fast now, the river in his temple stretching to its full length. "You have all the money you need, and this grant is for the betterment of the community, and *no*body but me is going to decide how to spend it. Not you, not *any*body. If you don't want to be part of this, you all can go back and play golf wherever the fuck you want to. I don't *need* to hear this bullshit." He sat back, the cords in his neck showing with each breath.

"Bob, it ain't that much money anyway," added John Stevens reasonably. "Compared to some grants, that ain't but chump change. Hire a few people, buy some equipment, and it's gone."

"Come *on*." Bob hunched forward, tried again for a sale.

"We've got four *hundred* kids out there for a whole summer and you've got what, fifty, sixty kids for ten weeks? Give me . . ."

"There's no comparison," Al snapped. "We're paying people, we're helping people, we got none of this bullshit corporate money—"

"Where do you think you got *your* money, Al?" asked Tina. "It's all corporate—"

"Will you let me finish—"

"No, let me finish—"

"Hang on a second—"

For the next fifteen minutes, the debate raged. Bob embarked on several unheard arguments; Greg tried, unsuccessfully, to karate-chop each side's case into digestible bits; Tina's voice kept rising until it topped soprano; Al stonewalled with "Because that's the way it is" and "Because I said so"—until finally the discussion collapsed under the sheer weight of unsustainable babble.

Afterward, Bob and Tina worked their way across a garbage-covered field toward Orleans Street. Not much had been accomplished. Al had not backed down. Bob remained unshaken.

"A lot of this bullshit happens because Bob and me are opposites," Al said later. "Bob believes in Christ, but I believe only in myself—no Jesus, just myself and some God beyond all this. I don't use the word 'trust' no more. People are *different*—you lay in a hole with some cat, you come out, and things change. I have faith, but I don't trust nobody but myself.

"That's always been the knack of white America," he continued, "taking over, taking over shit they don't know nothing about. That's the whole thing, white male dominance. Well, it ain't gonna happen with me, and it ain't gonna happen with that baseball program. Bottom line, they aren't out here every day. Last week, I was at Durso Park, running the tournament at four-thirty in the afternoon, when some cats drove by and started shooting on the court. Four-thirty! People are running everywhere, and this woman is trying to find her four-year-old baby, and everything's going wild! There's some boy—fifteen years old maybe—racing down the street, firing back at the car! A few nights later, I'm up with Mrs. Edwards, her daughter Laquanda shot in the head, fifteen years old, her brains all over the street. It's wildness, man, wildness. They don't see the wildness."

"They hate us," Bob had said as he left the meeting, not specifying whom he meant. "They fucking hate us." Kicking an empty liquor bottle, he had walked back to Carson Field without saying anything more.

"I don't know what makes Al so angry," Tina once said. "Did some white people call him 'nigger' a long time ago?"

When Alvin Carter was nine years old, one of his best friends was a skinny Sicilian boy named Virgilio Ontario. Virgilio lived across the street, and he would invite Alvin over for spaghetti about once a week. Alvin wasn't much for spaghetti or any of the other strange-smelling foods they cooked over there, but he went anyway. If he didn't, he figured, Virgilio might not be his friend, and Alvin didn't want that to happen. Being an only child, Alvin appreciated playmates.

When he was seven, Alvin had come down with a severe case of rheumatic fever. The doctor—a white man, he would remember with disdain—said that the fever had made his heart delicate, and told his mother, Zelphia, not to let him run around with other children, lest he overexert himself and die. So little Alvin stayed indoors, and on weekends Zelphia would take him on the train to the mansions of Kenilworth and Winnetka where she worked. While she washed steps and dusted, her skinny boy would play with her employers' children, teaching them how to shoot marbles and ride on the handlebars of a bike. Their mothers grew fond of Alvin as well, and would sometimes give him bags of hand-me-downs. Before long, he had built up quite a wardrobe and a reputation. People back home—

even Sicilians—would stop him and ask what it was like "up there." "I was the preppiest cat on Hudson Street," Al recalled. "People thought I was the greatest guy in the world, because I could go up there and come back, and they never left the neighborhood."

When Alvin was ten, his family applied for placement in the new Cabrini rowhouses on Chestnut Street, a block from where they lived. These were nice places, neat two-story apartments with separate doorways, and flower beds, and squares of grass between stoops. The Carters' was a respectable two-parent, one-wage-earner household (Alvin's father, Moses, worked in a paint factory), and their application was quickly accepted. Alvin liked his new home; it was cleaner and bigger than the old one, and it had a real bathtub—a big improvement on the tin tub he was used to. His parents even bought him a dog, a big brown chow he named Chico, which they picked up from the pound for eight dollars. What Alvin liked most, however, was the fact that the rowhouses had a baseball team, the Mohawks. Though his parents, still worried about the doctor's warnings, sent Al to spend months in Arkansas with relatives, the rest of the time he was a Mohawk. They were tough and smart, the cream of Jenner Elementary School, and they knew it. There was Butchie Boneface and Snooty; Columbus, Charlie, and Abraham; Duper, Wallace, Little Johnnie, and Mouse; they were coached by an old white man named Doc.

Despite or perhaps because of the doctor's warnings, Alvin grew into quite an athlete; he was still skinny, but muscular and fast enough to win quarters racing up the stairs of the new Cabrini Extension highrises being constructed up the block. Despite his build, he played back-catcher for the Mohawks and came across as a tough guy who wasn't afraid to tease opposing hitters from behind the plate. Sometimes he'd go a little overboard and somebody would want a piece of him, but when that happened Al would call for Chico to protect him. None of his teammates can remember an instance of his backing down. "Some boys have a hard head," his friend Tommie Johnson said, "but Alvin, with his dog and all, he got a *real* hard head."

In September 1955, Alvin, almost fourteen, had returned to Chicago from a summer in Arkansas and taken up a newspaper route. One day he spotted a story in the bundle of papers he was about to deliver. It was about a Chicago boy named Emmett Till who had been visiting relatives in Money, a town in Mississippi. He had gone into a store to buy candy, and had whistled at a white woman. Word got back to the woman's husband and his half brother, and the two men kidnapped Emmett at gunpoint. The boy's body was pulled out of the Tallahatchie River three days later; he had been beaten and shot and a gin-mill fan was wired around his neck. The two men were arrested, and at their trial admitted to having kidnapped the boy, but said they had let him go after scaring him a little. The all-white, all-male jury acquitted the pair after deliberating for sixty-five minutes. In an interview published in *Look* magazine a month after the trial, one of the men admitted that they had killed Till. "What else could I do? He thought he was as good as any white man."

Along with the Supreme Court's 1954 *Brown vs. Board of Education of Topeka* decision, which ordered desegregation of the nation's public schools, the Emmett Till killing and the acquittal of the murderers would be regarded as a turning point in U.S. race relations, forming a foundation for the equal rights movement of the next decade. For young Alvin, however, Till's murder had a more immediate effect.

"We were the same, him and me," Al recalled. "When I was down South, I did all the things he did—spit in the whites-only water fountains, whistled at white women. When I seen that picture of him, layin' in the casket beaten up so bad he didn't have no face left, man, I had some nightmares. I told my mother I wasn't ever going back down South, and I didn't, not until the Army. That Emmett Till thing traumatized me. He was like my clone."

When the Mohawks entered high school, they started drifting apart. They went out for different sports, they started to run with different crowds. Eventually, several met with considerable success. Columbus became the owner of ten Wendy's franchises in Newark. Butchie Boneface became a schoolteacher in Indiana; Snooty, the owner of a meat-packing plant on the South Side. Others didn't. Wallace was shot to death playing three-card monte in Minnesota. Charlie was murdered on the corner of Division and Larrabee when he was nineteen. Little Johnnie, who at age ten had a better fastball than any of them, hung out on Cambridge Street, not doing much of anything. Nobody knew what became of Doc.

Alvin, however, was ready to go further than any of the others. His four-minute, thirty-two-second time in the mile helped win him a full scholarship to Drake University in Des Moines. In the fall of 1959, he packed his bags, said good-bye to his dog, and left for school, wondering whether he'd ever return to Cabrini.

By March 1968, Al was back in Chicago, tired of everything. He had dropped out of Drake after three years, frustrated by his lack of progress in track, and had joined the Army. After two tours of duty filling fuel tanks in South Korea and Vietnam, he came home and drove trucks for United Parcel Service, then lost that job after trying to organize a strike. Now he was picking up a little cash driving cabs and trucks, but he didn't have much besides his wife, Barbara, a baby daughter, Cheryl, and a little apartment at 82nd and Racine.

He was waiting for a bus at the corner of 51st and Racine with Barbara when he heard a voice.

"Hey, nigger."

The voice came from down the sidewalk, and Al didn't look.

"That's right, nigger, we're talking to you."

Now he looked. Half a dozen white men with crew cuts, around twenty years old, were walking toward him and

Barbara. One of them had a German shepherd. Unbeknownst to Al, this was the same neighborhood that once had greeted Martin Luther King Jr.'s marchers with a hail of bottles and rocks. That had been more than a year before, but now these guys were looking for a fight.

"We might be making him angry," said the one with the dog. "We wouldn't want to make the nigger angry now, would we?"

Al stared straight ahead. He had met men like these before, mostly in the Army. It was full of white southern boys, and Al had never liked or trusted any of them. He had spent his time with black men from Mississippi, Alabama, and Georgia, had heard their stories about Jim Crow, the lynchings and rapes. He had started reading: *Muhammed Speaks, The Fire Next Time;* he devoured everything by Malcolm X that he could get his hands on, including tape-recordings of his speeches. For basic training, Al had been in Alabama and Kentucky, and had seen plantation-style homes that reminded him of the mansions his mother used to clean; he had heard townspeople dare black soldiers to come into town alone at night. He had converted to the Muslim faith, and had begun correcting friends when they called each other black; they were Moorish-American, he said. He moved, as the literature put it, into a higher consciousness.

In Yongi-gol, South Korea, he had had to deal with a southern-born officer who went out of his way to antagonize the black soldiers in his command. He had called them niggers, spit on their shoes, and hinted broadly that he was a member of the Ku Klux Klan. Al decided that something had to be done. One night, long after bedcheck, Al gathered six enlisted men. After polishing off a case of beer, they fashioned hoods out of pillowcases and pulled baseball bats from the rec closet. They burst into the officer's room, pulled the covers over the sleeping man's head, and beat him. "It was just like the Klan," he recalled. "We had bats, hoods, eyeholes, just like them. We beat the shit out of that guy, and it felt good. They ended up sending the cat back to the States. He was all fucked up, shoulder broke, stitches. But he had it comin'."

Even as Al lashed out, he was hit by greater blows. He was in Vietnam when he heard the news that Malcolm X had been assassinated. "I couldn't believe it—the King was dead. Every black man who took a giant step forward got killed. It proved to me that the system has a way of getting you if you step out of line."

The German shepherd barked. The crew cuts were only steps away, but so was the bus. It squeaked up to the curb. Al hustled Barbara aboard, and he probably could have made it in himself, but the crew cuts were close now, taunting. He faced them.

Words were exchanged, and then the dog was snapping, Al was kicking the dog, and one of the men was leaping at him. Before the crew cuts were able to land any serious blows, however, Al grabbed one man's collar with his left hand and started punching with his right. The others hit and pulled, and the dog tore Al's pants, but Al kept hold of the collar. If he let go, he knew he'd fall, and if he fell, he'd get stomped. The hitting finally stopped, and Al pulled away and dove onto the idling bus, his face covered with blood. He shoved the driver hard, telling him to move—now.

After a block or so the driver pulled over. A policeman had signaled to him to stop; he came aboard and ordered Al to get off. Al did, and saw that another officer was talking to the crew cuts. One of them held a handkerchief to his bleeding jaw. The white men went home; Al was arrested for battery and taken to jail. After Barbara bailed him out for fifteen dollars, he went to the hospital to get stitched up.

FIVE

"I got a call from somebody on the team the other day," Coach Bill began, "and they wanted to know about the trip to Iowa."

A soft buzz was heard from the players as they huddled around their coach at the end of Monday's practice. Everybody had been talking about Iowa—or as it was pronounced, Awwa—for the last two weeks. Bob Muzikowski had arranged the whole thing: Chicago teams played Iowa teams, took hikes in the woods, slept in an old Boy Scout camp, had a barbecue along the Mississippi, and spent an afternoon at a water park. Now, almost two weeks in advance, Rufus's gym bag was already packed with socks, T-shirts, and his green dragon water pistol.

"I told them," Bill said, gesturing for silence, "that I wasn't so sure going to Iowa was a good idea for this team." He let this sink in.

"I'm just not sure," Bill continued, "given the way you acted against the Bantus and again today. If you're going to keep whining and yelling at each other, we won't go."

The complaints welled up immediately: "Maaaan!" "Y'all cheat!" "You phony!" "All the other teams get to go!" But Bill ignored them. He wasn't kidding about canceling the trip. This day's practice had been a seamless continuation of the Bantus game, starting with a reluctant infield practice orchestrated by Coaches Kevin and Feets. But then Harold had shown up, and Feets, perhaps forgetting the sitdown strike during the Bantus game, had made the mistake of picking him first for an intrasquad scrimmage. *"See!"* Harold threw his arms up triumphantly. "They was actin' like they was gonna kick me off, but they *can't*! They *know* I'm too good!" Everything had gone downhill from there.

"Let's talk for a second about attitude," Bill said once the protests had subsided. "What does it mean, in one word?"

All was quiet.

"Control," volunteered Maurice. Bill gave a professorial nod.

"Not teasing," said Calbert.

"Not teasing," parroted Demetrius.

"Not yelling at each other," said Louis.

"There's one more word, and it begins with a *t*." Bill unfolded a long index finger and capped it with his flattened palm.

"Trophy," yelled Harold, rising.

"Sit down, Harold," said Brad. Harold didn't.

"Teamwork," said Louis.

"That's right," said Bill, "teamwork. That means encouraging each other. That means saying 'Good swing' and not calling somebody a buster. That means helping each other out instead of screwing each other up."

The players, sensing a lecture, started to move fitfully. Rufus drew circles in the dirt. Freddie tried to see if the knob of a bat would fit in his mouth.

"Okay," said Bill warily. "We've got something else to discuss." He pointed toward the outfield, where a tall, sticklike boy in an orange shirt stood waiting.

"Jalen and I were talking a few minutes ago." Bill folded his arms. "He told me that he'd changed his mind, that he wanted to come back on the team. I told him that it was fine with me, but that I had to see if the team wanted him back."

"Yeah!" shouted a jubilant Freddie. "Yeah, boy!"

Bill's hand went up. "Just a second. You may want him back on the team, but that doesn't mean everyone else will."

Bill paused, enjoying the silence. The players actually looked pensive, watching their self-exiled star backcatcher approach them slowly, his tough-guy walk reduced to a slow drag, a small dust cloud trailing each Scottie Pippen. When Jalen was close, Bill put a hand on his shoulder as if the boy might suddenly float away. Jalen shifted and kicked and tried to glare, but what came out was an embarrassed half-smile.

Bill looked solemn. "It's time to vote. If you think we should let Jalen back on the team, raise your hand."

Hands shot up, some more quickly than others. Three Busters, Louis, Calbert, and Rufus, sat on theirs.

Bill counted, then knitted his eyebrows in concern. "I don't think it means anything unless it's unanimous."

"C'mon, man," yelled Freddie, not wanting to lose his friend. "Lift up your *hand!"*

"I guess everybody deserves a second chance," said Calbert. The remaining holdouts raised their hands.

"Well," said Bill. "I think you all should dogpile on your new teammate."

"Yaaagh!"

Freddie dove at Jalen, and the others followed, forming a small pyramid of legs and arms. Jalen was on the bottom, giggling.

When the players eventually scattered, Bill hoisted the equipment bag on his shoulder and looked out on the scene. "Years from now," he said, trying to sound sarcastic, "they'll all look back on this meeting as the turning point in their lives."

*   *   *

On the afternoon Calbert was beaten up, the El tracks next to Carson Field caught fire. Track fires aren't particularly unusual in Chicago; sparks from the steel train wheels ignite dry trash on the wooden ties regularly. The fires are typically small, and are easily spotted and snuffed out.

But this fire, because of its location, was not immediately spotted. By the time the engines from the Division Street firehouse wailed over, the scent of acrid black smoke was mixing with that of pimiento from the Oscar Mayer smokestacks. The trucks screamed up, the hoses were unreeled, and the firemen scrambled up in their greatcoats and put out the flames.

Freddie and Jalen, who had been playing catch on the field, stood by and watched, gloves on hips, enthralled by the noise and action of the big equipment. Then they heard a voice behind them.

"It's been a cold summer so far," said the man in the "Boss" hat. The boys jumped. They had seen him many times before, shouting advice from behind the backstop, and like everybody else, they had ignored him. But now he was too close to ignore, with his yellowing eyes and whiskery face, cigarette smoke pluming from his nostrils. Freddie and Jalen took a cautious step back.

"This means the hot time's come," he said, bending forward and showing them his teeth. "And I'm tellin' you, it's gonna get hot."

Calbert was maybe twenty feet from Orleans Street when the Little Cobras caught him. They didn't have any trouble pulling him off his bike, because there were six or seven of them. They hit him in the face and the leg and went through his fanny pack, pulling out the $1.55 he had brought for pizza and pop after practice. They took his Bulls cap and his bike. They also found his blue inhaler, but they left that for him. Even Little Cobras had sympathy for asthma sufferers.

Woozy and scared, Calbert ran to Sammy's Red Hots

and called his mother, who promptly took him to Children's Memorial Hospital for overnight observation and asthma therapy. The X rays turned out to be negative, but that was of little solace to Calbert's mother. She felt betrayed; the coaches had told her that they would watch out for her son, and now he had been beaten. She phoned Bill and left a furious message on his answering machine, stating that it was all the coaches' fault and that Calbert had played his last game as a Kikuyu.

"And I'm gonna get . . ." The voice on the machine gasped for breath. ". . . a fucking . . . piece . . . of . . . your . . . *ass*."

"Holy cow," said Coach Cort, replaying the recorded voice for the third time. "I hope somebody knows a lawyer."

Bill phoned her the next morning. Calbert would soon be home, and she had calmed down somewhat. Bill listened to her story sympathetically and then told her his side, trying to be as rational as possible. The coaches had tried to keep an eye on every player and make sure they all got home okay, he told her, but in this case Calbert had lingered long after practice had ended, racing around on his bike. Any of the coaches would have escorted Calbert home had he asked, but he hadn't. Bill also told her that games were being played at Carson Field at the time, and that any one of a dozen or more coaches, umpires, and parents would have been capable of helping Calbert, if the incident had not happened just out of view. When you looked at the whole thing objectively, it was just a stroke of bad luck, a neighborhood misfortune over which nobody had control. "The important thing is that Calbert's okay," Bill said.

Calbert's mother remained angry. It was the coaches' fault. They knew that Calbert didn't know how to handle himself in that neighborhood, that he needed to be watched over. If they had paid any attention, Calbert wouldn't have had to go to the hospital and everything would have been fine.

Bill didn't push it. He wished her and Calbert well, said a polite good-bye, opened his manila folder, and started counting.

It didn't look good. Demetrius and Nathaniel were visiting relatives in the South, Louis was at Boy Scout camp, and Harold's attendance was questionable at best. With Calbert on the disabled list indefinitely, that made for a maximum possible turnout of seven for the game against the Xhosa on Thursday. Bill quickly volleyed, dialing the other coaches and Maurice and telling them to survey the neighborhood to try to recruit new players. Then he found a brand-new baseball and set it aside for the coaches to sign. They'd give it to Calbert, if his mother would let them.

In the last days of July, the wet weather returned with a vengeance, canceling the Kikuyus–Xhosa game and granting Carson Field a needed break. When the sun finally showed itself on the thirty-first, the place had changed. The rains had greened the brown edges of the weeds and exposed gumball-size rocks which now balanced precariously on the infield dirt like glacial erratics. Artifacts churned up by three months' constant sneaker-brushing—bottle caps, shoelaces, condoms, curlicues of plastic ribbon from the tops of Little Hug containers—were now rinsed clean. In the outfield the friction of bored feet had burned several telltale spots in the grass, but the infield was full, clean, and smooth, as if it had been laid down the day before.

There had not always been a Carson Field. From 1908 to 1979, the lot at the corner of Division and Sedgwick was the site of various secondary schools, the last of them a fortresslike vocational academy best remembered for the 1975 movie *Cooley High,* made by an alumnus of a nearby high school. Few mourned the school's demolition in 1979; by then it had become a dreary, outdated place to learn welding and carpentry, and a symbol of the city's inability to provide adequate education. "Kids who can read go to Waller High," went the saying at the board of education, referring to the neighborhood's other secondary school. "Those who can't, go to Cooley." The school came down, the students were sent to the new Near North Career Metropolitan High School, and the lot was left empty.

It stayed that way until 1981, when a Cabrini gang war left eleven dead and thirty-seven wounded in the first three months of the year. In a much-ballyhooed attempt to stop the violence, Mayor Jane Byrne temporarily relocated from her Gold Coast apartment to a security-fenced, body-guarded building at 1150–1160 North Sedgwick. Shortly after moving in, the mayor noticed the garbage-filled lot across the street and decreed that it be transformed into a recreation facility. In memory of the two officers slain at nearby Seward Park in 1970, the area—the field and the basketball courts across the street from it—was christened the Severin–Rizzato Sports Complex, and the field with its two diamonds was named after Frederick Carson, a local volunteer who ran sports programs.

The first baseball league was the idea of Byrne's husband, Jay McMullen. In the spring of 1981, he obtained uniforms, drew up a schedule, harassed the city parks commission into immediately sodding the field, and recruited dozens of children from Cabrini. By June, only a few months after the project had begun, all was ready. On Opening Day, dozens of city dignitaries came to laud the historic effort and to watch the mayor underhand the first pitch.

Twenty months later Byrne lost her bid for reelection. A few of her husband's volunteers attempted to sustain the league, but they were hamstrung without the financial and political pull of the mayor's office. The league folded, and the field reverted to a weed-filled trash dump, which is what it remained until Bob Muzikowski organized a cleanup party in the spring of 1991.

"What they let happen at Cabrini is one of the sorriest episodes in the history of youth sports in Chicago,"

McMullen said a few years before his death in March 1992. "We created a showcase program over there, and it was allowed to totally collapse overnight. . . . And nobody even shed a tear for it."

All that remained of McMullen's efforts were the scraps of black plastic netting that had held the strips of grass laid down for Opening Day. Now, after a rain eleven summers later, that same netting was still blowing around the field, clumping like cottonwood seeds along the chain link. If one looked closely, black plastic threads could even be seen sticking up amid the outfield grass, everlasting blooms of a league scuttled by politics.

There was a vague but persistent rumor that the demolishers of Cooley High had not done a complete job; that rather than extract the building's foundations, they had stopped at the basement ceilings and poured dirt over them. If the rumor was true, then the appearance of the netting signified that the players of the Near North Little League were slowly scuffing their way through the field's present skin into the bones of its past. That one day, perhaps, a shortstop might run back for a pop-up and be swallowed whole into the depths of a long-forgotten machine shop.

"I got, I got, I got . . ." Maurice shouted, racing toward the ball with his Ed Kranepool mitt unfurled before him like a spinnaker.

"I got . . ." The ball smacked off the heel of the big glove and fell to the ground. Maurice, in a well-rehearsed motion, scooped it up and threw it toward Bill.

"Tailed away at the last second," Maurice hollered. "Hit me another."

Bill shook his head. Practice had gone smoothly so far, and he wasn't going to risk a chorus of complaints if Maurice was allowed to field an extra ball. He hatcheted a grounder to Jalen. Moving reluctantly from his usual glove-on-hip ready position, Jalen scuttled sideways into the hole at shortstop, scooped up the ball, and winged it stiffly toward Freddie at first base. Jalen was like a marvelously coordinated senior citizen—never graceful, always efficient.

"Nice play, Jalen," Bill said. Jalen pretended he didn't hear, but a look of satisfaction crept over his face.

"Harold!"

The ball bounded into center field. Harold tried to be quick and casual at the same time, as he plucked the ball bare-handed and threw it to Rufus at second. The ball ticked off the smaller boy's glove and rolled back to Bill. But Harold, for once, didn't say anything.

It was tough to explain why everyone was behaving so well. Bill thought it might have been his threat to take away the Iowa trip, or maybe, with all the rainouts, absence had made the players' hearts grow fonder.

It also might have been the new faces. Maurice had come through with two recruits: Rassan, a scrappy, shrimplike boy who loved to run; and Jonathan, heavier and gentler, with long, feathery eyelashes. Neither had played baseball before. Bill handed them applications and told them to show up at the next game, against the Zulus. Both boys had been quietly thrilled. They looked up at Coach Bill with a mix of admiration and doubt, and held the applications as if they were the keys to the kingdom. The other Kikuyus looked on, aware of their own station.

"I'm fittina teach you how to throw a *palm*ball," Alonzo had told the newcomers. "Mine dips, then it breaks sideways across the plate."

"This how you stand at the plate," Maurice had instructed. "You step up and let the pitcher be fittina bust you inside, but then you step back, and *boom*—whack it to the gate."

Rassan and Jonathan nodded dizzily.

It was difficult to tell what effect, if any, Calbert's beating had had on the team. Bill had been prepared to inform the team and answer their questions, but he was too late. Word was already out.

"Little Cobras stole on Calbert," Alonzo told Bill before practice. "Took his bike, hit him with a lead pipe, *frac*tured his skull in two places."

"Yop." Freddie bobbed and weaved, jabbing the air. "They popped him, boy! They *stole* on him!"

"Listen up." Bill's voice rose. "Calbert wasn't hit with a lead pipe, and he doesn't have a broken skull. He's at home, a little shaken up, but feeling good. We'll wait to see if he'll be well enough to come back to the team, but the important thing is that he's okay."

He looked to see if anyone on the team seemed worried or upset, but no one did. Calbert's plight had already been reduced to a sketch like all the others. Anthony Felton waiting under a tree, popped in the chest by some GDs. Laquanda Edwards crossing the street, popped in the head by a sniper from the Castle. Bonita Hemphill, after words with VLs, popped in the face. Calbert beaten up by Little Cobras, bike taken. Same story; different details. Everybody knew people who got hurt; there wasn't anything special or unusual about this one.

Rufus tugged on Bill's T-shirt. "Calbert fittina go to Awwa?"

"We'll see," Bill said, hope in his voice. He didn't tell the team that a day or so before this practice, Calbert's mother had phoned him. Calbert had received the signed baseball, she told him, and he was grateful that they had been thinking of him. She said that Calbert wasn't counting on playing in any more games this season, but he might go to Iowa, if he was feeling well enough.

Calbert's mother wasn't the only one to change her attitude. Lately, a few of the Kikuyus had taken to phoning Bill at his office. Ignoring the beeps on his other line, Bill would have long talks with them about nothing in particular. Jalen divulged a secret omelet recipe, Harold rated the coaches ("Brad's too loud. Steve got the best ride"), and Bill was able to correct their belief that Little League coaching was a paying job. They and other players made wagers with Bill, betting for pizza and Cokes, that they would hit so many home runs or get on base every time at bat. Bill's desk was bristling with yellow notes covered with his bookie scrawl: "Xhosa, Jalen bat 1.000, half hits extra bases = 1 slice," said one. "Zulu game, Harold HRs 1 triple = 2 slices," said another. Bill got a big charge out of the calls, and he worked them subtly into conversations with other coaches. "Jalen called me the other day," he'd say, waiting for the inevitable, unbelieving, "*Jalen* called *you?*"

Now practice was under way, and Bill arranged the defense for situation ball, with Steve and Kevin filling roles as opposition baserunners.

"One out, nobody on," Bill called before chopping a grounder to third base. Alonzo, in his high-heeled ready position, lurched unsteadily toward the ball, grabbed it, and unleashed a sidearm toss that flew far over Freddie's head.

"Overhand," Brad reminded Alonzo.

"I *wanted* to throw overhand," Alonzo replied. "It's just that my arm wanted to throw *side*arm. It ain't warmed up yet."

Brad walked over and shouted into Alonzo's shoulder. "Hey, arm! Throw overhand!" Alonzo nodded approvingly.

"Get two, now," Bill shouted.

For the Kikuyus, practicing double plays was little more than an exercise in optimism, but they did it anyway. Bill rolled a soft grounder to second. Rufus tiptoed to the ball and trapped it in his glove while Steve, the runner on first, jogged slowly toward second. Rufus excitedly turned and tossed the ball to Jalen, who whipped it to Freddie in time to get the limping Kevin at first.

"Double play!" Bill yelled. "You're outta there!"

Steve and Kevin tossed their arms to the heavens, miming disbelief. Jalen and Rufus smiled.

"Nice play, Rufus. Nice play, Jalen," Bill called. "Great play all around."

Two El trains rumbled past, one headed north and the other south, and the glass on the sidewalk glittered and rearranged itself for the hundredth time that day. Sunlight from the west angled off the passing train windows and was transformed into a glimmering string of metal-bright reflections, small patches of light racing across the grass and dirt like so many ghosts, melting into one another, then continuing their separate ways.

On the last day of July, Al Carter stood on a Durso Park basketball court, in need of a referee. His tournament had been going on for three weeks. Now, however, he was looking at an afternoon slate of four games and an empty striped shirt.

"Damn!" he said, unable to find a qualified volunteer. "You get one thing going and then something else falls off."

In his charcoal sport coat, gray pants, and fashionable black loafers, Al may have looked out of place, like an NBA coach suddenly materialized out of thin air. But that was an illusion. He was at home here, perhaps more at home than he would be anywhere else. Sweeping shorties off the court with one hand, he used the other to summon a stocky, Jheri-Kurled teenager in a blue nylon jacket, one of the paid youth organizers. "Emmanuel, go to your building and find us a referee. He'll get paid—just make sure he's good."

Emmanuel nodded and strode off. As a Gangster Disciple shot-caller, he, with a cadre of his lieutenants, had been hired by Al to help run the games played. At the other site, Seward Park, Al had hired Cobras and Vice Lords. In concept, the basketball tournament was simple: one division for Folks, one for People, the winners of each to meet in an all-Cabrini final on neutral ground at the YMCA. In reality, bad weather and confused sign-ups had reduced the number of teams participating, and the rains had thrown the already cramped schedule into havoc. Still, Al didn't mind: "There's always something. What matters is getting it done, and that's what I'm doing."

Al had been doing this kind of work in Cabrini since the mid-seventies. Back then, in his job at the YMCA, he had single-handedly organized a track meet, outlining a 260-yard oval with flour, using Popsicle sticks as relay batons, and awarding three pennies for first place, two for second, and one for third. Cramped by the Y's bureaucracy, he quit and started his own foundation in 1978, and became Cabrini's best-known youth worker, each July staging his signature event, the Al Carter Cabrini-Green Olympics.

Occasionally in the late seventies and early eighties, dissatisfied with his work, Al had dabbled in radio—disc jockeying, hosting a local talk show, teaching broadcasting at a local school. But these careers never panned out, and he always had returned to Cabrini and his foundation. That, at least, was his. He ran whatever programs he thought the community needed—tutoring, counseling, computer classes, food giveaways—and he answered to no one. He solicited donations of supplies and money from Kraft, Apple Computer, Oscar Mayer, and other corporations. He obtained tax-exempt status for his organization in 1984, and successfully petitioned the Chicago Housing Authority for rent-free space, at first in the Castle, and then in a rowhouse on Hudson Street. Now, after fourteen years, one wall of his foundation office was covered with photographs: Al standing next to Mayor Harold Washington. Al being honored by Mayor Richard M. Daley. Most of the photos, however, were of children—a line of pigtailed girls running the hundred-yard dash, a reedy boy long-jumping, a group of kids eating hot dogs. There were more than three hundred photos in all, many faded and curling with age. Sometimes visitors would drop by and search themselves out amid the images, and talk with Al about old times. Al enjoyed himself immensely when that happened.

Recently some of Al's friends had been worried about him. He had been discontented before, but the new baseball league and all its controversies seemed to have brought out the worst in him. Since its inception he had become moody, tense, and defensive, and even more hardheaded.

"Al's having some kind of mid-life crisis," said Pat Hill, a close friend who had helped organize the league's African-

American educational classes and who was aware of the grant controversy. "I think it's a male thing—when you have certain goals and aspirations and you reach a certain age and you haven't attained them, you begin to doubt. Even Al doesn't understand why he does things. What other people take as challenges, he takes very personally. All these battles he's never experienced before—working with people, dealing with people of various backgrounds and status—he's saying no to that; he's retreating.

"Part of it is Bob and Tina," Hill continued. "They've got this missionary mentality: 'Hey, you little puppies, we'll help you.' And that doesn't help people—it's not honest. Al has a problem with that, as I do, but the difference is that he doesn't know how to deal with it, where I do."

Except for the exchange at the Seward Park fieldhouse, Al hadn't spoken to Bob, Tina, or anyone else from the league since the grant controversy had begun. He had heard about Tina's calls to The Chicago Initiative and Bill Seitz's slow drives past the basketball courts—to count players, it turned out. But Al did nothing. At one point during the Seward Park summit meeting, Bob had summarized his "evidence": TCI's write-up; Al's resignation from the Demicco board; the disproportion between the size of the grant and the participation in the basketball tournament; a report in the Demicco newsletter that, to Bob's reading, described the baseball league as if it had been paid for by the TCI grant—and challenged Al to prove him wrong. Al had declined. Perhaps, at the meeting and in the months to follow, he could have produced a budget, check stubs, the original grant proposal, something that would prove unequivocally to Bob and Tina and everyone else that each penny had been received in good faith and was being put to good use. But Al didn't. Out of pride or bitterness, or maybe for some other reason, he didn't.

"Let's go, let's go, let's get this thing moving." Al moved around the crowded basketball court like a traffic cop, pushing heads and shoulders to the sidelines so the game could start as soon as Emmanuel returned with the referee.

The kids knew Al, or at least sensed his importance, and they hurried out of the way with little protest.

Emmanuel arrived now, so quietly that Al didn't notice him. "Got one," he said, touching Al's shoulder.

"All right, let's go, let's go, let's go, let's go." Al was off instantly, in charge again, snagging the ball and passing it to a tall young man who had just pulled on a zebra-striped shirt. Soon, the ball was flying among the players. Al smiled, then checked his watch. Had to go. Somewhere to be.

"Keep it under control now." He shook hands with Emmanuel, touched a few of the shorties' heads affectionately, and was gone.

At midnight, after he put in his eight hours with the city, Al would go home to his apartment near State and Chicago. Usually his daughter was asleep, and that was just as well. When she was asleep, he could play his music.

Years before, between the Army and his work in Cabrini, Al had had a brief career in jazz. A fanatic since his teens, he never had been much of a musician, but he knew enough to talk himself into a spot as manager of the Thad Jones–Mel Lewis Orchestra. He had traveled with the group to New York, Tokyo, Brussels, Barcelona, and even hung out with Thelonious Monk, Dexter Gordon, and Dizzy Gillespie. When he finally had tired of hauling trombone cases and haggling with club owners, he returned to Chicago. But he still possessed a bit of that world in his thousand or so jazz albums. To a man without many close friends, they served as company: Lee Morgan, Gene Ammons, Sonny Rollins, Paul Chambers. His friends. Some nights when he couldn't sleep, Al would put on the old albums and just sit there, soaking it in.

"Music is the healing force of the soul," he said once. "It's like ducking a bullet. You can't let the bullet hit you, or you're through. You gotta keep on ducking."

AUGUST

I prefer to think of Iowa as I saw it through the eyes of a ten-year-old boy—the eyes of all ten-year-old Iowa boys are or should be filled with the wonders of Iowa's streams and woods, with the mystery of growing crops. His days should be filled with adventure and great undertakings, with participation in good and comforting things.

—HERBERT HOOVER

ONE

Four hours before the game against the Zulus, and Freddie and Jalen were playing catch under the El tracks. They normally would have been out on Carson Field, but with so much jumping off lately, that wasn't a good idea. Besides, it was hot and the shade felt good.

"Curve," Jalen yelled to Freddie, carefully gripping the ball.

"Come on, boy." Freddie bounced on his haunches, incapable of remaining still. "Heat or soft, it don't matter."

Jalen braced his Scottie Pippen against the brick that marked the pitcher's mound and threw. The ball bounced two feet in front of Freddie and hit him in the ankle.

"*Maaaan,* Jalen!" Freddie petulantly flung the ball back. It bounced three feet in front of Jalen, who picked it cleanly.

Jalen stiffened as he prepared a retort, then froze. He cocked his head, listening intently. Without a word, he dropped his glove and pulled himself onto the massive metal crosspiece that held the tracks up, wedging both feet in the notch where the crosspiece met the girder. Freddie scrambled and did likewise.

Seconds later, the track began to shake, then to rumble. As the noise grew louder, the boys put their fingers in their ears. Then, with a rush of wind, it was upon them, blotting out the light, obliterating their senses, sucking every loose molecule of air and dust upward. Their T-shirts fluttered. They smiled at each other.

"You feel it?" Jalen shouted. "Make your feet go all *funny.*" Though he could not hear his friend, Freddie nodded enthusiastically.

The shooting was more frequent now. The previous night, the thirteen-to-fifteen-year-old Ewes and Mau Maus had been forced to suspend their game midway through the final inning. Nobody knew just where the shots had come from, but they sounded close enough that everyone raced behind the equipment shed in the southeast corner of the field. Some said it was the Black Gangster Disciples on Division shooting at the Cobras; others, including the police officer who responded to a call, believed the shots were intended for someone on the field. Again, as always, it didn't matter which story was true. All that mattered was that it wasn't safe.

"I'm fittina pitch today," announced Jalen, jumping off the strut and motioning for Freddie to return to the rock that was home plate.

The shorter boy remained on the support, trying to climb up the incline to the top.

"I said, I'm fittina *pitch* today. In the *game.*"

Freddie hopped down, instantly suspicious of the older boy.

"You *lyin'.*" Freddie tilted his head back.

"Ax Bill. I talk to him on the phone this morning, and he ax me who I think should pitch, and I say me."

"Maaaan! Why he *do* that?"

Jalen's voice was light and girlish. " 'Cause I the best."

"Maaan!"

"You jealous." Jalen walked away and tucked his foot in front of the brick. He summed up the game situation. "Bottom of the ninth, two outs. Sox ahead of the A's three to two, Canseco up."

"Nah," said Freddie, "Mark McGwire."

"*Canseco* up," Jalen called tightly. "Jalen's on the mound. He winds, and he throws . . ."

Freddie sprawled to his left to keep the ball from flying into the fence.

"Strike three!" Jalen jumped away from the brick, hands in the air. "Sox win, Sox win, Sox win!"

"Yeah, boy!" Freddie was up, celebrating too, skip-hopping between the girders. The pitch was far outside, but that didn't matter to Freddie. With him, things didn't have to be exact.

Freddie liked playing with Jalen. Ever since his cousin Michael had gone away, the two had spent almost every moment of the day together—from eight in the morning, when Freddie rang Jalen's buzzer, to midnight and after. They played sock baseball, milk-crate basketball, Sega Genesis, and a tightrope game in which, on the count of three, they both leaped onto a narrow fence and saw who could stand there longer without falling. They sometimes fought, because both of them hated to lose, and then they would retreat: Jalen to Sega; Freddie to hopscotch games with some girls who lived in his building. But eventually one of them would give in, and they would start playing again. "I only had myself one son, but now I got two," Jalen's mother liked to say.

It wasn't far from the truth. In a family of four children, Freddie was the youngest by five years; the only boy. When he was younger, Freddie had been content to sit in the arms of his sisters for hours. But now that he was older, almost ten, he was lonely. "Too many womenfolk in the house," his mother put it: there was his mother, his grandmother, three sisters, and their five babies, four of them girls. Freddie's father came around sometimes, but he never stayed long. Too many womenfolk for him, too, he said.

When his fourteen-year-old sister, Jacquis, and her new baby needed their own room, Freddie's grandmother, a tiny, raisin-skinned woman of eighty, started sharing his room. She did the same things every day: sat in her creaky rocking chair, spat her snuff into a plastic cup, painted her nails, and peered out gauzy white curtains to the street below. Sometimes she told stories about the old days in Mississippi, when she had hoed cotton fields and worked in the house of a rich white woman. Freddie liked her, but he found her vaguely frightening. He missed his cousin Michael, who when he stayed over would always watch TV or play sock basketball with him. Michael had been away for more than a month now, and he wouldn't be back until Freddie was in high school. The way Freddie understood it, "some lady say he do something, but Michael didn't. He wasn't even *there,* but she be lying on him 'cause she hates him."

Freddie's mother wasn't sure whether it had anything to do with Michael's absence, but lately her youngest son's moodiness had increased. "Look at you, frowning all the time like that," she would scold. "I don't know what a boy like you has to frown about." Freddie didn't like it when his mother said that, and it only made him frown harder.

One afternoon when he was with his tutor, Freddie made Michael a card. He took a sheet of plain white paper and folded it over once. Painstakingly, he wrote a cursive *F* linked with an *M,* drew hearts around the edges of the paper, and filled each with blue and purple marker. Then he opened it up and began writing inside.

"I miss you Michael. I remember what you sade about baseball, and I'm doing good Love Freddie."

"You ever been to jail?" Freddie once asked a coach. When he was told no, Freddie's eyes widened, then relaxed as he tried to show his nonchalance. "My grandmama, she like *eighty,*" Freddie said, "and she ain't *never* been to jail."

*   *   *

Half an hour before the game against the Zulus, Maurice and his mother were standing on Sedgwick Street, waiting. They had been there for fifteen minutes or so, long enough for the broken-down soles of his XJ-9000s to heat up. He shifted his feet uneasily.

"We got to go—we gonna be *late*," Maurice said. "He's not coming."

"Ten more minutes. Then the game."

"What if he don't come?" Maurice hopped in alarm. "The game gonna start!"

They were waiting for Maurice's father. He was leaving for California that afternoon at five-thirty, headed for that job in Los Angeles. Maurice's mother didn't believe him at first, but then he showed her his bus ticket. He said he wanted to say good-bye to his son, and she said she'd bring him by. So here they were, standing outside the building where he was supposed to be staying, and waiting.

"He ain't here." Maurice's voice turned desperate. "We gotta go!"

His mother turned to look up the street. "Maybe he got held up or something."

"I'm *psychic*," Alonzo announced when he arrived at Carson Field for the game with the Zulus. "I already know if we gonna win or lose."

"Well, Alonzo," Coach Bill asked, "what's your prediction for today?"

Alonzo looked to the outfield, where a willowy left-hander was warming up for the opposing team.

"Not gonna say, but it's gonna be close." He winked at Bill as if over some shared secret. "Real close."

It didn't require a great deal of clairvoyance to know that the fortunes of the Chicago Research and Trading Zulus, like those of most teams in the league, rested chiefly on the shoulders of one player. With Lashon on the mound, they were tough. Without him, as they had been in their last game, against the previously hapless Nilotes, they were terrible. The Nilotes had destroyed the Zulus 32–1 for their first victory ever. Lashon's replacements had issued no fewer than thirty walks. Since league rules prohibited any pitcher from throwing more than six innings a week, the Zulus had lurched through much of their schedule, alternating wins and losses according to the availability of their star. Unfortunately for the Kikuyus, the Nilotes game was twelve days ago.

At ten minutes before five, Bill counted heads. Six Kikuyus, including eager new recruits Rassan and Jonathan. Bill scanned the small assembly of toddlers, shorties, grandmothers, sisters, and other ballplayers behind the backstop—no luck.

At four fifty-five, Harold sauntered up to the field, pants at three-quarter mast. Bill thumped a glove in his chest and told him to get to third base, pronto. Three minutes later, Maurice and Rufus ran onto the field, their mother laboring a few hundred yards behind.

"Sorry we're late, Bill," Maurice breathed. "Had to run some errands." He spoke quickly, formally.

"Maurice, take shortstop; Rufus, take second," Bill said, relieved to be able to fill in nine blanks on the scoresheet.

As he wrote the lineup, Bill did a quick mental inventory of players: Nathaniel was still visiting relatives, Louis was at camp, Calbert was, as Bill put it, on "injured reserve." Two names remained—Otis and Samuel. One lived in the Whites, from where shooting had come the previous night; the other in the Castle. Then he counted the Zulus—only eight. At least the Kikuyus weren't the only team having problems coming up with players.

From the start, the game was an exciting, seesaw affair. The Zulus hit Jalen for three runs in the top of the first; the Kikuyus answered with three in the bottom. The Kikuyus surged ahead on homers by Maurice and Harold, 8–3; the Zulus came back in the top of the third, 10–8; Harold countered with a patented three-overthrow homer, and the Kikuyus edged ahead, 11–10.

"Bill!" Harold shouted as he returned to the dugout. "You owe me now. We bet and you lost—so who's gonna tell me that I ain't the best hitter on the team?" He placed his face squarely into Maurice's, an inch away. "*You* gonna say you better than me?"

"Shut up," Maurice said under his breath.

"*What?* You little buster tellin' *me* to shut up?" Harold waggled his head in mock outrage. "Maybe you want to push me and see how much of a buster I am." He stuck out his chest and held Maurice's hand on it. "Come on, boy, come on, why don't you give it a try?" His voice dropped to a whisper. "Come on, motherfucker, see what happens."

Brad stepped in and pulled Maurice's hand away. Harold was triumphant.

"Coach got to come and save you, little buster baby." He looked around the dugout, making sure that everybody was watching. "Look at little Maurice with his raggedy hair. . . ."

"Shut up, Harold!" Brad grabbed him by the shoulders.

"Get your *dusty* hands off me." Harold pushed away and walked to the other end of the dugout, still talking.

Bill, observing the exchange, decided to try something. He turned to Kevin and asked him what he thought about putting Harold in to pitch, to quiet him down. After all, it had worked with Jalen and Demetrius.

Harold crowed upon hearing the news. "See? They know who's the best. Now they asking me to . . ."

"Shut *up*, Harold," three coaches said.

Harold had never pitched before, and he quickly settled on a makeshift technique: he took a little skip off the rubber and flicked his arm as if he were swatting flies. His pitches would have been easy to hit, if they had been close to the plate. He made it through his first inning allowing

only one run. The next inning, however, one of the Zulus'
coaches told his players to wait until they got a strike, and
they started walking.

"*Maaaaan,* Harold!" Freddie yelled as the third run
came across the plate. "Why you *do* that?" The shorties behind the backstop began to mock him, imitating his form
and laughing. Harold grew frustrated. He slammed the ball
into his mitt and glared mutely at his adversaries.

"Hey, hey," said Kevin. "Look at Mr. Talkative now."

But before long, Harold found a solution. He got proud.

"That's right!" he yelled after a Zulu dove away from one
of his errant pitches. "That's right, get you dusty ass out the
way!" He turned to the crowd, a wicked grin on his face.
"They afraid because I'm too *wild.* I'm outta control—OC,
baby!"

With the score 14–11 in favor of the Zulus, Bill pulled
Harold and waved Maurice in from shortstop.

"We gonna loo-oose," sang Rufus.

"No we aren't," answered Demetrius, slipping into his
best white voice. "Just keep trying and everything will be
okay, buddy."

"They can't handle my heat," Harold yelled to no one in
particular. "Who's gonna tell me I ain't the wildest?"

As Maurice set himself on the mound, a short, skinny
man in a turquoise sweatsuit walked down Scott Street toward the backstop. He wore old Nike Cortez running
shoes, wraparound sunglasses, and around his neck, a rosary of white plastic. He nodded coolly to Maurice's
mother, but didn't approach her. He placed his plastic grocery bag on the sidewalk, then took a post at the center of
the backstop, directly behind home plate.

When Maurice was halfway through his warm-ups, the
man dropped down into a catcher's stance, as if trying to
check the location of the pitches. Maurice tugged on his
cap and shifted nervously on the mound, but didn't say
anything or indicate in any way that he saw the man. Then
the umpire was saying "Play ball," Maurice was squinting
toward the plate, and the skinny man in the turquoise

sweatsuit was hunkering down in his crouch, his white rosary swinging over the pavement. Father and son, neither acknowledging the other, pantomiming a game of catch.

Maurice didn't start well. He gave up two walks and a single to bring the score to 15–11.

"He's trying to throw too hard," said Coach Steve, the baseball expert. "He's kicking too high, and it's throwing him way off balance."

"Hey, Maurice," Bill called. "Take a little off. Throw strikes."

Maurice followed the advice. He got a strikeout and, with the bases loaded, caught a short pop-up.

"Nice going," Bill said, patting him on the arm. "Attaway to throw."

"Thanks," Maurice said, looking not at Bill but toward the sidewalk, where the man in the turquoise sweatsuit had risen and was walking away, grocery bag slung over his shoulder. Maurice's mother later guessed he was embarrassed. "He's shy," she said. "He loves Maurice and all, but he just don't know how to show it."

In the bottom of the fifth, the Kikuyus rallied. Freddie led off with a walk, and Jalen and Rude Dude doubled him home; Maurice walked, and Harold doubled him home and scored on a subsequent wild pitch to even the score at 15, and that was where it ended. Though it was only a tie, the Kikuyus were jubilant, perhaps because several players thought that, batting last, they had won the game. The coaches did not go out of their way to correct them.

TWO

The caravan wouldn't leave Carson Field for another hour, but already at eight-thirty this Thursday morning a small mountain of luggage had accumulated at the curb. On the bottom were Alonzo's beige vinyl suitcase, three T-shirts and two hats inside, and Maurice's black duffel, containing Lux soap, comb, towel, and cologne. Then came Rufus's identical duffel, with his green dragon squirt gun tucked in at one end, and Demetrius's blue suitcase, with four pairs of underwear and a Hulk Hogan flashlight. Atop it all, holding everything in place like a giant tarpaulin, was Calbert's gray vinyl suit bag. He had returned to the team for the Iowa trip, and the contents of his luggage suggested that perhaps he planned to stay there for a while. He enumerated: "I got ten shirts, five pairs of shorts, two pairs of pants, one flashlight, some underwear and stuff, five Cheetos, four 7-Ups, ten Now and Laters, some cheese, my radio, three tapes I made myself, three Bahama Blues—

oops, I already drank one, make that two—and a box of doughnuts. Want some?"

"Geez," said Greg, a coach for the Zulus, who were accompanying the Kikuyus on the four-day trip. He looked from the pile to the trunk of his rented car, and back to the pile. "You'd think we were going to the other side of the world."

He wasn't far off. The teams were headed to the Four Mounds Foundation preserve, sixty acres of bluffland overlooking the Mississippi River just north of Dubuque. The foundation's program director, Sam Mulgrew, a friend of Bob Muzikowski's, had set up a weekend of activities including nature walks, visits to water parks, and baseball against Dubuque's Little League teams. Already this year, the foundation had hosted six Cabrini teams, and all had returned with tales of wild cows, snakes, and mysterious hillbillies. By departure time, most of these stories had been fashioned by repeated telling into a substantial mythology.

"They got cows in Awwa," said Rufus. "If you get in their way, they stomp you."

"They got a rich man's mansion where some teams get to stay," said Jalen. "They *better* be fittina let us stay there."

"I heard that one of the Mau Maus got his Air Jordans took by a hillbilly," said Freddie.

"I ain't afraid of no Awwa cow," Alonzo said, poker-faced. "I just duck under their legs, jump on their back, and ride 'em." He thought about this for a moment. "I'm a *cow*boy."

"Yop, but you best be 'fraid of them hillbillies," Freddie said, insistent. "They *grab* you and take you away with them."

"When I'm in Awwa, I'm fittina get me a slingshot and kill me a hillbilly," said Jalen.

"When I'm in Awwa, I'm fittina sneak into a cow field and tip over a big old cow," said Demetrius.

"When I'm in Awwa," said Harold, mocking his team-mates' excitement, "I'm fittina kick you all in the dick."

Bill sent Harold a disapproving look and counted heads. The buzz had inspired an unprecedented turnout: eleven Kikuyus, everyone except Nathaniel, who was still in Mississippi; Samuel, who had said that he would try to come; and Louis, whose mother had called and said that he would be a little late.

Louis had a good excuse. He had landed a second audition for the television program *Star Search*, which was holding tryouts for its Midwest regional talent contest. Of more than two hundred in the first round, Louis had been one of only twelve to receive a callback.

"He blew their minds," his mother said. "He brought in his little keyboard and played a hymn, then they had him play two more. Then this man from California, the one running the whole thing, asked him if he had written anything himself. So then Louis does this song, and they loved it. I mean, they *loved* it. I don't want to get his hopes up or anything, but they told me that if he does well this second round, he would go on the big show with Ed McMahon and everything."

At nine-twenty, just as his mother had promised, Louis strolled down the sidewalk in his unhurried heel-toe walk. He wore pink-framed sunglasses and carried a small portable television under his right arm.

"Howya doin' there, Mr. Star Search?" said Bill.

Louis whirled. "Who told you that?"

"Your mother." Bill's voice dropped. "Hey, I think it's great, but if you don't want anybody else to know, then—"

"Right," Louis interrupted. "*No*body."

The cars were quickly loaded up. Window and front passenger positions were highly prized, so it took a while to arbitrate seating arrangements, but after a few impassioned rounds of rock-paper-scissors, five cars, twenty-one players, and five coaches were ready to go. Doors slammed, kids yelled, arms emerged from every open window, prepared to play with the rushing air. Calbert produced a Kris Kross tape and soon the shocks of the car he was in were bouncing lightly to the beat of "Warm It Up."

As the caravan rolled out of Cabrini, Maurice hollered at his driver to stop the car, *now,* as if there were some vital emergency.

"What the . . ."

Maurice was leaning out the window, waving to a heavyset woman walking a baby along Division. "Hey, LaRelle," he called.

The woman did a double take. *"Maurice?"*

He leaned back in the car, smiling and nodding. "Yop, my auntie saw me."

The drivers fell in line and headed out on the Kennedy Expressway. Framed in the open windows, the city scrolled past: the bricks of the old industrial sector gave way to the steeples and walk-ups of the near West Side, the baby sky-scrapers of the suburbs, and the impressive bustle of O'Hare Airport. The boys oohed and aahed as they drove beneath a McDonald's built over the highway, and yawned through the long stretch of cookie-cutter neighborhoods. Within an hour, some of the children were farther from home than they'd ever been. Those who had traveled, or at least those who said that they had, played tour guide.

"See that?" Alonzo pointed to a tall industrial sandpile alongside the highway. "They're fittina make that into another Mount Rushmore."

"Really?" asked Rassan.

"Yop, except that it's with more modern presidents, starting with Eisenhower. They add one on whenever somebody dies."

"Oh." Rassan looked back at the sandpile with new interest.

The suburbs gradually gave way to cornfields. The brown haze of the city disappeared, traffic thinned, and the cars kept a seventy-mile-per-hour pace. Now and then one would surge ahead, and the children in the other vehicles would exhort their driver to catch the leader. Whenever a driver took the lead, his passengers would celebrate and wave to the slower cars; whenever a driver fell behind, his passengers would sulk and announce how, at the next rest stop, they would switch to a car that wasn't driven by a buster. And now that they were out of the city, it was apparent that the day was beautiful: eighty degrees, high skies, not a cloud in sight.

Though they didn't mention it to the players, a few of the coaches found it ironic that they were headed toward a town best known for its ongoing racial controversy. Dubuque's troubles started in 1989, when a white high school student burned a cross in the yard of one of the city's few black residents. In response, the city council instituted a plan to help diversify the ninety-eight-percent white city by recruiting twenty minority families a year for five years—a move that sparked a small but much-publicized rash of hate crimes in the fall of 1991. Bricks were thrown through windows. Graffiti appeared on public buildings: NO NIGGERS. WE DON'T WANT THEM. The national media had flocked to Dubuque and portrayed the circumstances in the quiet river town of 58,000 as the epitome of middle-class midwestern racism. The furor had since died down, but tension remained. In the twelve months before the Kikuyus' visit, twelve more crosses had been burned.

The Cabrini teams that already had come to Dubuque had encountered no hostility. On the contrary, most residents made a special point of welcoming them. There had been a few touchy moments, as when a family in a pizza parlor stared so long and hard at the visitors that a Bakongo player became unnerved. "What's your problem?" he asked them. "You motherfuckers ain't never seen no niggers before?" But for the most part, relations had gone smoothly.

At Rockford, Illinois, the cars peeled off the interstate onto the narrower blacktop of State Highway 20. Soon they were in the country proper, rolling past one-stoplight towns like Winnebago and Pecatonica, Eleroy and Stockton. The kids shouted when they saw cows, and wrinkled their noses at the smell of a pig farm. They passed so many red barns that Maurice had to be reassured several times that they weren't traveling in circles. They stopped to buy candy and pop at a gas station and, later, to pee in an open field, where they stood shoulder to shoulder for fear of snakes and lofted thin, crystalline parabolas far into the sorghum.

At the town of Woodbine, three hours into the trip, the land began to rise, at first almost imperceptibly, then with a graceful and ever-increasing rhythm as they approached the Mississippi River. The road threaded through clusters of oak and maple, rose to reveal views of rich farmland, and dropped smoothly into gladed hollows. Cows leaned into hillsides for purchase. As they approached Galena, the picturesque resort town where Ulysses S. Grant was born, one coach wondered aloud why there were so many hills near the river.

"Pipes broken?" Demetrius offered.

"Close, but nope," intoned Alonzo. "The concrete is all old and bumpy-like, and that's what makes hills."

"Oh."

Jalen intercepted Coach Bill's car as it pulled up to Camp Burton.

"Don't get out," he said, reaching through the driver's-side window and covering the lock with his palm. "This place is phony. We ain't staying."

They had come to this heavily wooded hollow in farmland a few miles north of Dubuque, and were now looking at their billet: an ancient two-room cabin with a leaky tar-paper roof, sagging wooden siding half engulfed by ivy, and four small screen windows, two of them torn. Beside it were a fire ring and a water pump, and a few dozen yards down a dark path was an outhouse. The cabin was used by Dubuque's Boy Scouts as a base for winter camping trips. In the summer, presumably, they had better places to go.

"There ain't no electricity!" Louis held his portable television out, unbelieving.

"I ain't going to the bathroom in no lighthouse," Rufus said.

"Take me home," said Calbert, opening a can of 7-Up.

After more protesting and a group version of Bill's man-to-man talk, however, it was agreed that the teams would stay. As the sun set, twenty-six worn mattresses were un-stacked and arranged like dominoes in the main room, then covered with the nylon sleeping bags the league had purchased. The coaches, acting on the instructions of Sam Mulgrew, locked their cars as precaution against anyone seeking a room upgrade. Within half an hour, everyone had settled in, Zulus on one side and Kikuyus on the other, some in their pajamas. When word went out that the coaches were about to venture on an exploratory walk, panic ensued.

"Man, what they *do* that for?" Freddie, in his underwear, leaped up and ran for the door.

"You leave us, we gonna sue you!" shouted Jalen, hoping the coaches would hear.

"I ain't *goin'*," Rufus said defiantly. He changed his mind as soon as it became apparent that he would be left alone. The cabin's screen door banged, and all twenty-one boys ran swiftly, their sneakered feet noiseless on the grass, on a narrow trail into the darkening woods.

Once they were inside the forest, everything changed. The sky disappeared, replaced by a curtain of oak, elm, and maple. Brambles and ferns rose up to touch bare skin. Sneakers slipped on mud; legs were caught in the unfamiliar trip wires of roots; the coaches felt the clutch of small hands on their shirttails. Flashlight beams bounced to nervous chatter.

"Man! I got poison ivy!"

"Shut up, man, you got *gay* ivy."

"Maaan! Straight up, I seriously got bumps all down my leg."

"Big Bird, big-nose, pigeon-neck . . ."

"Who pooted?"

"I can't wait until we sue them coaches for taking us here. It'll be like, *See* ya, wouldn't wanta *be* ya."

"Wasn't me."

"Harold, you can let go of my shirt now."

"I ain't *got* your shirt. *Tell* me not to beat you up, Brad."

"Be quiet, Harold. Hey—*everybody,* be quiet." Bill paused. "Turn off the lights and listen."

The coaches switched their flashlights off, and one by one, so did the players. Everything fell into blue-black. Sounds welled up: the rapid clicks of crickets; the ratchet spins of cicadas; the high-pitched buzzes and rattles of thousands of insects—the forest switching over to the night shift. There was no wind. One of the Zulus slapped a firefly, pinched off its tail, and stuck the still-glowing mush to his earlobe.

"Straight up," Demetrius whispered to a coach. "This *scary.*"

Bill, who was in the lead, flicked on his flashlight and panned back along the trail. In the beam of light he could see Demetrius and Alonzo clinging to coaches shirts. Rassan and Freddie held hands, as did Rufus and Maurice and some of the Zulus. Harold stood with his back against a tree, wielding a broken branch against unseen menaces. Someone murmured that he wanted to go home.

"Sam told me there was a river down here," Bill announced. "Who wants to keep going?"

"Not me."

"Man, we should go back and light a fire."

"It's too *dark* in here."

"I need some marshmallows."

"Let's keep going, Bill," said a voice behind him.

Bill turned his beam to identify the lone explorer.

"Come on," said the biggest buster on the team. "Don't you want to see the river?"

Nobody said anything.

Calbert put his hands on his hips and squinted past the glow of Bill's flashlight into the darkness beyond. "Well," he said, more than a little exasperated, "I don't know about you all, but me and Bill are fittina go."

After the group returned from the river, actually nothing more than a small stream, they sat around the fire and then went to bed. Before Harold and Jalen had even finished complaining about the cheap sleeping bags and the phony mattresses, Calbert was fast asleep.

The Awwa boys wore their stirrup socks high. They had blue hats and button-up polyester grays with "Dodgers" across the chest, just like the major leagues. Most of them were big, most of them were blond, and a good number of them wore glasses. All of them wore spikes. Their appearance suited their home park, a large, well-kept complex of diamonds with a batting cage, lights, restrooms, and a candy shack. In the Dubuque Independent League, which had just closed its season, the Carpet Shack Dodgers had finished in third place.

"*Third?*" Jalen shook his head as he watched their pitcher warm up. "Man, these Awwa boys is *hard*."

A few minutes before game time, the Dodgers took the field. Bill, John, Trent, Jason, J.C., Chris, Andy, Jim, Mike: the coach spoke their names and they sprinted—sprinted! —to their places and immediately dropped into knees-bent, glove-forward, butt-down ready positions right out of *How to Coach Little League Baseball*. They whipped through a choreographed blizzard of grounders, flies, and effortless cut-off plays. The Kikuyus' coaches couldn't help but feel a twinge of embarrassment. Surely, their team would look like a soccer riot by comparison.

"All right, let's go get these guys now," shouted Bill hopefully as he tried to gather the team to give them the lineup.

Demetrius looked at him, opened his mouth to say something sarcastic, then decided it wasn't worth the effort.

In the top of the first, the Kikuyus went down in order—a groundout and two strikeouts. Freddie's first pitch in the bottom of the inning was hit into deep left field for a home run. The next was hit closer to the Coors Light sign in center. The Dodgers' cleanup hitter, a hulk of a lad named J.C., turned on Freddie's best fastball as if it were sitting on a tee and knocked it clear to the Drive One Home Truck Country sign. Shortly after Louis tracked it down, J.C. was exchanging low-fives in the dugout.

The final score was 10–2. Had the Dodgers not eased up, it easily could have been 100–2. But as the game progressed, something curious happened. The Kikuyus behaved themselves. They didn't complain or throw tantrums or blame the umpire. In fact, they behaved a little like the Dodgers. Though Freddie was hit hard for two innings, he never lost his composure. Demetrius dropped into a ready position for the first time in recent memory. A few players even hitched up their stirrup socks to look more like the home team. By the Kikuyus' half of the third inning, Harold and Maurice had made their way to the Dodger dugout and were hefting their Louisville Slugger TPXs and comparing gloves. After some small talk, Harold went on one of his vainglorious monologues, claiming to be the best and complaining about his buster teammates. By the Dodgers' reaction it was one of the funniest things they had ever heard; he was just like that trash-talking Wesley Snipes character in *White Men Can't Jump*, they said.

"This guy is cracking me up," said big J.C.

Maurice was more serious, checking out the Dodgers' spikes and saying he was trying to decide which kind to buy. "I like the Nikes, but Pumas is pretty good, too. Maybe I buy them both."

Then, from the woods surrounding the field, three deafening gunshots. Some of the Kikuyus fell on their bellies; others crouched and moved warily away from the sound, looking for a place to run.

"*Deer hunters*," shouted the Dodgers' coach when he saw how frightened the Kikuyus were. "Just deer hunters— they're not supposed to be back there. Don't worry."

"Hunters, guys, just hunters." The Kikuyus' coaches made calming gestures with their hands. "Nothing to worry about."

The Dodgers looked on the visitors with new curiosity. It was clear that they hadn't been told much about this team from Chicago.

"Don't worry about them," Maurice said, making his okay sign with exaggerated nonchalance. "Sometimes they get a little scared of loud noises. They just not used to life in the country, that's all."

The Dodgers nodded. That made sense. They went back to showing Maurice the soles of their shoes.

Toward the end of the game, the Kikuyus did score two moral victories. In the top of the third inning, Calbert smacked a clean single to center, his first hit of the season. "Man," said Rufus, wide-eyed. "Calbert got him a stick!"

And then, in the bottom of the same inning, with Dodgers on first and third, Freddie pitching, and Maurice back-catching, Maurice called a meeting at the mound and told Freddie to be ready. Sure enough, the trail runner broke for second, Maurice threw, Freddie cut it off, and the lead runner was out at home. The Dodgers looked at the Kikuyus with new respect: they hadn't expected them to know a trick play.

"Yeah, bay-*bee*!" yelled Freddie, punching the air. "We *got* them Awwa boys!"

The stories had started on the league's first Iowa trip, in June. Around the campfire one night, Bob Muzikowski and Sam Mulgrew had invented a simple yarn about kid-snatching hillbillies. By the time the Kikuyus and Zulus arrived, the tale had grown into a richly detailed legend, which Sam passed on to these latest visitors with great solemnity.

Hillbillies, he informed the boys upon their arrival, lived in shanties hidden within the trackless hollows of Iowa river country. They were simple, peaceful folk, making their living by brewing moonshine and sneaking corn from neighboring fields. They were short, a little taller than children, but with long, wiry fingers and drooping, raggedy beards like the guys in ZZ Top. (*Who?* the kids asked, but Sam kept going.) On balance, they were peaceful and quiet, not likely to cause anyone distress. Except for Old Man McGlariddy.

Old Man McGlariddy, Sam said, lived in a little hut near Camp Burton, and rarely emerged during daylight. He was grieving, you see. Forty-one years ago this very week, he had lost his only child—an eleven-year-old boy—when one of his overall straps was caught in a corn combine and he was dragged to his death. It had been a terrible, bloody accident, and ever since, Old Man McGlariddy had kept strictly to himself, seldom leaving his shanty, never talking to anyone. On certain nights, Sam said, when the moon was full and he had been tippling the moonshine a little, the old hillbilly would wander the woods searching for his lost son. He had forgotten just what his boy looked like, but that didn't matter—any boy would do. He came at night, sneaking from the hollow, stealthy as a cat, and he would snatch sleeping boys by the heels and drag them to his shanty before they could utter a word. In fact, just the week before, a second baseman for the Mau Maus had awoken down in the hollow to find Old Man McGlariddy unlacing his Air Jordans and asking him in a creaky, rattly voice, "Why do you wear these things on your feet? Don't you want to go barefoot like me?" The boy managed to escape; the old man had been tippling too much that night. He had, however, kept the Air Jordans.

"I *heard* about that boy," Freddie said, bolting upright.

"Yop." Alonzo nodded knowingly. "He lucky."

Sam told the story well, perhaps too well. By the first full day in Iowa, every twig snap, every birdcall, every shadow on the trail became the sign of a hillbilly. Gradually, all the boys became amateur anthropologists, querying one another on the habits, home life, smells, strengths, and strategies of the common Awwa hillbilly. They had long, vociferous debates over whether a hillbilly could beat Freddy Krueger (no) and whether four hillbillies could beat four players with bats (maybe—depending on whether they fought in the open or in the woods). But the most important hillbilly science was conducted in the evening, when the boys would map out strategies to minimize their chances of being snatched by Old Man McGlariddy. Mattresses were dragged close to coaches and away from doors; branches the length of golf clubs were secured and kept at the ready; the precise location of windows was memorized. The idea of a preemptive strike, in which the entire team would embark on a hillbilly hunt, was considered, but then abandoned when it was concluded the hillbillies would have too many advantages in the forest. All the boys were deeply scared, but rather than dwell on their fear, or complain, or cry for their parents as some children might have, they busied themselves by trying to solve what for some was a familiar problem: making sure they lasted the night.

Privately, some of the coaches questioned the wisdom of frightening these mostly fatherless children with such a tale. But despite twinges of guilt, they felt strangely reassured. There was something encouraging in the children's reaction, the way it stripped away the tough-guy veneer, overshadowed the definitions of Buster and Home-Run Hitter, and made them need their coaches as they never had before. Kids from Cabrini didn't believe in Santa Claus or the Tooth Fairy, but on a moonlit night in Awwa, every one of them believed unwaveringly in Old Man McGlarridy.

As darkness arrived on Saturday, the team's last full day in Iowa, players and coaches drifted toward the fire ring outside the cabin. Calbert dug into his suit bag and extracted his last bag of Chee-tos. One of the Zulus' coaches produced marshmallows, and the kids ran to get sticks. Coach Brad pulled out his guitar and strummed.

It had been a long, exhilarating day, beginning with a 6–3 victory over the Braves (the coaches didn't mention to the kids that the Braves had finished their season with an 0–22 record). Later, as the temperature rose, the Kikuyus and Zulus had gone to a water park, where the players wore themselves out on the slides and high dives, slowed only slightly by the fact that only a few of them knew how to swim. There were some memorable moments: Calbert leaped optimistically off a diving board, sank like a stone, and had to be rescued by the lifeguard; Maurice caused a mild panic when, after attempting his first-ever underwater somersault, he nose-vomited cherry Kool-Aid into the shallow end. It was Harold, however, who made the greatest impression on the citizenry of Dubuque. For no less than ten minutes, he stood on the edge of the high diving board attempting to summon the courage to leap. Five minutes into his ordeal, people below took notice, and soon it seemed the entire water park was chanting, "Jump, jump, jump." He finally did so, sprawling spider style into the water and waving victoriously to the cheering crowd as he dog-paddled to poolside.

"This was the best day so far," Maurice said, his cheeks bursting with marshmallows. Everybody else agreed.

The children looked at home here, bare-chested in the glow of the fire, uniform pants pushed above their knees, tired backs leaning against oak logs. They knew their way around; they were comfortable on the trails and in the cabin. Some of them even went to the outhouse alone.

"I could see living in *that* one . . . *that* one . . . or maybe *that* one." Jalen had pointed out houses as the group's cars wound their way through a Dubuque neighborhood. "Man, I could see living *anywhere* here."

Bill and Kevin listened intently as Harold taught a vocabulary lesson. " 'Musty' is like where you ain't showered in a while. 'Dusty' is when you all dirty, like after a game.

But 'rusty,' that when the skin on your elbows and back get all dry and it start looking like you got rust on you."

"So," Bill said, "right now you could be a little rusty, but you wouldn't be dusty or musty."

"You a smart guy, Bill."

After the marshmallows were roasted, Sam Mulgrew stopped by to give his farewells. He thanked the boys for coming and for being such considerate guests, and wished them well for the rest of the season.

"Oh, and one more thing," Sam said. "Don't worry about Old Man McGlariddy tonight. If he hasn't come out yet, he's probably hitting the moonshine too much to bother anyone. Good night!" He waved, and as the taillights of his truck disappeared, unease settled over the group.

"Maaaaan! Why he *say* that?" asked Otis. "I forgot about them billhillies till then."

"Hillbilly come up to me, I'm just gonna run," said Demetrius.

"I do a karate move on his head," offered Rufus, chopping the air tentatively.

"I'd give him Freddie," said Jalen.

"Man, shut *up*!"

"He come up to me, I'm gonna slap his face and kick him in his hillbilly balls," said Harold. He mimed the maneuver and made everyone break up in nervous laughter.

Bill ran a hand through his hair. "Coach Brad, how about a little music?"

"All right, Coach Bill." Brad propped his six-string Goya on his knee and started in on Jerry Garcia's "Friend of the Devil." The guitar hummed and rocked gently, and everybody leaned back and listened, surprised at first by the sound, then slowly growing accustomed to it, as if it had been there all along. Brad sang the refrain, and a couple of coaches joined in, affecting the required high, nasal voice.

"Shhhh!"

It was Maurice, sitting on the log nearest the edge of the clearing.

"Be quiet!" His voice dropped to a whisper. "I *heard* somebody."

A dozen flashlights sliced into the darkness beyond the fire, their beams turned liquid by wood smoke. They revealed the first layer of leaves, but would penetrate no further. After a tense moment, Brad resumed playing, and everyone turned inward again to listen.

"There!" Maurice yelled. "I heard it again!" His voice shook.

Bill had started to say, "It's probably just a rabbit or something," when the screams began. A hook-nosed old man leaped into the clearing, quick and low, making grasping motions with his hands and shouting in a small, twisty voice. "I want my son back! Give me my son!"

Pandemonium. As if hit by an electric shock, children levitated and flew for the cabin door, screaming all the way, the fleeter clawing their way past the less speedy in a frantic struggle to get away from the fire, across the yard, onto the porch, behind the screen door to safety. Harold and Jalen were the first inside, followed by Freddie, Maurice, and a pileup of players. One Zulu wet his pants, and though many knew, no one teased him.

Sam let them stay scared for a few seconds, then pulled off the mask. "Hey, hey, you can come outside now. The hillbilly's gone."

A panicked voice called from inside, "Sam! Hurry! Hillbilly's gonna get you!"

"No, no, come out, it's okay, there is no hillbilly. It was me in a Halloween mask. Really."

The door remained shut. Several flashlights clicked on simultaneously and pointed at Sam, who stood with his arms outstretched holding a rubber mask.

Harold was the first to recover. "Man," he said, flinging open the screen door and striding toward the fire. "We sure had those fools running, didn't we?"

"*Right,* Harry," said Kevin, laughing.

As the boys trickled out of the cabin, Sam handed the mask around so each boy could feel the rubber and the fake black hair. He sat down with them around the fire. Some boys' knees were still shaking.

"There's two things to learn from this," Sam said, holding the mask like a hand puppet. "The first is the tradition that whenever you go camping, you have to tell scary stories. The second is that a lot of things you're frightened of are just like those rubber masks. From far away, they look scary. From up close, though, there's nothing to them."

The boys nodded, most of them claiming that they knew it was fake all along and had gone along with the joke to fool the others. Sam then swore them to secrecy, and they resolved to tell the teams back in Chicago that one boy—a Zulu who lived in the Whites—had been dragged off.

"Look." Maurice held the mask out to Rassan, who was still scared. "It ain't nothing—it's just rubber." Though Maurice would later be awakened by nightmares, right now he wanted to calm his friend. "Here, feel it for yourself—it's nothing to be scared of."

Relieved and exhausted, the group once more sat around the fire to listen to Brad's music. He did some blues tunes, led them in a few campfire standards, and then groped for songs they might know. After a few unappreciated attempts at James Taylor, he settled on "Swing Low, Sweet Chariot," and perhaps half the children joined in, recognizing the song from church. Another coach pulled out a harmonica. Talking ceased. Demetrius put his hand on the guitar to feel it vibrate. Rassan, spent from all the excitement, fell asleep with his head against a coach's shoulder. The coaches nodded conspiratorially to one another, anticipating the case of beer they had chilling in the trunk of a car. As soon as the kids went to sleep, they would break it out. But for now, they sat and listened.

"These is buster songs," Harold said loudly. "Y'all don't know nothing but all these slow, boring—"

"Shut up, Harold," Bill said.

In the growing silence, Brad turned to the old Buffalo Springfield tune "For What It's Worth." It was a song the kids wouldn't know, but Brad played it often on camping trips. His voice was smoky and resonant:

> "There's something happening here,
> What it is ain't exactly clear,
> There's a man with a gun over there,
> Telling me I got to beware.

> "I think it's time we stop, children, what's that sound?
> Everybody look what's goin' down. . . ."

The players picked up the chorus. By the second time through, some were singing, tapping on logs with the beat.

"Man," said one of the Zulus when it was done. "I like that song."

THREE

The day after the Kikuyus returned from Iowa, they held their best practice of the year. Coach Kevin, whose take-charge manner and gravelly voice worked well from a distance, stood at home plate calling out baserunning situations and hitting fungoes. Steve and Cort roamed the infield and outfield, holding private tutorials and reteaching the cutoff and other plays. For once, the coaches did more talking than the players.

"I want to see dirt every time you scoop that ball, Alonzo."

"Hands up high on the cutoff, Otis."

"Calbert, were your eyes open on that one?"

"Two hands, Maurice, always two hands."

Improvements were evident. Demetrius stayed in front of the ball more often. Rassan was looking like a good acquisition, fearless at the plate and a quick learner in the field. Rufus had matured into a quietly dangerous hitter, surprising opponents with quick wrists and opposite-field line drives. The coaches were proud of such a dramatic change, but they could not claim all the credit: Maurice and Rufus had been practicing every day at Seward Park, playing strike-'em-out against a brick wall. Even Calbert, flush with his Iowa successes, was less of a Buster. During batting practice, Steve discovered that Calbert was stepping toward third base, instead of the pitcher, whenever he swung. Though he had a compact, powerful swing, his bat was covering little of the plate. When his habit was corrected, Calbert peppered the infield with hard line drives.

"Man!" said an awed Rufus. "I *told* you Calbert got him a stick."

Coach Bill pulled out the manila folder. A week remained in the regular season, and the Kikuyus' schedule was crammed: The defending-champion Ewes the next day, the Northern Trust Maasai on Wednesday, the Frain Camins & Swartchild Pharaohs on Saturday, the makeup game against the Merrill Lynch Watusi on Monday, and at some point, completion of the Zulu tie. Seven days, five games, then playoffs—if they made it. The latest word from the league was that it planned to include more teams than the previous year's four, but that did not assure the Kikuyus a spot. Tina Muzikowski had just handed out a standings update:

Conference A		Conference B	
Pygmies	13–0	Ibos	11–2–1
Bantus	12–1	Bakongos	7–5–1
Ewes	9–3	Fantes	7–6
Watusi	7–4–1	Kikuyus	6–4–1
Pharaohs	7–6	Mau Maus	6–8
Zulus	6–5–1	Mandinkes	4–7–2
Maasai	2–9–1	Hausas	3–10–1
Xhosa	1–9	Nilotes	1–9–1

As things stood, it seemed the Kikuyus would finish somewhere between second and fifth in their conference.

The Ewes were good—they'd have to be lucky to beat them. But from the way the Kikuyus were playing, the rest of the games looked winnable.

Toward the end of practice, Bill took Maurice aside and asked him what position he wanted to play the next day against the Ewes.

"Pitcher." Maurice didn't hesitate.

"Okay." Bill wrote something on a piece of paper. "Who do you think should backcatch?"

Maurice absentmindedly picked at his hair. "Jalen. If I get into trouble, we can switch. That way we can save Freddie for the Maasai game."

"That sounds good." Bill looked pleased.

All season long, Bill had taken players' opinions into consideration when assembling the lineups. But this was different. He wanted to acknowledge Maurice's role as a team leader openly, to see how he acted in a position of responsibility. Over the next few games, Bill would try this with other players, and it would not always be as successful. But on the eve of the big game, with Maurice, it worked. The boy came up with a solid, workable strategy; more important, he felt in a way what it was like to be a coach.

"Maurice on the hill, Jalen backcatching." Bill penciled the names on the scoresheet as other players gathered. Bill's eyes narrowed with interest. "Who do you think should play first base?"

A violent thunderstorm rolled through Chicago the next morning, complete with forty-mile-per-hour winds and tornado warnings. By early evening, though, the storm had spun itself out on Lake Michigan, leaving only a few pink clouds and a light breeze that dispersed a faint vinegary smell from the Oscar Mayer smokestacks.

A few of the Kikuyus who had arrived early went to a narrow lot on Scott Street to play alley ball, their compact

version of baseball. Past the windows was a single, past the
stump a double, to the cars a triple, and over the oak tree, a
homer. A few minutes before seven, Bill spotted Maurice
and asked him where everybody was.

"We havin' a warm-up over there." He pointed.

Bill's eyebrows rose. "Warm-up? How's it going?"

"Real good." Maurice's hand gave his okay. "Everybody's ready to play."

"*Really?* Nobody's yelling or complaining? Nobody's
quit?"

"Nope," said Maurice. "Everybody's thinking as a team."

Bill walked over to see for himself.

Jalen stood on the curb, waving Rude Dude menacingly
and saying that they were all faggoty gay motherfuckers.
Harold was yelling at Rufus. Demetrius was poking Freddie
with a stick, and Freddie was calling Demetrius a monkey
and saying he was going to kill him. It took Bill ten minutes
to get the team quieted down and onto the field.

"*This* is thinking as a team?" Bill asked, and Maurice
shrugged. After helping with the lineup, he was feeling special. He hadn't wanted to say the wrong thing.

Warm-ups on Carson Field went well. Though the outfield had to be jiggled around when Louis didn't show up,
Maurice's lineup looked good, producing only five or six
miscues in a fifteen-minute infield practice. Bill sat with
Harold on the bench, and explained to him that while he
would get to play part of the game, he couldn't start, because he had missed practice the day before. Bill braced
himself for the inevitable outburst, but none came. Suspicious that there was some misunderstanding, Bill repeated
the news. Harold nodded. Then Bill saw the reason. Behind
the backstop, watching them casually, stood a slim bearded
man in a white button-down shirt.

"Harold, that wouldn't be your father over there, would
it?"

The boy squirmed. Bingo. Bill immediately walked over
and introduced himself. Later he said he had enjoyed the

conversation, but more than that, he enjoyed the way their talking had unnerved Harold, whose eyes never strayed from them.

The Ewes, meanwhile, had taken the field. With game time a few minutes away, they confidently decided to forgo their infield. "Ready when you are," called their coach, Charles Hudson.

"We might just have a chance today," Brad told Kevin. "These guys look a little phony."

"But if their skin were dry, they'd be rusty."

"If they hadn't taken a shower in a while, they'd be dusty."

"If they pooted, they'd be musty."

"Man!" said Jalen, having difficulty dredging up much vehemence. "Y'all *play* too much!"

The Ewes scored six runs in the top of the first; the Kikuyus went down in order. The Ewes scored four runs in the second; the Kikuyus scored none. The Ewes scored five runs in the third; the Kikuyus scored one.

It didn't stop. Maurice threw as hard as he could, but was driven to tears by the Ewes' good hitting and his own team's lack of defense. After a few good games, the Kikuyus' fielders seemed rattled by the importance of this one. At least half the Ewes' runs came on overthrows, and most of those resulted from attempts to throw out runners who were going to be safe anyway. "Hold on to the ball," the coaches yelled, "run it in," but still the players kept throwing, hoping valiantly to erase past mistakes with a single great play. Lemon, the Ewes' rangy pitcher, threw so hard that it made some question the age of the Ewe players.

"They cheatin'," cried Rufus after striking out for the third time. "He too *old*."

There were a few bright spots, though. Calbert hustled in left field throughout the game and prevented a few grounders from turning into home runs. Harold, too, played well and, moreover, kept his mouth shut. Quiet Otis, whose mother introduced herself to the coaches before the game, had two hits and a nice play in the field. Moreover, Bill was pleased at the way the team, even in defeat, had begun to manage itself. In the later innings, players negotiated their own defensive changes, Demetrius moving to pitcher, Maurice to third, Freddie to catcher, and Jalen to first. "Look at that," said Bill, smiling broadly at the sight of the infield convened on the mound, not a coach within ten yards, discussing who was going to play where.

After the game, the Kikuyus departed quickly, most of them asserting valiantly that they had won the game by forfeit because of the Ewes' overage players.

Otis, however, stayed behind with his mother. She was talking to one of the Pygmies' coaches, a medical resident at Northwestern. After a few minutes, the coach pulled out his wallet and gave Otis a ten-dollar bill. "Hope this helps," he said.

Otis's father had died the day before. Tuberculosis, it was said, from AIDS. He'd checked himself out of Cook County Hospital, gone to his apartment in the Reds, and died. His name was Jimmy; he had been a truck driver before he got into dope and left the family. Even when he was a junkie, he seemed a nice guy, quiet, never a harsh word to anybody. When people heard about how he'd died, they said that was just like him; Jimmy never did want to cause anyone any trouble.

"Otis knew his daddy was gonna die," said his mother, who shared her son's soft voice and steady manner. "I kept telling him, 'Hush, honey, he gonna get better,' but Otis wouldn't listen. He kept sayin', 'He gonna die soon—I know it.' "

Otis was collecting money for his father's funeral. His mother hadn't asked him; he had wanted to do it. Now he had a sixty-dollar lump in his sock.

After the game, word of the boy's effort got around

quickly. One by one, the Kikuyus' coaches and others offered him a few dollars. Otis's mother watched, nodding appreciatively.

As he pulled a crumpled five-dollar bill from his shorts, Brad told Otis, "Hey, I'm sorry about what happened."

The boy looked up, surprised.

"I'm sorry to hear about your dad." Brad extended the money. "Are you doing okay?"

Otis gave an odd, forced laugh, and looked at Brad questioningly, trying to gauge in his expression whether or not he was joking. It was the response of a child unsure how to respond to sympathy. Brad had to be joking—of *course* Otis was okay; it was his father, not he, who had died.

After Calbert and Samuel, he was the third player on the Kikuyus to lose a father in the season of 1992.

Cabrini seemed to quiet down somewhat at the end of August: Though there was still the usual shooting between Folks and People, the click between the GDs and the BGDs had been worked out. The Vice Lords and their West Side reinforcements were holding the Castle. For Rat and the Slick Boys, it was business as usual. The Emp was said to be holding out the possibility of a People–Folks treaty; police felt he was less interested in peace than in the increased sales that a truce would bring. The closing of the Public Housing North police station had been postponed until fall or later for several unspecified reasons, one perhaps being that local activists had gotten word of the proposal and had promised a hurricane of community protest if the station was closed.

There was plenty of random shooting, and weekly fights and feuds. Residents blamed most of those on young gunslingers, twelve- and thirteen-year-olds who weren't being stopped by the gang leadership. And in fact, neither Rat nor the Emp had been seen around Cabrini in more than a month. "They lettin' the shorties run wild," said one resident. "Ain't nobody around who can instruct them, tell them how to behave."

Some of the younger teens weren't showing the proper respect toward the Slick Boys, for instance. Older gang-bangers knew that it didn't pay to mess with police; they held the power to make life difficult through constant patrols and "bad paper," lightweight charges that, though they might not stick in court, would put you out of business for a few days. Some gang members had even developed what amounted to good working relationships with the Slick Boys. "I make an agreement with the leaders," said a thirteen-year veteran Cabrini officer. "I treat them with respect. If your boy goes and shoots somebody and he fucks up—let's say ten people see him do it—then I expect you to give him up. If your boy goes and shoots somebody and nobody sees him do it, I don't expect you to tell me. Let me find out the hard way."

If a Slick Boy played dirty, however, the gangs had ways of dealing with him. Since shooting a police officer tended to provoke a furious response, the gangs instead spread rumors or lobbied with other officers for a change; if those methods didn't work, they played dirty. Slick Boys and gangsters alike knew the tale of a certain white officer who abused his privileges by beating dealers up, confiscating their dime bags, and pocketing them for his own use. One morning he was found dead at his kitchen table. Rumor was that he had smoked rat poison that somebody had cooked up to look like a rock.

Now, not only did the young gangbangers not respect the police, they were stupid enough to shoot at them. On the third Monday of the month, an 18th District squad car was pinned down by sniper fire at Hobbie and Larrabee; several minutes passed before the officers were able to escape. "That *had* to be some young slingers," said one officer. "Why would they do that, when they know that if an officer gets killed, the shit's gonna come down here like the wrath of Khan."

The young shooters hadn't always been such a problem.

Rat's predecessors had kept the shorties in line because they were more visible leaders, presences in the community. They sold drugs, sure, but they weren't about drugs. They were about power. In the late seventies and early eighties, one of them, Bo John, walked the neighborhood in his long coat and wide-brimmed gangster hat. He always had three bodyguards, two by his side and one across the street, and he would call meetings out in the open. Everybody in the Reds knew who he was, and his word was law. Now, Rat wore a leather belt buckle that said "Rat," and still there were plenty of shorties in the Reds who didn't know him from Adam. He just wasn't around much. "Fuck Rat," some of the young gunslingers would say. "He ain't no top dog."

Most of the old-time regents were long gone. Bo John opened his front door one day and was killed by a shotgun blast. Gus stepped down after one year, when he got too much heat from the Slick Boys. Jimmy G. was shot and injured by a fellow gang member, then sent to prison. Fat Daddy was killed by order of his own brother after he stepped on too many toes. Kelvin and Red Dog were still hanging out, still banging. Rat, though, was a different breed. He didn't make enemies; he knew how to work around the Slick Boys. He was a businessman. And he might have the juice to last longer than any of the old-timers.

FOUR

Ten minutes before the Northern Trust Maasai game, Coach Steve walked up to Coach Bill with the news.

"The bribes are down."

"Good. Pizza?"

"Yep. And a ride in the Blazer to my place to watch movies."

"You're a brave man, Coach Steve."

Bill and Steve stood atop the dugout bench, watching the team warm up. It was the night after the loss to the Ewes, and the Kikuyus were preparing to face the 2–9–1 Maasai. It didn't seem this would be a tough game, but at 6–5–1, the Kikuyus couldn't afford to take any chances. Freddie would start on the mound, and Steve would aggressively pursue his role as primary bookmaker for the team's burgeoning incentive program. Throughout warmups, he had negotiated an unprecedented number of deals: Hit a homer, get a slice of pizza. Hit a triple, get a Coke. Play well as a team, get a field trip to Steve's apartment.

There had been one such trip, and it was the stuff of legend: pizza, Nerf footballs, a sports bloopers video, several two-liter bottles of Coke, a balcony where you could go to yell at the people passing by on the sidewalk. "Steve is the *best* coach," Jalen pointedly told Bill afterward.

At first, some of the coaches had been skeptical about offering rewards for good play. It cheapened the relationship, they thought, it compromised whatever disciplinary leverage they were gaining on the children, and it was intrinsically tilted against the Busters, who rarely would play well enough to earn any goodies. All of these were valid arguments; but they ignored one inescapable fact: Bribery worked.

"Bet me, Steve, bet me." Alonzo held out his hand, ready for the ceremonial pinky-shake. "Piece of pizza if I don't strike out; whole pizza for a homer."

Steve held back. "Grand-*slam* homer."

Alonzo studied him, poker-faced. "Three run or more."

They shook. Alonzo skated off, telling the other players about his wager. It didn't matter that he hadn't hit a homer all year; only that, in the bet, there existed the distinct possibility that he might. The bribes were a distraction, yes, but at least for now, they seemed a healthy one.

As it turned out, Steve would regret making so many bets. The Kikuyus scored the league-set limit of ten runs against the Maasai in the first inning, then added nine in the second and eight in the third. Freddie was almost untouchable, giving up only two hits and striking out eight in three innings. Throughout the game, it seemed the Kikuyus could do no wrong. With the bases loaded in the third inning, Rassan lofted a harmless pop-up to the infield. Four infielders collided, the ball dropped to the ground, and when the Maasai stopped throwing the ball around, Rassan stood triumphantly on third base.

When the Maasai were up in the same inning, their lead-off batter hit a triple and the next batter walked—but the team's cheers had hardly died down when Maurice and

Freddie pulled their trick play, and nailed the lead runner trying to score.

"Yeah, bay-*bee*!" Freddie slam-dunked the ball on home plate and swung into an abbreviated rendition of the Electric Slide.

With the score 27–2, coaches on both sides were well into a damage-control mode. The Maasai coaches substituted freely and offered boundless encouragement to avoid any glove-throwing scenes. The Kikuyus coaches constantly reminded their players not to showboat. "Remember, guys"—Bill brought up an example of sportsmanship from the city's recent basketball rivalry—"be like the Bulls, not like the Pistons."

The coaches' greatest asset in these matters, however, was the home-plate umpire. A muscular man with a coalblack biblical beard, he approached the game with extreme seriousness, bellowing "Ball" and "Strike" with an undisputed authority. While many umpires would have enlarged the strike zone to hasten the end of such a one-sided game, this man called each pitch with equal precision, leaping out of his crouch to punch a strike or wave at a ball. Between innings he laughed and joked with the crowd, but once the game started, he brooked no disruptions. When the shorties behind the backstop made fun of the Maasai pitcher, he silenced them with a sharp look. Later the coaches found out that the man was one of the people Al Carter had hired with his grant. His name was Anthony Garrett; around Cabrini he was called Fly. He had been in the Army a long time back, he said, and lately he had been hanging around the neighborhood, doing this and that. When Al asked him if he wanted to umpire for a few dollars a game, Anthony jumped at the chance.

"I like working with kids," he said. "I ain't always been straight in my life, but if I can keep a few of them out of trouble, then I done my job."

After the game the coaches lined up to shake Anthony's hand, appreciative that he had brought them through without major incident. Like every other coach, Bill had heard Bob and Tina complain vehemently about how unreliable Al's umpires were, how they had been seen drinking before games. But for this afternoon, Al's controversial employee was something of a hero.

"I never saw him drinking," Bill said the next day. "And if he did during a game, then he probably made a stupid move. But as far as I'm concerned, Anthony's the kind of guy who needs to be involved in this league—a guy from the community who knows the kids. I always assumed that the point was to turn the league over to the community some day. If that's the case, then the Anthony Garretts are the guys we need to find and keep."

Whether because of the motivation provided by Steve's pizza bets or for some other reason, the Kikuyus kept playing well. The next Saturday they won the completion of the Zulu tie, 17–16, then went on to defeat the Frain Camins & Swartchild Pharaohs 16–8, thus boosting their record to 9–5.

The Kikuyus won mainly because they hit everything that came near the plate. In the two games, Maurice was 2 for 2, with another grand slam; Jalen and Rude Dude went 4 for 4; Harold was 4 for 5, with a homer; Otis, 3 for 4; and Freddie, 4 for 4. Even Jonathan got a hit, a dribbling single up the middle.

"This is unreal," said Cort. "When they get into a groove, they *all* get into a groove."

Not everything, of course, went as smoothly. Louis didn't show up for either game, having given a vague excuse about having to be somewhere else. Harold acted up in the Zulus game when he was hit by a pitch, mad at being deprived of the chance to be the hero. Jalen also took a turn for the worse, threatening to quit when Bill asked him to play first base. Bill dealt with each outburst patiently and fairly, but it was overwhelming even for him. The same anxieties that existed before the Iowa trip had resurfaced, and now seemed stronger than ever. Maurice, too, was affected. Frustrated when Harold refused to pick up grounders during infield practice, he directed his anger at Bill. "Why you *do* that?" he asked. "You let them get away with everything!"

The turmoil, however, was eased somewhat by the announcement that the league would include five teams from each conference in the next week's playoffs; this decision assured the currently third-place Kikuyus a spot. The playoffs would have a single-elimination format, and would start with a wild-card game between the fourth- and fifth-place teams in each conference. A tournament would follow: wild-card winner versus first-place team in the conference; second-place team versus third-place team; conference final between the winners of those games; and finally the championship game between the conference winners.

"Guys, it looks like we're in the playoffs," Bill announced at the huddle after the win against the Pharaohs. "What do you think of that?"

"Don't matter," Jalen said quickly. "We ain't *never* goin' to the 'ship with all these busters."

One hot day in the Reds, Alonzo and J-Nice were in their usual haunt: the small playground set in a nook of their building. It wasn't a particularly nice playground, but since the July shootings had cut down on forays to Grasshopper Field, it served their purposes. Home plate was an orange spray-painted X; bases were a defunct swing set, monkey bars, and a pizza box. A three-foot fence surrounded the infield, and beyond it, in right field, rose a hedge dotted by white and yellow flowers the size of buttercups—"the Green Monster," Alonzo called it. A cracked hump of concrete surfaced near first base. It once had been the base for a teeter-totter, but it now served as Alonzo's administrative office, from which he oversaw the activities of his baseball league and its two principal members.

All afternoon, Alonzo would run the games. Most of the

players were younger kids who came down from the ramps dragging dolls or pedaling Big Wheels, looking for something to do. Alonzo would quickly explain the rules to them: Off the fence was a ground-rule double, off the monkey bars a ground-rule triple, over the buttercups was as many runs as you could get. Alonzo was all-time pitcher, except for when he deigned to bat.

"My father started this a long time ago," Alonzo explained, looking into the distance, as he often did when he made things up. "But since he gone to California, that makes me the league commissioner. I have a lot of my childhood memories on this playground, so I call it the Memory Playground League. Right now, I got 'round 'bout seven hundred . . . make that seven hundred fourteen homers." He looked at J-Nice. "Don't I."

J-Nice was picking at a scab on his elbow.

"That makes me tied with Babe Ruth," Alonzo continued. "Then I'm fittina catch Hank Aaron, then I'm alone in first place. Of course, my father hit more home runs than that—he hit 'round 'bout seventeen . . . make that nineteen hundred. His career was longer."

Alonzo walked to the pitcher's spot and yelled at J-Nice to get ready.

"Double reverse palmball," he shouted, carefully gripping a balding tennis ball. J-Nice nodded, waving the toy bat that had been a promotion at a Cubs game.

Midway through his elaborate windup, Alonzo stopped and motioned J-Nice a step closer to the plate.

"You can't hit it if you're way back there," he said, striding up to the smaller boy and moving him forward with a thump on the back. He adjusted his stance, moving J-Nice's front foot and repositioning his hands.

Alonzo stepped back to admire his work. "Now you got to put your weight into it and keep your eye on the ball. *That's* how you get to be a home-run hitter."

Alonzo wound and threw, J-Nice hit a looper over the buttercups, and by the time Alonzo could find the ball, J-Nice had scored three runs.

FIVE

He was in the dugout before anyone recognized him. It shouldn't have taken so long. The outfit was the same: Miami Hurricanes jacket, Miami Hurricanes cap, tattered black glove held together by shoestring, tattered Air Flights. But it wasn't until Samuel had been sitting on the bench a few minutes before the start of the Kikuyus' last regular-season game, against the Watusi, that Coach Bill's eyebrows rose.

"Hey, is that who I think it is?" Bill lifted his voice in mock surprise, then let it fall. "Naw, it couldn't be."

Samuel stared straight ahead. He appeared taller than he had in June, and heavier too. His belly, no longer protruding with a babylike cuteness, looked broad and heavy; his shoulders were rounded and hunched forward. Even his hands looked like an old man's: tightly bunched clusters of muscle, covered with a spiderwebbing of dry, white hatch marks.

His face looked older, too; his cheeks had broadened and flattened; the three vertical scowl lines on his brow were deeper, more permanent. It was hard for Bill to see his face, because Samuel wore his cap low over his eyes, in an oddly menacing fashion, not set back on his head as it had been when Bill last saw him. But when Bill pushed the hat back, he could see that Samuel's eyes were the same: giant, wet saucers whose only expression was an unnerving blankness.

Bill put his hands on his hips, playing the interrogator. "Is there any way that you can prove that you're really Samuel, and not some impostor?"

"Uhh." The toe of the boy's sneaker traced a figure eight in the dust.

"Well," Bill feigned resignation. "There's only one way I know of to tell if it's really Samuel or not."

Bill leaned over and put his hands on either side of the boy's torso like pincers. Samuel looked up, alarmed, and tried to scramble away from the hands suddenly clutching and grabbing at him. It took him a panicked few seconds to realize he was being tickled.

"Well, maybe that's not the Samuel I knew," Bill said, a little chagrined. "*That* Samuel was ticklish."

Throughout the game, the other players treated their old teammate with a combination of wariness and neglect. Few spoke with him; when they sat next to him on the bench, they gave him several feet of room.

"He ridin' with the Vice Lords," Alonzo whispered to Brad. "When he on the street, he wear his cap to the left and a earring."

Brad peered at Samuel's earlobes. "Come *on*," he said, highly doubtful that such a meek ten-year-old could be in a gang. "There's no hole."

"Clip-on," said Alonzo, disgusted at Brad's naiveté. "He wear the long-sleeve coat to hide his tattoos, too."

"No way," said Brad, but he sounded halfhearted.

The Watusi game was a quick one. Knowing he needed to save pitchers for the playoffs, Bill started Maurice for two innings, brought in Jalen for two, and then Freddie for one. The defensive lineup changed inning by inning, as players took the management-by-committee philosophy to new heights; Rufus moved to third base, Alonzo tried shortstop, Calbert and Demetrius attempted center field in Louis's continued absence. Samuel played the entire game in right field and struck out the three times he batted.

The Kikuyus trailed throughout the game, and most of the players were blasé about the impending loss. The coaches tried to stir up enthusiasm with talk of the playoffs, but their efforts were feeble and ineffective. Dating back to the Iowa trip, the Kikuyus had now been together for eight of the last twelve days. They were weary of baseball and of one another. The final score was 14–8, and thus the Kikuyus ended their regular season at 9–6, good for third place in Conference B.

As they slapped hands with the Watusi, a group of kids lined up to throw to each other in right field: the Bakongos, second-generation disciples of Bo Schembechler, holders of an 8–5–1 record, and the Kikuyus' opponents in Saturday's first-round game.

Brad noticed them and nudged Cort, smiling. "Look at that," he said, pointing toward the tightly ordered phalanx of players, each throwing short, accurate pop flies to his counterpart.

"Then . . ."

His arm swept to the infield. Demetrius had stolen Calbert's cap, Harold was threatening to crack the dome of every Watusi player, and Freddie and Jalen were biting the tips of their fingers and then putting their hands in a prayer position, howling with pain and surprise as the flesh pushed against their compressed fingernails.

After the game, Steve cemented his position as Dream Coach by inviting the team over to his apartment for pizza. Alonzo brought along J-Nice, who said he wanted to be the team's batboy.

"He's little, but he'll be good next year," Alonzo said. "I taught him everything I know."

"*Super*," Kevin whispered to Brad. "He knows how to strike out."

By eight o'clock, J-Nice was denting Steve's carpet with groin-smash dance moves, Demetrius was standing on the couch wearing a plastic Viking helmet, Freddie and Jalen were on the balcony, aiming their spit at passersby, and Alonzo stood at the kitchen counter, mixing several kinds of soda into a drink he called a "suicide." Samuel sat amid the chaos, not saying a word, pushing a battery-powered truck back and forth across the hearth. He wore a short-sleeved T-shirt. Brad had been relieved not to see any tattoos.

"Heyheyheyheyhey." Bill motioned for silence. No one paid attention.

"*Hey!*" He stood up and slapped his hand on a football, and everyone started. Bill smiled.

"Everybody have a seat." His hand traced a circle around the room. "Let's get in here and talk a few things over."

Slowly, the kids gathered, pushing each other to gain space on the couch. Bill waited until things were calm, then, as was his habit, waited a little longer.

"The playoffs start this coming weekend," he began. "I want to know from you guys what you think it's going to take to win." Bill held up the football. "There's one rule in this meeting: The only person who can talk is the person who has the ball."

He tossed the football to Rufus, whose eyes widened in shock and dismay that Bill could expect him to go first. He let it sit in his lap, untouched, until Harold grabbed the ball and spoke into it as if into a microphone.

"I only hope that all you busters, Calbert, Alonzo, Samuel, Jonathan . . . Demetrius, Maurice"—he pointed at each one as the room erupted in denials—"I hope you all hit a home run like me."

"Thanks, Harold," said Bill, his words tilting with

sarcasm. He removed the ball from Harold's grasp and handed it to the next player. "What do you think, Jalen?"

Jalen took the ball, but turned shy. He smiled, without saying anything.

Next was Demetrius. *"Beat Bakongooooos,"* he screeched, doing a pelvic thrust into the football.

Maurice reached for the ball and stood up. His hair made him look tall. It hadn't been cut since the season started, and now it tufted wildly around his face, swirling here and there into miniature Rasta curls. Maurice cleared his throat and spoke in a soft voice.

"I hope all the busters get a hit, and that includes me. All of us is busters sometimes, 'cause ain't none of us perfect all the time."

Bill tried not to smile. "Maurice, I'm not sure if everybody heard that. Why don't you repeat it for them."

Everybody listened. Even J-Nice stopped doing groin-smashers on the floor.

"I *said*," Maurice's voice rose, "I hope all the busters get a hit, 'cause all of us is busters sometimes."

Then Freddie grabbed the ball, J-Nice danced, Harold yelled at Demetrius, and everything started up again.

Forty-five minutes later, Bill and Samuel were parked on a narrow street next to the Castle. On one side, the burned-out shell of an El Dorado teetered on a low concrete wall. On the other sat two squad cars, blue lights spinning.

"Do you want me to let you off out front?"

"No!" Samuel's mouth stayed on the "o."

"Won't the police make sure that you get home safe?"

Samuel spoke softly. "I don't got no key."

"You don't have keys?" Bill was incredulous. Keys, carried on a chain necklace, were an essential part of a Cabrini child's outdoor wardrobe. "How do you get in when your mom's not around?"

Samuel shrugged.

Bill sighed and shifted the car into drive. It was nine-thirty now, half an hour since the party ended at Steve's, and he and Samuel had spent the greater part of the time driving around Cabrini looking for his mother. First they had gone to the Castle and called up to her window—no answer. Then they had driven by her sister's place on Larrabee—but her car wasn't there. Then to her other sister's place in the Whites—still nothing. Now they had struck out at the Castle again, and there was nowhere else to go.

Bill was antsy. He didn't like to be in Cabrini at night, especially in a shiny red Saab. He drove with caution, rolling through intersections, careful not to rev the engine too much lest it be taken as a sign of aggression. When two cars in front of him blocked the road so the drivers could hold a conversation, Bill had no trouble fighting down the urge to honk. The windows of the Saab stayed rolled up. The radio stayed off, better to hear any outside sounds.

Cabrini looked different at night. There weren't many streetlights, and those that weren't broken sent out pools of dirty, rusted light that lent little definition to anything within their reach. Bill now witnessed the clusters of paperbaggers by the liquor stores; the committees of junkies and gossipers out on the dirty-lit stoops of rowhouses; the casual handoffs of boosters selling baby clothes and sneakers out of the backseat of their cars; the young men walking self-consciously with bags of Pampers; the pipehead dancing crazily in the glare of a police spotlight; the music thumping from windows; and everywhere, children. Dozens of children, grouped in twos and threes and fours, jumping rope, leaping off curbs, climbing on cars, throwing rocks, riding bikes, running. As the unfamiliar outline of the Saab rolled past, teens and adults looked casually, but with squinted eyes that revealed curiosity. The children, however, stared.

On the third lap, Samuel spotted his mother's car outside his aunt's building. Bill pulled up near the entrance and stopped the car. He leaned over and looked at his passenger. "Are you going to be okay?"

Samuel wasn't listening. He was looking anxiously out the window, assessing the terrain. Fifty feet or so separated him from the doorway, then it would be another thirty feet to the stairwell, then four flights to his aunt's apartment. Three tall kids in hooded Duke and Georgetown jackets leaned against the building watching Bill's car with interest. Samuel zipped his jacket to his neck and straightened his cap. He looked out the window again.

"We'll see you Saturday, right?"

Samuel looked at Bill blankly.

"Saturday. Two o'clock. The playoff game against the Bakongos. Be sure to tell your parents."

Samuel squinted, still puzzled.

"I mean, your mother."

Samuel nodded.

"If the game's at two, when should you be there?" Bill fiddled with the Saab's fan control to give the boy time to solve this problem.

Samuel's brow furrowed. "Three?"

"Close," Bill said patiently. "One-*thirty*."

"One . . . one-thirty," Samuel repeated.

"We'll see you Saturday."

"Uh-huhhh."

Samuel got out of the car, ran through the doorway, and disappeared.

Late that night, Bill's phone rang. He was already in bed, so he let the machine pick up. He heard his voice on the pre-recorded message, then a long silence. Then a little boy's voice.

"I . . . I made it home okay."

By the time Bill got to the phone, Samuel had hung up.

SIX

Saturday dawned clear and cool. Dew coated the specks of glass on the sidewalks and basketball courts, turning them into fields of diamonds. Wrinkles had crept into the blue flowers of the chicory, but everything else—aspens, elms, fernlike trees of heaven, even the much-trampled weeds of the field itself—looked full and healthy in the morning light. Sea gulls that had hitched over on the lake breeze walked Carson Field alongside the pigeons. On Sedgwick Street, two boys squashed ants with a billiard ball.

In a small, tidy bedroom several blocks from Carson Field, Louis stood in a shaft of sunlight eyeing the yellow laundry basket that served as the hoop for his imaginary basketball league. "Laser brings it upcourt," he announced. "Guarded by Chain. Chain reaches in . . . but Laser is too quick. . . . He drives . . ."

Louis pirouetted, slowly, using his bed to shield himself from his imaginary defender. He didn't have to worry about traveling: in the Louis Basketball League, there was no dribbling.

"He fires . . ."

The ball bounced weakly off the front of the basket.

"It won't go! Chain pulls down the rebound!" Louis snatched the ball off the floor and walked back toward the bed imitating the goonlike stride of the biggest, meanest X-Con. LBL rules were strict: Rebounds went to the defensive team unless they led by more than ten points and/or the carom came off more than five feet.

Since his *Star Search* audition, aside from the Iowa trip, Louis had spent most of his time here. When coaches phoned, wondering why he hadn't shown up at games, he told them that he had been visiting relatives on the South Side, that he was out of town, that his mother had put him on punishment, that he was sick, anything but the truth: that he had been home waiting for the phone to ring, waiting for the news that he had landed a spot on the show.

Louis couldn't stop thinking about it. After all, the try-out had gone so well. The nice producer had told him that he had done a terrific job and that the people from the show would be in touch real soon. His mother, as she always did, told him not to count on anything, but he couldn't help it. Every time he saw a TV show, he pictured himself on it. With construction paper and pencil, he designed houses he would build with the money he earned.

Louis's mother told him to forget about it and go join his teammates, but out of embarrassment and hope, he couldn't. He threw himself into his private games and emerged from his room so infrequently that he thwarted the Kikuyus' intelligence network.

"Who knows where Louis is?" Bill asked one day, looking at Jalen.

"How we fittina know where Louis at all the time?" Jalen shouted angrily. "We ain't his *daddy*."

It was fifteen minutes before the Bakongos game, and Coach Bill had his hands on his hips.

"Chuck E. *Cheese*?" he asked Jalen. "He's skipping the game to go eat pizza?"

"That's what he say. He say he sick of baseball."

"Sick of baseball?" Bill crossed his arms. "Does Louis know this is the playoffs?"

Jalen shrugged. "He say he goin' to a birthday party."

Having already sent Jalen to Louis's house once, Bill decided not to push it. He had more urgent matters to deal with, the lineup for instance. On the diamond, the Bakongos were running through their drills like clockwork, the pitcher scooting to back up all throws to home.

"Attababy," their coaches yelled, and clapped. "Attababy now."

Most coaches had already mapped out their playoff strategies, and the majority of them hinged on two simple facts. First, teams advancing to the final would play three games (wild-card teams would play four) in eight days; second, that the six-inning-a-week pitching limit was still in effect. Each coach, therefore, was faced with a decision: Do you play conservatively and pitch your ace in the first game, or do you take a chance and go with somebody else, saving a trump card for a more important contest? In Saturday's early game, Bob Muzikowski's Pygmies had made their strategy apparent: they had used their second-best pitcher and defeated the Watusi, saving the fireballing Shondrae for the semifinal against the winner of the Ewes–Bantus game.

"I love it," said Bob. "We take a gamble early on, then go best-against-best in the semis. Then, if we make the finals, it's all up for grabs. Both teams will probably be out of pitchers, and whoever's deepest overall will win."

The Kikuyus, on the other hand, didn't really have a strategy. With the notable exception of the 12–3–1 Ibos, their Conference B opponents looked to be of roughly equal caliber to the Kikuyus—which was to say, thoroughly average. If they could sneak past the first two rounds while the Bantus, Ewes, and Pygmies (combined record: 38–4) slugged it out in Conference A, they might have a chance. As for pitching, the coaches came to a consensus that Freddie should probably start, but with his shaky temperament, he couldn't be counted on to go the distance. Bill hoped to go a few innings with Freddie, then bring in Maurice or Jalen, and stick with whoever was throwing the best. "Of course"—Bill alluded to his players' penchant for switching positions—"I could be overruled."

Elsewhere in the field, Bill had made a few changes. Otis was moved from left field to third base, where his good hands would stop any run-producing overthrows, and Demetrius from shortstop to center field, not so much for his glove but for his speed, which could back up Alonzo and Rassan in left and right. The changes had gone over with a surprising smoothness. Not to say that Alonzo and Demetrius didn't complain and threaten to quit, as banishment to the outfield was tantamount to public declaration of Busterhood. But their protestations had been weak, almost a formality. Before long they were taking their new appointments with great solemnity, dropping into ready positions that the coaches had not seen in weeks. Warm-ups took place without the usual jeering and catcalling. Harold, playing shortstop, didn't even yell at Rufus when the two tangled on a throw to second.

"What's the matter with them?" Cort asked Brad as they stood together on the bench. "I mean, everybody's so quiet."

Brad tilted his head toward the backstop. Besides the usual assortment of mothers, grandmothers, and shorties, a few new faces were visible. Jalen's mother stood there wearing a brilliant white blouse and dark sunglasses; Harold's father stood nearby. Maurice and Rufus's mother was there, too, ensconced in a lawn chair that the coaches had given her as thanks for her faithful attendance. This was the biggest crowd the Kikuyus had seen all year.

"I think they're a little scared," Brad said.

Along the right-field foul line, Kevin warmed Freddie up, teaching him a new pitch. Normally he wouldn't teach anything new the day of a game, but Freddie wasn't like other players.

"Kick your leg real high, like you're going to throw it fast." Kevin pantomimed. "Then just throw it slow."

Freddie nodded. He tried one.

"Perfect!" shouted Kevin. "One more."

Freddie kicked and threw. The ball floated in for a strike. Kevin got up out of his crouch and walked over to the little pitcher.

"That's called a change-up. You want to throw that with two strikes, okay? And don't throw it very often, because if they're waiting for it, they'll hit it."

Freddie nodded. He hissed a narrow thread of spit between his teeth. "Like I'm gonna fake 'em out."

"*Right!*" Kevin was ebullient. "Like you're gonna fake 'em out!"

*   *   *

When boys of widely varying abilities play a difficult game such as baseball for a long time, probability dictates that in the course of the season one or two crystalline moments will emerge when, in defiance of the law of entropy and every established pattern, everything will go perfectly. In that scheme, the Bakongos game ranked supreme.

In the top half of the first inning, the Kikuyus erupted for nine runs on seven hits, seven of the runs coming on two Andre Dawson–style homers by Maurice. In the bottom half of the inning, Freddie struck out the first three Bakongo batters, the final one on a knee-buckling full-count change-up that had the other Kikuyus' coaches high-fiving Kevin in the dugout. Freddie came off the mound with a cool hitch in his step, all confidence, while the Bakongos' coaches rolled their eyes.

"A change-up?" one of them shouted over to the Kikuyus' bench. "He throws a *change*-up?"

The rest of the contest was for the most part an afterthought. Freddie, then Jalen, then Maurice mowed through the demoralized Bakongos, each of them striking out five in two innings' work. On offense, the Kikuyus hit the ball as if they were in batting practice; on defense, they played flawlessly. Harold homered twice. Maurice threw out one of the Bakongos' rare baserunners trying to steal second. Otis had two hits and made a nice play on a grounder at third. Freed from their pregame jitters, the players fell into their new habit of negotiating position changes. Bill sat back, watching his team run itself and empathizing with the Bakongos' coaches as they tried to manufacture enthusiasm and effort in a team that knew it was beaten. By the end of the third inning, the score was 15–0; the final would be 18–1.

"We'd better enjoy this while we can," Bill said.

Inside ten minutes he was proven a prophet. In the top of the fifth, Kevin casually asked Harold to help him pick up several pairs of uniform pants lying on the ground and throw them into a bag.

"No," said Harold, who had spent most of the game in a

bad mood. Though he had homered twice, he resented the way the coaches directed most of their attention to Freddie, Maurice, and Jalen. Harold wanted to pitch, he wanted to be the hero.

"C'mon, Harold, give me a hand."

Harold purposely stepped on one of the pairs of pants.

"Pick up the pants, Harold." Kevin's voice rose.

"I *ain't* picking up your laundry." Harold walked away.

Bill followed him and asked him to pick up the pants.

"I'll do it later." Harold smiled to let Bill know he wouldn't.

"Do it now, or you sit." Bill pointed to the pants, crumpled beneath the bench.

Harold crossed his arms and stared mutely at the coaches. Heads in the dugout turned. He couldn't back down now.

"Pick up your own damn laundry."

On reflection, Bill would say that he didn't mean to cause such a confrontation. After all, it was just a pair of pants, and Harold had doubtless gotten away with much more serious insubordination. But now, with the team rolling along, everybody on the same page for once, Bill wasn't going to let Harold seize control.

"Pick up the pants," he said slowly, "or your pants will be on the bench."

"You *blackmailin'* me!" Harold shouted as he pulled off his jersey. "I'm the best player on this team! I hit the most home runs! Who's gonna say I'm not the best!"

"We're not blackmailing you, Harold. We're not cheating you. We just want you to pick up the pants."

"I'm *gone,*" Harold said, and walked out of the dugout. "Y'all know you just lost your best player," he yelled from the street. "Best player in the motherfuckin' league!"

As Harold walked down Scott Street, his insults disappearing in the breeze, the mood in the dugout lifted. Calbert and Rufus smiled slightly as they watched him go. Jalen, who normally would have stuck up for Harold, said nothing. Maurice looked at Bill and nodded approvingly.

Freddie was the only one to give voice to the team's emotions.

"Man"—he shook his head—"Harold *talk* too much."

Most of the team was in the stands later that afternoon when the wildcard Linnco Mandinkes upset Keith Melanson's favored Ibos, scoring three runs in the top of the sixth and playing clutch defense to win 11–8. These Mandinkes were a different team from the one the Kikuyus had played in June. They had a diminutive pitcher, Derrick, who resembled Freddie, a fleet outfield, and a solid defense that erased three Ibos on plays at home plate. They also had a brigade of supporters led by Pumpkin, an appropriately named woman who screamed almost unceasingly throughout the game. When it ended, players and coaches, parents and children rolled around the infield in a great, joyous clump.

"Man-dink-uh," they chanted, *"Man-dink-uh!"*

Behind the backstop, the Kikuyus joined in the dancing. They knew *they* wouldn't have stood much of a chance against the Ibos, but the Mandinkes? The buster team that Alonzo kept referring to as "the Dinky Men"? They had thrashed them 21–13 the first time, and they figured they could do it again.

"We goin' to the 'ship," Jalen and Freddie sang, spraying each other at the water fountain and dancing. "We goin' to the 'ship."

SEVEN

 Early in the morning after the Kikuyus' win over the Bakongos, Bill's phone rang. The caller didn't wait for a hello.

"You got three-way?"

"Juh . . . Jalen?"

"You got three-way?"

"Uh, I think I do, but I don't know how to use it."

"Hang on."

Bill heard a pleasant beep as Jalen went to work. Seconds later his voice returned.

"Okay, Harold's mom is going to get him. I'll do the talking. You just back me up."

Bill, amused, agreed. Jalen, who had been unwilling to stick up for his friend in the dugout, had inserted himself as a diplomat in an effort to get Harold back on the team.

For the next twenty minutes, the three of them talked. They covered familiar ground: responsibility, respect, and leadership. Bill could picture Harold on the other end, transformed into his gentlemanly self, his aquiescence sending a clear message: He was sorry and wanted to come back.

Bill was hesitant. Allowing Harold back on the team without punishment might antagonize the other players, not to mention the coaches. It would reinforce the idea that actions need not have consequences; that the individual could be bigger than the team. Besides, history had shown that the team played well without Harold in the lineup, freed as they were from his constant verbal assaults. Objectively, it was a simple problem. The team was probably better off without him.

But Bill again had to admire the boy's deep intelligence, the way he built his argument, the way he knew how to elicit sympathy. Bill knew he was being manipulated, but he gave Harold credit for the undeniable quality of the manipulation. And at the heart of it, Bill rationalized, the guy wanted to play ball. Throwing him off the team would be denying the better half of his personality; it would be treating him as if he in fact *were* the smart-ass troublemaker he pretended to be. The question inevitably arose: What would be the cost of that? In the end, it was an easy decision. The team would stay together, for better or worse, or it would split up.

"Practice is tomorrow at six-thirty," Bill said. "Be there."

"Thanks, Bill," Harold said sincerely. "You're a good coach."

Practice on Monday was an unmitigated disaster. After only five minutes Harold was fighting with Demetrius. Moments later Jalen decided that not enough balls were being hit his way, and he walked off. Rufus, growing increasingly bolder, threw a rock at Alonzo, who picked up a bat and threatened to brain the smaller boy. Even Maurice and Rassan joined in, complaining and crying when they didn't get to be first in batting practice. Some of the coaches considered offering a few incentives for good team behavior, but the idea was discarded. Things were too out-of-control to be solved by sausage pizza.

"What's going *on* out here?" Cort asked no one in particular.

Bill tried to handle each dispute with his customary even humor, but his assistants could not be so patient.

"I have *had* it with you, Demetrius," said Kevin. The veins in his neck bulged purple as he walked toward the boy holding a bat like a firebrand.

"What the *hell's* going on?" Cort repeated as Jalen stomped away for the second time. "This is *contagious.*"

Practice ended with the players hopelessly scattered around Carson Field and the coaches collecting the equipment. Nobody said much. There wasn't anything to say.

Half an hour after practice, Bill sat on the curb near the field staring at the brick expanse of the Oscar Mayer building.

Bill pointed up. "How tall is that?"

Jalen answered without looking. "One thousand three hundred eighty feet."

"Really." Bill squinted. "Seems only about eight, nine stories to me."

"I know how tall it is," said Jalen, suddenly angry. "I been in there. On a *field* trip."

"Easy there, chief," said Bill, gazing up again.

It was dark now, and the building looked tall indeed. It loomed over the field, a monolith of industry, blocking out all but a violet rectangle of sky. From inside, Bill could hear the faint hum of thousands of sausages and wieners being formed. It was a comforting presence, the humming factory, shielding them from Cabrini, the steady glow of its mercury-vapor lights pushing back the encroaching darkness.

Bill didn't know why he was hanging around. The other coaches had left as soon as practice had ended. But he didn't want to go home. There was too much to think about at home. He had just received the news that his company was being discharged as the manager of North Pier; there was a decent chance that his job would be terminated. As a potential casualty of the recession, he felt a vague obligation to update his résumé, call a headhunter, start networking. But right now he didn't want to do any of that. He just wanted to sit on the curb in the dark. After a while Freddie joined him, along with Jalen.

"If my bat is phony"—Jalen was resuming a debate he and Bill had begun several days earlier—"then how come I hit so many home runs with it?"

Bill leaned back on his elbows and tilted his head at the sky.

"Jalen, if you had been the coach, what would you have done differently this year?"

Jalen didn't say anything at first. He began hammering Rude Dude's handle on the concrete. He did so for several seconds, then spoke. "I'd take the team out for pizza after every game."

"No matter if they won or lost?"

"Yop, and I'd . . ."

"I'd buy 'em lots of pops and candy and stuff," Freddie yelled.

"But," Bill persisted, turning toward Jalen, "what if they acted up and talked back when you did things for them? What if all of them always wanted to bat first, and they all called each other buster, and they all complained that they were getting cheated when things didn't go their way? What if no matter what you did, it was never good enough for them, and they always found something to complain about?"

"I'd *still* take 'em out for pizza," Jalen said. "And if they argued over who was gonna bat, I'd make 'em play rock-paper-scissors for it."

Bill mulled this over. All season he had been confronted with discipline problems, and all season he had chosen to solve them not through the benchings, push-ups, and suspensions used by virtually every other coach, but simply by doing what he did best: talking. Sometimes it had worked marvelously; other times, as with Harold, not so well. Now, as Bill sat on the curb at the end of the season, it was apparent that he could not have behaved in any other way; that Bill could no sooner be a strict coach than he could sprout wings. Perhaps it had something to do with his own distant relationship with his father; perhaps it was a deep empathy with these children, perhaps it was something else. Whatever the cause, Bill, the unshakable, all-capable coach who never showed his emotions, could not bear, even for a moment, to have one of his players angry with him.

There was one encounter especially that Bill liked to recall. Toward the end of a late-season practice, Jalen had threatened yet again to quit. Before he could walk off the field, however, Bill put a hand on his shoulder.

"Why are you quitting?"

"Because you don't care." Jalen had avoided Bill's gaze.

"What don't I care about?"

"The players." He spat out the words and looked up, wearing his best indignant expression.

"Hold on a second." Bill sat down on the grass. "Are you telling me that I don't care, even though I took you to Iowa, took you to the batting cages, went bowling with you, tutor you in the off-season? Are you saying that I don't care about you? If you are, that really hurts my feelings."

Jalen's head dropped. "I guess I didn't mean that."

Bill lifted his chin, signifying a change of focus. "Do you care about me?"

Jalen shifted uncomfortably. "I dunno."

"Do you care about Coach Cort?"

"I dunno."

Bill continued naming the coaching staff, and received the same answer. Then he asked Jalen if he cared about Freddie.

"Yop."

"Do you care about Maurice?"

"Yop."

Bill went through the entire roster, and Jalen, sitting on the grass next to him, answered yes to all of the names, even Nathaniel's and Calbert's. Jalen, grouchy, cranky, impenetrable Jalen, Bill's most worthy opponent, had actually said yes.

Bill now rose from his seat on the curb and walked to the low fence protruding from the sidewalk behind him. It was an unremarkable structure: about three feet high, made of hand-worn plumber's pipe two inches in diameter. It served no ascertainable purpose other than to mark the boundary between two adjacent lots, but Bill knew of another use. He had seen Freddie and Jalen playing the balancing game in which they tried to stand on the pipe without falling or touching the other.

His bad knee creaking, Bill stepped up on the fence and reached out to grasp the eave of a nearby house for support. Freddie and Jalen quickly hopped up, grabbing his arms and twisting like surfers to gain their balance. Then, on the count of three, they let go.

The old man sitting on the stairs of the house put down his Little Hug and sat up. Two willowy teenage girls in sunglasses stopped and stared. A baby who had been playing in a rectangle of weeds peered up, mouth open. Everybody looked, then laughed at the sight, a tall man in a white T-shirt standing on a pipe fence with two little boys, all windmilling in the darkness, trying to keep their balance.

EIGHT

On Tuesday, the day of the conference championship, the wind began to blow. Garbage swirled down the street; pigeons took cover under the roof of the Seward Park fieldhouse. A man selling pinwheels, his stock humming furiously inside his cardboard quiver, huddled next to the abandoned Church's Fried Chicken. A few leaves blew across the infield.

"This ain't no good," said the man in the "Boss" hat, swaddling an old cardigan around him and squinting at the stormclouds to the west. "No good at all."

At ten minutes to six, the Mandinkes still hadn't shown up.

"We win," proclaimed Rufus. "They forfeit."

"Hold on there, chief," said Coach Bill. "Give them a little time."

The Kikuyus had been warming up for a half-hour, long enough for their initial nervousness to give way to a few outbursts. Demetrius announced that he wasn't playing if he couldn't play shortstop, Rassan said he was quitting if he couldn't play center field, and Jalen claimed he had a head-ache and lay curled in the open hatchback of Bill's Saab wearing an enormous pair of yellow-framed sunglasses he had found in a gutter.

"Looks like everybody's in top form," joked Coach Kevin.

The storm that had threatened the afternoon sailed safely to the south, but it brought with it a brisk tailing wind. Fortunately for the Kikuyus, they had been assigned Carson Field's northeast diamond, set in the shelter of the Oscar Mayer factory. The semifinal, between Bob Muzikowski's Pygmies and the defending-champion Ewes, was being played on the other diamond, and these teams weren't so fortunate. The Kikuyus could see dust devils wheeling about the southwestern infield.

At five minutes before six, an old yellow station wagon pulled up on Scott Street. Players in yellow jerseys started getting out. And getting out. And getting out.

"It's like one of those clown cars," said Coach Brad.

Finally, ten Mandinkes stood on the sidewalk along with five assorted parents and coaches. The Kikuyus con-tinued their warm-ups, but all eyes turned to watch when their opponents gathered outside their dugout, arranged themselves in a circle, and started to pray.

"Uh-oh," said Kevin.

"We gonna loo-oose," said Rufus.

The Linnco Mandinkes arrived by car because they were the only Near North Little League team not from Cabrini. They were from a poor southwestern Chicago neighbor-hood, North Lawndale; they had been assembled by an ac-quaintance of Bob Muzikowski's who worked for a church in that troubled community. Because the team was put to-gether at the last minute, they had played sloppily early on. In fact, when they had lost to the Kikuyus 21–13, it was only the second time they had been on the field together. Now, after some three months, the Mandinkes had

improved immensely. While part of their improvement
had to do with fine athletes and good coaches, much of it
could be traced to their outsider status. As foreigners, the
Mandinkes were impervious to the catcalls of the shorties
behind the backstop and immune, at least temporarily, to
most local strains of divisiveness. They might have bick-
ered at home, but when they piled into the yellow station
wagon and drove to Cabrini, they hung together, no matter
what. Earlier in the season, when a Hausa player accidentally ran over their first baseman, umpires and coaches had
to intervene to stop the entire Mandinke team from jumping the offender.

Their head coach, a muscular Eurodollar trader named
Allen Eaton, ran a tight ship. Coach E, as he was known,
handed out benchings frequently and forbade the Mandinkes to jaw at other teams. He could be generous, too; he
rewarded one player who said "Excuse me" with a start at
shortstop. But late in the season his greatest asset had been
Pumpkin and her cheering section, a group of parents and
relatives who attended every game. They had shown up
only sporadically at first, but after a July game in which the
Mandinkes came from ten runs down in the last inning to
beat the Watusi, Pumpkin and her crew became regulars.
With her rattling the backstop, Coach E's boys won five of
their last seven regular-season games, thumped the Hausas
in the wild-card game, and upset the Ibos. Now they felt
fairly invincible.

"One, two, three, *Mandinke!*"

The yellow jerseys broke out of their prayer huddle and
took the field. Their cheering section, which had expanded
to a group of about a dozen, hollered wildly from behind
the backstop. Coach E, impassive in sunglasses, stood outside the dugout with his arms folded. Pumpkin rattled the
chain link and gave a piercing wail.

Also behind the backstop was the Kikuyus' cheering
section: Maurice and Rufus's mother, seated in her new
chair and wearing a dazzling purple shirt; Harold's father,
Jonathan's mother, Demetrius's corn-haired girlfriend, all

except Harold's father monitoring assorted babies and toddlers. The number of backstop shorties was about double the usual, filled out by players whose seasons had ended.

"Come on now, Kikuyus," Maurice and Rufus's mother yelled. "Don't listen to them none."

Brad shouted out the lineup. Freddie, leading off, pitching; Otis, batting second, at third base; Maurice, batting third, backcatching; Harold, cleanup, at shortstop; Rufus, batting fifth, at second base; Demetrius, sixth, in center field; Alonzo, seventh, right field; Jonathan, double cleanup, left field; Jalen, ninth, at first base.

"Ninth?" Jalen looked ready to explode. *"Ninth?"*

"Relax, chief." Bill took Jalen aside and explained that he had switched the lineup to spread out some of the good hitters. This way Jalen could be on base when the meat of the order came up; it was like the White Sox did when they had Ozzie Guillen bat ninth.

"Ozzie Guillen a *buster*." Jalen retreated behind his yellow frames.

"We gonna lose," repeated Rufus, wanting to say something.

"Yop," added Rassan, who, unlike Jonathan, had learned how to complain. Already he had threatened that he would be playing for the Pygmies the next year. "I bet *anything* the Mandinkes win."

Freddie whirled. "Man, shut up!"

"He's right," Harold chimed in. "We gonna lose because I can't bat for y'all, because y'all is a bunch of busters."

"Man, shut *up*!"

"Hit me if I'm wrong!"

"We ain't gonna lose," said Maurice loudly, turning his head to make certain Bill heard. "We gonna win."

"We gonna loo-oose," sang Louis under his breath, taking his solitary post at the end of the bench. In all the commotion, few had noticed that he had returned to the team. He sat there as he had in the first game, arms folded, eyes set straight ahead as an invitation for sympathy. His pretended anger, however, couldn't hide his happiness. That morning he finally had received a call—not from *Star Search,* but from his old piano teacher, who wanted him to join a youth gospel band she was putting together.

"They're gonna pay us fifty dollars each time we play, at least," Louis breathlessly described later. "I get a new tuxedo outfit and my teacher says they put a big jar on the piano and I get to keep all the tips. There's five other kids in the band—we don't have a name yet, but they're all supposed to be real nice and everything, and she says there's a chance we might even make a *record.*"

Though there were six LBL games on the schedule for Tuesday, Louis decided to skip them and come to the game. But he still played hard-to-get.

"Don't put me in," he told Brad when the rest of the team took the field at the top of the first. "I don't feel like playing today."

"Okay, Louis." Brad pretended to make a note in the scorebook to that effect. "You got it."

A minute later Louis got up and walked toward Brad, then touched his sleeve to get his attention. He looked not at Brad, but at the sky, half smiling as if he knew something his coach didn't.

"You know how I told you not to play me this game? . . ."

Freddie, cap tugged low and stirrups pulled Awwa-high, threw the first pitch for a strike. The next pitch was hit on the ground toward first base. Jalen scooted over and reached down, and the ball squirted past him into right field.

"Maaaan!" Jalen looked around for something to blame and settled on the sunglasses. He ripped them off and frisbeed them into the dugout.

"No problem, Freddie," Coach Bill called, anxious to avert any meltdowns. "Forget about it. Get the hitter."

A few pitches later, with one out and runners on first and second, Freddie's pitch bounced past Maurice. The runners, as expected, took off—but the ball ricocheted off the backstop and into the glove of Maurice, who recovered quickly and threw the ball to Otis at third. The lead runner, seeing that he was about to be out by ten feet, put on the brakes, as did the runner behind him. Suddenly everything froze. Both runners were stuck between bases, and a new third baseman held the ball.

"Oh, shit," said Coach Kevin, knowing how infrequently Little League teams execute the delicate throw-catch-tag of a successful rundown. If history was any lesson, the Kikuyus were about to engage in a frenetic fifteen seconds of throwing the ball around the infield, and both runners were going to wind up safe, if not score.

But this time was different. Otis ran toward the lead runner, pushing him back toward second, then threw to Harold, who applied the tag and then threw to Jalen at first, who slapped the tag on the trailing runner. Brad marked down a 2–5–6–3 DP in the scorebook, and the bench cheered.

The bottom of the first started well for the Kikuyus, with two singles and an error loading the bases with no outs and Mr. Home-Run Hitter himself coming to the plate. But Harold was nervous and swung too hard, and popped out weakly to first base. Then, with Pumpkin and her crew chanting and rattling the fence, little Derrick induced Rufus to pop out and Demetrius to strike out. Bases loaded, no outs, and the Kikuyus hadn't scored. The Mandinkes went wild.

As the dispirited Kikuyus trudged out to start the second inning, their coaches unholstered the usual truisms.

"No sweat, guys, lot more where that came from."

"Hey, hey, got five more ups, lot more chances to hit this guy."

"Little defense now, hold them. We got this game."

But in the top of the second, everything fell apart. The first Mandinke batter hit a harmless trickler to Rufus that went off his glove. The second batter hit another dribbler, in front of home, that Maurice couldn't find a handle on.

Now there were runners on first and second, nobody out. The third batter, a tall center fielder named Keith, hit a grounder that Rufus, now unnerved, misplayed. One run in. Still nobody out.

"Why you do that, Rufie?" Freddie lost control, as tears welled up in Rufus's eyes. "Why you *do* that?"

"No sweat, Freddie," Kevin yelled. He tried to distract his pitcher with specifics. "Take your breath, step right toward the glove."

It didn't work. Freddie walked the next batter, loading the bases, then gave up a comebacker that he turned into a force at home. He settled down to strike out the number-nine hitter for the second out of the inning, and for a moment it looked as if the Kikuyus would escape as the Mandinkes had.

"One more, Freddie, right to the mitt."

"Come on, Freddie, take your breath now. Step to the glove. Rock and fire."

The leadoff hitter worked the count full and drew a walk, forcing in a run. The next batter, Terrence, a lanky left fielder, hit a worm-burner to short that Harold misplayed, and two more runs scored.

Then, slow catastrophe. A hard single to left. A single up the middle. A blooper to right. A cheap infield hit. With each blow, the Kikuyus sagged. Gradually, the defense abandoned any semblance of a ready position and stood straight up, as if casual posture would reduce the chances that the ball would be hit to them. Harold began to jaw with the Mandinke runners, and soon was exchanging jacking-off gestures with their entire dugout. Freddie hurried his motion, kicking his leg halfheartedly to get the inning over with. After the sixth run, Bill motioned Maurice to the mound to calm Freddie down, but Freddie would have none of it.

"You shut up, man! You keep messin' up!" Maurice, chastised, retreated.

Finally, a diminutive Mandinke named Ed waved at a high pitch to end the inning. The Kikuyus walked slowly to the dugout, hurling their gloves before them. Freddie sat alone, sniffing back tears, his face a mask of anger. Maurice looked as though he might cry as well. The coaches abandoned any attempts at cheerleading; assuming damage-control formation, they paired off with players and quizzed them about the batting order, discussed how best to hit the pitcher, asked them about their families—did anything to distract them from the fact that they were now behind 8–0.

"Game's over." Harold smiled to show he didn't care. "Twenty-two homers this season, and I'm still the best on the team."

"Shut up and watch the game, Harold," said Brad.

The bottom of the second began well enough. Alonzo drew a walk, Jonathan was hit by a pitch, and Jalen singled, loading the bases. But then Freddie, still glowering, struck out, and Otis popped out to second. Pumpkin, sensing another closeout, started a chant.

"Man-dink-uh, Man-dink-uh."

Maurice walked to the plate, tapped the outside edge, and began moving his hands in the familiar Andre Dawson waggle.

"Man-dink-uh, Man-dink-uh."

"That's it," yelled Harold from the on-deck circle. "Maurice gonna fan, he gonna strike out now, baby." He pulled off his batting helmet and set it with exaggerated daintiness on the ground.

Not wanting to make any more of a scene, the coaches let Harold ramble. But this latest offense was too much for Maurice's mother. Levitated from her lawn chair, Mary appeared at the dugout fence, eyes glinting.

"*Why* you say that? Huh? Why you always talkin' your *trash* like that?" A red fingernail jabbed through the chain link. "You think you can't beat these boys? Is they better than you?"

"Yes," said Harold, slightly taken aback. "They *is* better than us. The score like twenty to nothin'."

Mary's palm rose, cutting off any argument; her voice rang as loud as a police siren.

"Don't give me that. *Last* time you beat them, and if you can play like you did last time then *you'd* be whuppin' *them* instead of *them* whuppin' *you*." She leaned back and gave a rhythmic shake, daring Harold to say anything. He didn't. She turned away.

"Come on, Reese!" she shouted. "Whack that ball good now!"

Maurice lined the next pitch past Reggie's head, a run-scoring single. While the dugout cheered, Maurice's mother aimed a fingernail at Harold.

"Come on, now," she said, pointing to his helmet. "Time to quit all your talkin' and go *do* something."

Harold smiled, but he seemed nervous. "Watch this," he said. "I'm fittina whack it to the *gate*."

He swung too hard on the first pitch and then topped a weak grounder to the third baseman, who stomped on the bag to end the inning. Harold jogged back to the dugout without a word. After two innings, the score was 8–1, Mandinkes.

Bill brought Jalen in to pitch the third, stanching Freddie's tears by moving him to backcatcher. Maurice grabbed the Ed Kranepool mitt and took Jalen's place at first base. Kevin tried to suggest that a smaller, less ancient glove might serve better, but Maurice dismissed him. "This a first baseman's glove," he said, as if that were all the rationale he needed.

Jalen pitched well. Though the Mandinkes loaded the bases with one out, he got Derrick to pop out and fanned the cleanup hitter. As the Kikuyus came off the field, the coaches clapped and reached for handshakes. They didn't get many in return. There was no satisfaction in holding them scoreless; they needed some runs.

"Lotta time left, guys, lotta time."

"Let's get this guy now, a few hits and we're right back in this thing."

"We *still* gonna lose," decreed Louis.

The bottom of the third began auspiciously. Rufus, rocking impatiently in the batter's box, grounded a single to right field, and Demetrius followed with a double to the same spot. Then Alonzo, who had had only a handful of hits since his big Opening Day, surprised everyone with a long fly ball to center field which, though caught, was sufficiently unlikely to make everybody take notice. After the out, the coaches welcomed Alonzo back to the dugout as if he had hit a homer; he accepted the congratulations gracefully.

"Hey, hey," said Brad, sensing the significance of the event. "Everybody hits this inning, everybody hits."

Jonathan, smiling nervously, walked on four pitches, loading the bases for reluctant ninth-place batter Jalen, who employed Rude Dude to bounce a two-run single up the middle that barely eluded three gloves.

"Everybody hits," called Bill, picking up on Brad's idea. "Everybody now."

The Kikuyus' cheers ebbed when Freddie, still upset from his pitching performance, fanned for the second out. But then Otis hit a hard shot that the Mandinke shortstop misplayed into a double, scoring Jonathan and putting runners at second and third for Maurice. With half of the dugout on its feet, and half playing disinterested, Maurice walked confidently to the plate.

"Here we go." Steve elbowed Bill, remembering the previous inning. "Maurice's got this guy's number."

But Coach E was looking at Maurice, too, and checking his scorebook. He yelled out instructions—walk this guy, pitch to the next one.

"Intentional walk?" Brad couldn't believe it. Yet it made sense: Maurice had hit the ball on the button in both his at-bats; Harold had swung awkwardly and had hit into two easy outs with the bases loaded. So Derrick threw four balls, and Maurice flipped his bat and trotted modestly to first.

As Harold came to the plate, Pumpkin's cadre rattled the fences and chanted.

"Man-dink-uh, Man-dink-uh."

"Don't worry about them, Harold," yelled Bill. "Hit your

pitch." Harold looked over and tilted his head, as if to say, No shit.

But he was worried. He dug in, hitching his shoulders and looking around at the crowd, trying hard to appear casual. He hacked wildly at the first two pitches, fouling them off. Then he let two close pitches go by, the crowd oohing in sync with the umpire's call. Coach E clapped and nodded to his pitcher. The strategy was working.

The fifth pitch was a strike, and Harold realized it too late. He swung weakly, and fisted a baby flare down the right-field line. Much deeper, and the fleet right fielder would have caught it. Any shallower, and the first baseman might have made the play. But it floated between them like a perfect tennis lob, dropping softly on the grass a few inches inside the foul line. The runners, moving on contact, spun around the bases. Harold, who briefly considered it beneath his dignity to run out such a buster hit, slipped and fell rounding first, sending up a great cloud of dust and eliciting raucous laughter from the crowd. But when the dust settled, there stood Harold, on second, three runs scored, and the Mandinkes' lead was down to one. The Kikuyus' dugout went crazy.

"Yeeeah, bay-*bee*!" Freddie punched the fence, rejuvenated by the chance play. "We gonna *win*!"

Rufus, who had started the rally with his single, was the next up, and he waited patiently through a full-count walk. Demetrius followed with the inning's hardest hit, a two-run line-drive triple down the left-field line. Sprinting around the bases on long legs, Demetrius would have had a home run, had he not had to slow down to avoid passing his teammate. Rufus chugged along at his own pace, feet barely raising dust as he rounded third. A smile of private delight beamed on his face as he stomped home with both feet, oblivious to the left fielder's too late throw and the teammates and coaches who engulfed him and Harold in the dugout. Nine to eight, Kikuyus.

"That's my baby!" shouted his mother. "That's my baby!"

"We *winnin'*, man, we *winnin'*!" Freddie danced.

Even Alonzo's strikeout to end the inning couldn't dampen the enthusiasm. He waved at three straight pitches, then strode back to the dugout with a sly look on his face, as if he had perpetrated some enormous joke on all of the Mandinkes.

"Nice cuts, Alonzo," said Brad. Alonzo winked at him.

In the fourth, Bill brought in the subs. Louis replaced Alonzo in left, and Rassan replaced Jonathan in right. Play deep, the new outfielders were told; block everything. Better to give up a hit in front of them than to let something get by.

The strategy paid off immediately. With two outs and a man on first, the Mandinkes' big third baseman rocketed a line shot into the left-center gap, a hard bouncer that, if not stopped, undoubtedly would have rolled to the fence. Demetrius couldn't get it, but Louis, running with abandon, blocked it goalie style with his shin and quickly returned the ball to the infield to hold the lead runner at third. While Pumpkin and Coach E clapped for the double, the Kikuyus' coaches howled with delight and surprise— Louis had saved two runs. When Jalen struck out the next batter to end the half-inning, the Kikuyus' coaches leaped out of the dugout to greet their left fielder. He tried hard to keep a straight face, but eventually let loose with a smile.

The next inning and a half were as tightly played as any game all season. The Kikuyus loaded the bases again in the bottom of the fourth, but Derrick pitched out of it, getting Otis on a comebacker and striking out an overanxious Maurice. The Mandinkes put men on first and second with no outs in the top of the fifth, but were held scoreless when Otis made a rare Little League play—fielding a hot grounder at third and throwing out the batter—and Jalen again came through in the clutch, fanning the fourth and fifth hitters.

Across the field at the other diamond, the Pygmies—

Ewes semifinal was a blowout. Every few minutes one of Bob Muzikowski's undersize outfielders would scamper into the Kikuyus–Mandinkes game, chasing a long hit. Bob could be seen visiting the mound several times to counsel his ace, Shondrae, as Ewes circled the bases.

"Sixteen to five," a shorty behind the backstop shouted. "Ewes *whackin'* Shondrae's stuff."

The Kikuyus' coaches, however, couldn't be bothered. They were too busy, reminding the players of ready positions, moving the outfielders deeper, telling everyone to block the ball, and attempting to cover their growing excitement with nonchalance. After all, no sense making any players more nervous than they already were.

"Nice snag," they called when Harold caught a high pop fly in the tip of his webbing after colliding with Otis.

"Way to scoop," they told Maurice after he captured Otis's throw with his eyes firmly closed.

"Good system," they told Jalen after he explained a discovery: Whenever he turned to check on the Pygmies–Ewes game, he threw a ball; whenever he didn't look, he threw a strike. "So I just don't look," he said.

"Holeeee shit," the coaches told each other privately.

In the bottom of the fifth, the Kikuyus added an insurance run when Harold got aboard on an error and Demetrius slapped a routine grounder that went under the Mandinke shortstop's glove and past the left fielder. Going into the top of the sixth, the scorebook read 10–8, Kikuyus.

"Come *on*," Maurice yelled as the team took the field. "We fittina win."

In the Mandinkes' dugout, Coach E gathered his team. "Wait for your pitch," he said. "Watch the ball, meet the ball, and good things will happen." Then they put their hands in a circle and yelled—"*Mandinkes!*"

The first Mandinke batter hit a looping line drive to the right side of the infield. Rufus took one step back and gave an off-balance leap, the heels of his XJ-9000s rising perhaps only three inches off the ground. It wasn't enough.

The ball grazed his mitt, and landed in short right field for a single.

"That's all right now, honey," his mother yelled, but Rufus looked as if he might cry.

The next batter was Ed, the short second baseman, who had struck out twice and walked. He took his place nervously. Jalen, seeing that the boy was too frightened to swing, tried to lob the ball in. Ed walked on a full count, and Jalen slammed the ball into his mitt. Tying run on first, leading run at the plate, nobody out.

"Man-dink-uh, Man-dink-uh."

"Throw hard, Jalen. Just you and Freddie." Coach Bill tried to sound casual.

"Step to the glove," yelled Coach Kevin. "Right at the glove."

Jalen struck out the next batter, but his teammates made no noise. The coaches pumped their fists and called out advice, wary that silence would freeze their players.

"One out one out one out one out." Kevin signaled.

"Man-dink-uhhh, Man-dink-uhhh."

"You and the glove, Jalen, just you and the glove."

"Nothing gets past you now, infield."

"Watch the ball now, get in front of everything."

Before the Mandinkes' next batter, the swift right fielder Kinje, came to the plate, Coach E took him aside, placed his hands on the boy's shoulders, and whispered in his ear. Kinje nodded and walked securely to the plate. Jalen stared at him. He seemed cool for a ninth-place hitter, definitely no buster.

"Hit the glove, Jalen. Don't worry about the runners, just hit the glove."

Jalen's first pitch was high and outside by two feet. The runners took a step, but Freddie flung himself out acrobatically, caught the ball, spun around, and came up ready to throw. The runners stayed.

"Tell Freddie, if they steal, not to throw," said Coach Steve, the strategist. "Overthrow, that's two runs."

"No throws!" shouted three coaches at once, pointing to Freddie. He nodded.

"Swing if it's there, Kinje, swing if it's there."

"Let's go, big Jalen, you and the glove."

"Run if it's on the ground, hold up if it's in the air."

"Man-dink-uhhh, Man-dink-uhhh."

"Come on, Jiffy," Freddie yelled, his high voice cutting through the noise. "Show 'em yo heat!"

Jalen wound and threw. Kinje swung—*plink*. The ball scooted off his bat and toward first base, a hard, low hugger. Maurice shifted easily to his right, the Ed Kranepool held low as Cort had taught him. Ed, the Mandinke on first base, hesitated, making sure that the ball was on the ground. Then, as the ball neared Maurice's glove, he turned and took off.

Ed, the ball, and the Ed Kranepool mitt collided at a point about one inch off the ground and fifteen feet off first base. The entire infield—Jalen, Rufus, Harold—and even Demetrius in center—ran instinctively toward the spot, forgetting their positions, hoping to make the play and save the game.

Suddenly the ball was rolling into the outfield grass, where it came to a stop on a tuft of weeds twenty feet from the nearest player. Everyone was yelling. Coolly, Coach E windmilled his lead runner around third.

"Home home home!"

Jalen was first to the ball. He grabbed it with his bare hand, whirled, and threw, too late to get the lead runner, who slid home in a cloud of dust. Ten to nine, Kikuyus still ahead.

Freddie caught the ball, then looked up to see that Ed had rounded third too eagerly and was now stranded between home and third. Pumpkin screamed. The Kikuyus' coaches hollered advice, most of it intended to stop the bleeding.

"Run him back!"

"Don't throw it!"

But Freddie couldn't resist. Ed was just standing there

off third, practically daring Freddie to throw the ball. Now he was supposed to just hang on to the ball like some buster?

Freddie pump-faked twice, then threw a strike to third. Harold, who had commandeered third base from Otis in an attempt to be the hero, sneaked up behind the runner to take the throw. The ball and Ed arrived at the same time, there was another tangle, and then the ball was rolling away toward the Mandinkes' dugout and Ed was up and sailing for home. He slid in just ahead of a throw that sailed over Freddie's head and into the backstop with a resounding clang. Tie game.

There was a moment of quiet on the field as the Kikuyus absorbed the impact of what had happened. Then tears began to fall.

"Why you do that?" Freddie stared at Harold, flinging his mitt down into the dust, unmindful of the lead run, which now stood on third. "Why you do that?"

The other Kikuyus spun around, frantically looking for an explanation for their pain. Jalen pointed accusing fingers of both hands, and shouted at Maurice and Harold for losing the game. Harold advanced on the Mandinkes' celebration, his fist cocked menacingly. Rufus stamped in the dust, angry but unwilling to draw much attention to himself lest someone remember the hits that had deflected off his glove. Louis nonchalantly turned to watch the Pygmies–Ewes game. Maurice, his eyes overflowing, yelled that the Kikuyus had been cheated, that the runners kept getting in the way, that they were getting robbed. Pumpkin and the Mandinkes shook the fence and screamed with joy.

"Easy come, easy go," said Cort, straining to sound as if he really meant it.

Brad was first to notice the umpire. He had run in from behind first base early in the play, waving and trying to get everybody's attention. Now that things had calmed down, he picked up the ball and walked to the mound, signaling the head coaches and the home-plate umpire to join him for a conference.

"They *cheatin'* us!" Maurice grabbed Bill's arm as he strode to the mound. "They takin' the game away!"

"Relax there, chief," Bill said. "Let's see what this is all about."

The conference on the mound lasted five minutes. When it ended, Bill was trying to hide an unbelieving smile, and Coach E was slamming his hand against his clipboard.

"No *way*," the Mandinkes' coach kept saying. "No way. If that happened, then how can you let play continue? No way. This game is being played under protest."

Bill gathered the Kikuyus on the mound and explained what had happened. Kinje's ground ball had hit Ed's leg, and according to the rules, Ed was out and the ball was dead. Everything that had happened after that—Jalen's throw home, the rundown, Harold's throw to the backstop—didn't count. The situation, therefore, was this: Runners on first and third, two outs, no runs scored.

But try as Bill might to tell them, the Kikuyus wouldn't listen. They remained convinced that they had lost, convinced that they were being cheated.

"I'm gonna bust his dome," said Harold, pointing to Ed. "*Tell* me I won't."

"But they *robbin'* us, Bill," Maurice's cheeks were wet.

"You cryin', Maurice," Jalen pointed out.

"I ain't *cryin'*," he sniffled, "I'm just angry."

Bill tried a different tack. He knelt down, hoping he could catch everyone's gaze. "Okay, guys. The bottom line is this: Get this guy out, and we win." Bill looked at Jalen. He understood. Bill repeated it for everybody.

"Get this guy out, and we win."

Noses were wiped. Positions were retaken. The Mandinke runners, the dust of their celebration still coating their skin, were ushered by reluctant coaches to their places.

The next Mandinke batter was Terrence, the left fielder who had not been retired during the whole game: three walks and the hard grounder that Harold had misplayed back in the disastrous second. Terrence dug in at the plate, confident and loose. Behind him, face pressed to the backstop, a skinny bearded man called out.

"Watch that ball, son, hit it if it's there."

Terrence heard, but didn't look back. Until a few weeks before, his father had been on the pipe. Now he was in a rehab program, trying to straighten himself out. Terrence's coaches had noticed the change a few games back—new haircut, clean clothes, a shave. He had begun attending the games, and had even helped coach a little. After the Mandinkes had upset the Ibos in the conference semifinals, Terrence's dad had been the first on the field, attempting to hug the whole team at once. Now he stood outside the backstop, biting his knuckles.

"Come on, boy, hit that ball now."

"You and the glove, Jalen, just you and the glove."

"Swing if it's there, son, only if it's there."

"Man-dink-uhhh, Man-dink-uhhh."

"Get this guy, and we go home."

Careful not to look at the other diamond, Jalen came set and threw. Terrence swung hard and met the ball solidly. Another half-inch, and he might have had a home run. But the ball shot straight up, arcing to the right side of the infield. Instantly, Maurice was calling for it, glove up, waving his brother out of the way with his free hand. The ball hung high in the air, then dropped into the heart of the Ed Kranepool.

"I was gonna catch it with two hands, like you taught us," Maurice told Bill later, "but I wanted to end it with style."

Rufus danced. Jalen smiled. Louis threw his mitt into the air. Harold stopped picking a fight for a few seconds and grinned. Demetrius did pelvic thrusts. Freddie raced from person to person, sticking out his tongue, yelling, "Goin' to the 'ship, bay-*bee*!" Maurice stood on the mound, doing the play-by-play of his final catch in announcer's tones. Bill gathered the team and told them that the championship game would be Saturday against the Ewes, who had defeated the Pygmies 20–9; there would be a practice on Friday at six o'clock.

Alonzo, hanging back in the dugout, tugged on a coach's sleeve.

"Remember the butterfly?" Alonzo held out his index finger as he had on that rainy day in May. "I *told* you that was good luck."

SEPTEMBER

I feel bad about what happened this morning.

I am scared to go to school.

I do not feel safe around Cabrini Green.

I feel if it could happen to love ones, it could happen to me.

I thought My life will be better than what it turned to be.

I want God to cover me for years and years.

—From an essay by Karen McCune,
Edward Jenner Elementary School fourth-grader,
October 13, 1992

ONE

 On Thursday, Jalen phoned Coach Bill at the office.

"Whatchu want?"

"I don't know, Jalen," Bill said. "You called me."

"I was just thinking: If we got a little hitting, and if we played good defense, and if the Ewes were all nervous . . ."

"You were thinking what?"

"I was thinking that maybe . . ." Jalen's voice trailed off dreamily. Then, abruptly, he came back to earth.

"Naaah. We gonna get kilt."

On Friday, the day before the championship game, Carson Field lay empty. A cold wind was blowing in from Wisconsin, rattling the chicory bushes and sending up a last fuzzy cloud of dandelion seed from the outfield. A skinny man in a tattered Bulls jacket slept on a dugout bench, his arms wrapped around himself against the chill, his knee gesturing toward the blue sky. Four pigeons, unmindful of the visitor, shopped busily in the infield grass.

After four months, 230-odd games, and untold practices, the field didn't look much the worse for wear. Aside from a few bare patches, the colonies of weeds and grasses were treaded into a thin but even covering. The infield, thanks to frequent rains and Bill Seitz's faithful watering, had not blown into Lake Michigan, but was congealed into hard pack. Now, as the wind scrolled back the uppermost layer of loose dust, the foundation was revealed, a rocklike surface etched with thousands of footprints, long gouges, and shallow squiggles—exact hieroglyphics of panicked rundowns and homeward slides. In a few days, the sun and the chafing winds would rub the marks away, but for now they remained, the exact imprint of a season almost past.

School had started, and neighborhood streets were unusually silent, temporarily sedated by an unfamiliar absence of children. Playlots stood vacant. The basketball courts across the street from Carson Field were left untended. The usual clusters of men in front of the liquor stores on Larrabee appeared more isolated, surrounded only by blowing trash. In front of one highrise, two preschoolers whacked an aluminum can with tree branches, the harsh music echoing off the bricks.

There hadn't been any shooting in the past few days. The police weren't sure why—the start of school, like its end, was a time for gangs to recruit fresh members and renew battles. But lately nothing had jumped off, not even at the Castle. Perhaps the rumors were true, that the Emp and Rat had made their peace. Perhaps it meant nothing, simply a temporary lull. But each morning and afternoon, as children came and went, a squad car stood parked along Oak Street by Jenner Elementary School, just in case.

Rat hadn't been seen lately. Word was that he had done well this summer despite the shooting and the General Assistance cutoff. As usual, much of his earnings had to be plowed back into the business, or paid as tribute up the line to his bosses at Vienna prison. But Rat did all right.

One day in late August, he drove up alongside an old friend and palmed him a thick roll of hundreds and fifties from the glove compartment of his van. He offered his friend a job. The friend, who was trying to ease out of gang business, shook his head, and Rat said fine.

"A lot of top dogs would have tried to bogart me back into the game," the friend said later. "But Rat, he cool. He know that if I don't want to work, then I ain't gonna do good work for him, and he ain't gonna do good work for King Hoover. When it come down to it, Rat a businessman."

At five-fifteen as usual, the man in the blue "Boss" cap sauntered up to the backstop. He was disappointed to see no baseball, and more disappointed to hear that the season was almost over, for this would be his last at Carson Field.

"They closin' this here, come December." He jerked a weathered hand at the bricks behind him, the last working meat-packing plant in the city of Chicago. "They say they don't need no more sausage an' spicy hot dog from here, that the plant up in Wisconsin can pick up the slack." He leaned forward, confidential. "I say they just wanna shut this place down an' get some money out of it. The land valuable, you know? *Gold* Coast. Can't say as I blame 'em neither. Why pay me some seventeen dollar an hour to make hot dog when they could build some fancy hotel an' charge people to eat hot dog?" He chuckled at his joke, and lit a Tareyton.

"Myself, I'm gonna retire. I'm fifty-eight now, ain't no more spring chicken. Got some land down in Greenville, Mississippi, a small log cabin my daddy built. I got some grandbabies, I'm gonna take them with me. Next summer the oldest gonna turn eight, and that's when it's time to get children out of this city and onto a farm. Gonna buy each one of them a horse, put up some fences, live right. Gonna eat lots of fish—I like fish, any kinda fish. I could eat fish three hundred sixty-five days a year and twice on Sundays.

But you can't get no good fish 'round here." He paused and blew smoke onto the field.

"I'll miss this baseball. It is an enjoyable thing, watching the young people play the game, even if most of them do have hard heads and won't listen when you tell 'em to do something. I expect I'll probably find another field in Greenville or somewheres where I can stand and watch."

About a week before the championship game, Al Carter and Bob Muzikowski had run into each other at Carson Field. It was a sunny Friday afternoon. Bob was preparing to practice with his team for their playoff game. Al was standing on the bleachers with a few people from the neighborhood; they seemed to be holding a meeting.

"Must be a white-bashing session," Bob theorized archly from across the field.

Al had dropped out of sight since the previous board meeting at Seward Park. Bob, however, had not given up trying to prove his allegations about the grant money. Bill Seitz continued to drive past the basketball courts at Durso and Seward parks to count the number of teams in the tournament, and Tina compiled a list of the Near North Little League's expenses and revenues to be sent to all the coaches to prove the league's fiscal propriety. Greg White, perhaps the only moderating voice in this controversy, had been on a monthlong trip in South Africa since shortly after the meeting. Bob was left to stew. "Near as I can tell, there's only a handful of teams in Al's tournament," he said. "Forty kids, tops. And then we're out here with four hundred kids, taking them to Iowa, buying trophies, holding banquets, all for way less than thirty-five thousand dollars? Come on."

Now that Al was around again, apparently organizing neighborhood residents and black coaches, Bob was curious: Was he starting another league? Planning to disrupt the playoffs? Bob decided to go talk to him. He picked a glove out of the equipment bag and, head canted upward for a friendly greeting, walked slowly toward the backstop, popping a ball into the mitt.

In a few seconds the two men were arguing.

"Why don't you just go get some more of this," Al said, pulling some change from his pocket and jangling it in Bob's face. "You already bought all the kids anyway."

"It's not about money, Al." Bob pulled his sweatsuit away from his chest and placed the glove over his heart. "It's about what's right *here*."

"Yeah, yeah." Some of the shorties hanging around the field were taking notice now.

" 'Yeah' is right." Bob thumped his chest with the glove.

"Right," said Al vehemently. In the same moment both men turned away, Al toward the street, Bob toward the field.

"Okay," Bob shouted to the kids. "Let's play some ball."

Bob walked to the mound and began an impromptu batting practice. He threw gently, sending out words of encouragement. After a few pitches, Al hopped off the bleachers, grabbed a glove, and came onto the field. If Bob could play baseball with the kids, he seemed to be saying, then he could, too. He took up a post at third base, and proceeded to catch a few grounders. Bob, encouraged by this potential thaw, smiled broadly.

"All *right*," said Bob, his voice somewhat forced. "Let's show them what a couple of old guys can do."

If Al heard, he didn't show it. Instead, he took a boy aside and gave him some tips.

"You got to keep your glove *down*." Al pushed on the boy's back, leveling it. "You can't be fielding like you catchin' roaches—get your body in *front*."

This went on for a few minutes, Bob on the mound and Al in the field, each coaching the children with considerable skill. Then Al decided he wanted to hit. Tossing his glove to a shorty, he took a place at the front of the line and stepped to the plate. He selected a small wooden bat and swung it a few times, checking his muscles against the unfamiliar heft. His form was stiff-armed but quick. He settled in, unsmiling.

"All right," Bob said, forcing a grin. "Gonna show 'em what a couple of old-timers can do, eh?"

Al nodded but said nothing. Bob wound and threw.

Crack! The ball flew over second base.

Bob watched it, then threw again, this time a little harder.

Crack! A short hopper back to the mound. Bob speared it and, winking at Al, tossed it to the shorty who was covering first.

"Gotcha."

The talking slowed and then stopped, as both men became hypnotized by the rhythm of the game: throw-hit, throw-hit, throw-hit, 'round and 'round. They paused only to take a breath and prepare for the next confrontation. The harder Bob threw, the more furiously Al swung—pop-ups, line drives, fly balls, grounders.

In the following months, the split between Al and Bob would widen. At Tina Muzikowski's urging, a representative from The Chicago Initiative made a visit to Cabrini in late August. The investigator, Nolan Shaw, observed the basketball tournament, interviewed Al Carter and Demicco Youth Services personnel, and concluded that no further action was needed. Shaw did not conduct an audit or examine any financial records. ("We're a new organization with hundreds of programs—we can't thoroughly investigate every complaint," he explained later. "We understood that there was some confusion between some existing programs and the one funded by TCI. I basically went out there, talked to some people, and made sure that there was in fact a basketball program. That's all.") When asked by a journalist to release the financial paperwork related to the grant, Demicco executive director Julia Burgess declined, saying the organization was not obligated to respond to the Muzikowskis' "slanderous and childish rumor-mongering." Burgess also had

Demicco's lawyers draft a letter warning the Muzikowskis that if they continued their behavior, they would be sued.

While Bob and Tina remained utterly convinced of their case against Al, in the end they were left with two pieces of evidence that could be regarded as circumstantial at best: TCI's write-up on the grant describing "baseball and basketball" and Demicco's newsletter discussing the ways in which the TCI grant funded Al Carter's athletic programs—though the article carefully stipulated that the baseball league was an "already-organized program." Later, Bob and Tina would add two more items to their tally: first, the account of a recently estranged friend of Al's, who told Bob that Al had tried to involve him in the Demicco grant and that Al had given some of the money to several other friends who had nothing to do with the basketball tournament; second, the effusive expression of gratitude toward Demicco made at the year-end banquet by John Stevens, who gave the keynote speech when Al failed to show up. Although neither was proof, Bob wouldn't see it that way.

"Why else would he thank them?" he said after the banquet. "Demicco hasn't given us one penny or sent over any volunteers or done shit in the last two years. The only reason he would want to thank them is that they think the grant money went to the league. No other reason."

After a fleeting reconciliation over the winter, Bob's near unanimous election as league president made Al sever all ties to the Near North Little League and reestablish his African-American Youth League. A few days after the election, Al sent an open letter to the Cabrini community (including the La Salle Street Church, of which Bob was a member) likening Bob's election to European colonists' seizing of Native American lands, mistakenly asserting that La Salle Street Church had taken over the league, and announcing that the African-American Youth League baseball program would be back in business the following summer. Bob responded with a volcanic twenty-five-page packet sketching out his allegations about the grant, enumerating occasions on which Al's paid umpires had failed to appear, and providing samples of what he said were Al's "blatantly racist remarks against the volunteers" as well as transcripts of the several threatening phone calls he had received since the split.

"You don't have to be Columbo to figure this out," Bob's six-page cover letter concluded. "A handful of incredibly inept people have received dollar compensation for doing what all the *volunteer* coaches do for free. (In fact, we *pay* to coach.) *THEY STILL CANNOT BELIEVE AND ACCEPT THAT WE DO THIS FOR FREE.* That is why so many other well-intentioned people have left this area. What a shame!"

"I don't know what exactly is going on here," Coach Cort would drawl as he paged through the packet, which had been hand-delivered by Tina and Bill Seitz to every head coach in the league. "But I could probably coach without knowing all of this stuff."

After a great deal of haggling through the spring, the two leagues reached an agreement by which they would use Carson Field on alternate days throughout the 1993 season. It remained to be seen how long such a system could last, but the upshot was that Cabrini-Green, for so many years without a baseball league, would now have two.

On Bob's last pitch, Al lined a shot past second base. The shorties scrambled, but couldn't reach it.

"Niiice," said Bob, but Al didn't hear. He was already rounding first, trying to stretch it into a double, shoes sending up puffs of dirt in his wake.

TWO

For the first twenty minutes of the team's final practice on Friday evening, nobody played baseball. Bill shadowboxed with Jalen and Freddie; Cort and Louis thumb-wrestled. Kevin fielded questions about trophies and banquets; Maurice and others reenacted the key moments of the game against the Mandinkes, already transformed through repeated tellings into instant nostalgia, won not because of an umpire's accurate call but by an almost impossible collection of heroic acts: Jalen's pitching, Harold's double, Otis's play at third, Louis's stop in left field, Maurice's game-ending catch, now rewritten into a leaping, tip-of-the-mitt grab. Several players dug out their green-and-yellow foam caps for the first time in weeks, battered proof to the shorties hanging around the backstop that they were the Kikuyus, that they were going to the 'ship. The blue equipment bag lay on the dirt outside the dugout, but nobody touched it, as if opening it meant acknowledging that they had to play a game the next day. It was more fun just hanging out, fooling around, watching the kids on the street stare in envy, sharing that unspoken knowledge that the team, despite an average record and an average talent, had come within one victory of winning it all.

"He fittina play on the team next year," Alonzo announced, putting his hand on J-Nice's shoulder. "I'm training him to take my spot when I move up to the big leagues."

"Rassan gonna play my center-field position next year," said Maurice, pointing at the smaller boy. "He's fast, like me, and can catch good. He's still a buster at hitting, but he fittina be *good*."

"Louis, that was one heck of a play you made in the outfield yesterday," said Kevin loudly.

The boy looked at him without expression.

"Come on, Lou. You save two runs and now you don't remember?" Kevin jabbed him in the ribs. "You're modest."

"I guess it *was* a pretty good play," Louis said warily, as if unsure whether Kevin was making fun of him or not.

"Good? Try *great*."

Calbert tugged on Bill's sleeve. "How big's the trophy? Because I got a shelf all set aside and there's another shelf above it and if I can put it there that'd be good because it'd be out of the reach of French Fry—that's my brother—but if not my mom say we can always put it on top of the TV." Calbert took a breath. "But a TV's *not* my idea of a good display case."

Finally somebody opened the blue bag, and reluctantly, the balls and gloves were dug out. Bill leaned against the fence and watched as the team paired off to play catch: Harold with Jalen, Maurice with Freddie, Demetrius with Otis, Rufus with Louis, Alonzo with Rassan, Jonathan with Calbert. Home-Run Hitters and Busters. Some things hadn't changed.

But some things had. One day, on a hunch, Brad had asked Jalen about Harold's grades. Jalen was offhand.

"Oh, he get all *A*'s."

"Straight A's? Never any B's or C's?"

Jalen thought. "I think he got a B once in fifth. But everything else, A's."

Brad checked Jalen's story with Harold's father, and he confirmed it. Harold, the original bad-ass, was an ace in the classroom. Harold, the bully who didn't care about anything or anybody, did homework. Brad would learn later that Harold had benefited by being held back a grade, but that did little to diminish the impact of the discovery. Most of the coaches had figured that Harold wouldn't go far; now they saw a previously unimaginable breadth of possibility: scholarship, high school, college, job, house, family.

"I do okay," Harold said when Brad asked him about his grades.

A few days before the end of the season, Brad and Harold had a long talk. They discussed school, the coaches, the team, the neighborhood, and Brad came away impressed. "Harold is a *great* kid," he said, shaking his head in disbelief. "Maybe it's just a matter of getting him alone, away from the other kids, away from where he feels he has to prove himself all the time."

Another revelation came after Bill asked Freddie how he had enjoyed his first days back at St. Joseph's.

Freddie avoided Bill's eyes. "Ain't goin' yet. Gotta wait till the check come."

"So when," asked Bill, catching on, "is the check going to come?"

"Mama say sometime next week." Freddie shimmied away.

The exchange started Bill thinking. From what he knew about area schools, St. Joseph's ranked among the best. It was a private Catholic, uniforms-only institution on Orleans Street, a block outside Cabrini. Its fifty-dollar monthly tuition and high-quality programs attracted pupils from all over the city. To Bill, who had heard the horror stories about Jenner and other public schools, it seemed vital to keep young, impressionable Freddie

enrolled at St. Joseph's. And yet here he was, sitting at
home because his mother lacked fifty dollars? "We spend
that much in a night at the bars," Bill told another coach.

A few days later Freddie was back in school. Bill had
written a $300 check to St. Joseph's, and drawn up a one-
page agreement for Freddie on his computer:

> I agree and promise to do my best in school, to
> study hard, to listen to my elders, teachers, and
> tutors, to not miss school or tutoring, to pay atten-
> tion, to always do my homework, and to stay out
> of trouble. I agree to be patient, helpful, honest,
> determined, and thankful.

Bill printed out three copies of the contract, and had
Freddie and his mother sign it. Soon after, Bill received a
note from them. "To My Coach," it was addressed, and
there followed a heartfelt message of appreciation from
Freddie and his mother. After showing it to a few friends,
Bill slid it into the tattered manila folder, where, along with
the certificate from Maurice and Rufus, it was preserved
carefully, like a piece of valuable evidence.

After practice was rained out one night not long before the
season's end, the Kikuyus' coaches had convened at a restaurant, Twin Anchors. As they polished off massive serv-
ings of ribs, slaw, and fries, the conversation turned, as
theirs inevitably did, to the kids.

There were the usual tellings of anecdotes ("Alonzo told
me that to get ready for the game, he was going to hang
upside down from the top bunk of his bed like a fruit bat—
it helps him see better") and vocabulary ("Supergranny is
what everyone calls their great-grandmother—supergranny"), and then the conversation took a more serious
turn. The coaches contemplated what each child would be
doing in ten or fifteen years. The kids hadn't been much
help on this front; all save Louis testified that they would

be playing professional baseball, football, or basketball, or in Maurice's case, all three. Nevertheless, the coaches tried to match each player with a future.

"I could see Maurice making it out of Cabrini, being a coach or counselor or something."

"Demetrius . . . How about a salesman, with all the angles he knows how to work . . . or maybe a con man."

"Calbert could be a newscaster. Or a teacher—except none of his students would ever get to talk."

"How about Jalen as an engineer? Construction foreman? Whatever he does, he'll have to be the boss."

As for Louis, everybody agreed: "We'll all be working for him."

"Alonzo? I just want to hear what he comes up with when we ask him twenty years from now what he's doing." Kevin dropped into a poker face as he mimicked: " 'I'm an *astro*naut!' "

Some names were avoided, those for whom the guesses could not have been molded so optimistically, those that evoked worry and fear. The coaches worried about Freddie, so gifted and vulnerable. They were afraid for Harold, so full of grown-up gangster bluff that someone might take him up on it. They worried about quiet Otis and delicate Rufus, and when they thought of Samuel, they were sad. "He's already gone," one coach said. "You hate to say that about a ten-year-old kid, but I think it's true."

The coaches stayed at Twin Anchors for a long time on this night, trading stories and predicting destinies. It was easy for them to imagine that most of the kids might beat the odds and make it out of Cabrini. This was, they knew, probably a naive sentiment—after all, even if the relationships created on the team produced higher test scores or better study habits or job connections, even if the few hours a week for a few months out of the year did make a difference, the odds were still long. As Al Carter had said once, "You got fifteen kids on a team. Ten years from now, you'll have a couple hired by one of these corporations, two will be dead, two will be in the joint, two will move away, and the rest will be hanging out collecting their checks. If we save one, then this league's a success."

But the coaches had to be optimistic. They didn't have a choice. They weren't teachers or youth workers or professional counselors—they were volunteer coaches with a baseball team. In April they had met many of their players for the first time, and now they were friends. They played games. They called one another on the telephone. They bugged one another. And in some way that was at once impossible to measure and impossible to ignore, they changed one another.

After thirty minutes of talking and fooling around, the last practice finally got under way. Coach Bill moved the team into positions for the usual defensive drill, and as if on cue, they started to complain. Demetrius didn't want to play shortstop; Freddie didn't want to play center field; Alonzo would rather rejoin the Wildcats than take a turn in right field. It would have been nice if they simply had done what the coaches requested, or if they hadn't called each other buster, or if the coaches had had some absolute power with which to threaten them into compliance. But that wasn't the way things were with the Kikuyus. The coaches yelled and cajoled until their faces were red, the players yelled and cajoled back, and slowly, grudgingly, both sides came to a compromise. Then they practiced until it was too dark to see.

THREE

They were called the Tigers. They wore white uniforms of stretch polyester with red and black piping, black hats, and black stirrup socks pulled taut as guitar strings. Some fifteen years before the First Chicago Near North Kikuyus and the J. P. Morgan Ewes, the Tigers had been the best baseball team in Cabrini-Green.

"We were the *shit*," remembered Marvin Tolbert, the shortstop. "Everybody in the neighborhood wanted to be a Tiger, hang with us. We were good guys, we came from decent upbringings, we had a good coach, and they could see that. We weren't into gangbanging and that mess. We were *about* something."

On the night before the championship game, three former Tigers were gathered in a small room of the Seward Park fieldhouse. Over a greasy Chester's pizza and RC Colas, they reminisced about the days when they were the most feared ballplayers on the North Side.

Marvin—or Rusty, as he was once known because of the

dry skin on his hands—sat at the head of the table, his muscular arms testing the fabric of his black T-shirt. He had close-cropped hair and a neat goatee, and his teeth were sharp and white. A beeper hung on a belt loop of his stone-washed jeans, reminder of his position as a community organizer for a local youth agency. To Marvin's left sat Foogie, a solid ball of a man with long, slicked-back hair. He wore a Bulls T-shirt, and his reserved, thoughtful manner was amplified by the fact that he had played poker until five that morning. Foogie had been working for the CHA until the previous May, but was now between jobs.

To Marvin's left, fidgeting slightly from the two forty-ouncers he had drained that afternoon, sat Domino. As a teen, he had been called Wilbur Wood, after the stocky White Sox pitcher. But now it was difficult to imagine that this almost painfully slender man with papery skin and large, expressive eyes had ever been chubby. He wore torn jeans, battered Air Flights, and a stained T-shirt that advertised the Illinois Lottery. Before commencing on the meal, Domino, who had spent some time working as a street preacher, solemnly said a short grace:

"Dear Lord, we thank you for this food and for the good people and love in the world. Amen."

Then they started to tell stories.

They told of the days when life in Cabrini-Green seemed good, and when the best thing about life was baseball. Each building had its own team—the Tigers in 1150–1160 North Sedgwick, the Reds in 1117–1119 North Cleveland, the Twins in the rowhouses. The teams didn't have sponsors in the traditional sense, but they raised money by swarming the ramps with thirty-six-count boxes of Baby Ruths and Slow Pokes. They found their own coaches, too, enlisting fathers and older relatives for practices and scheduling games. On summer nights, hundreds of people would filter out of the highrises to cheer on their teams at Seward Park, some trundling picnic baskets into the outfield grass, or setting up cut-barrel barbecues overflowing with pork and beef. The smell would drift for a mile or more, drawing more people to the field, until ropes had to be strung along the foul lines to keep the game going. The gangs came, too, the Disciples in their blue tams and the Stones in their red tams, and though the rivals sometimes taunted one another, they never fought during the games. There was an unwritten rule against gangbanging during baseball. "If they saw you was a baseball player, then you was something," Marvin said. "They respected that, and they would leave you be."

They told of old teammates: Gym Shoe, who was so fast that he could round the bases on a high pop fly, and Smiley, the tough little backcatcher who wanted to play for the Tigers so badly that he moved in with his grandmother at 1150–1160 North Sedgwick and endured the scorn of his friends in the Castle. They told of their coach, a seventeen-year-old gospel singer named Melvin, and how he would make them run to the trees of Lincoln Park and back for conditioning. They told of fathers who would come out to help, how they would pop the kids with belts if they played around or argued too much. They told of Ty and LeRoy, brothers who were so different from each other— Ty intense and quiet, LeRoy loud and combative—and of the unforgettable summer day in 1977 when LeRoy was found dead in his apartment with a bullet in his head.

"He died right away." Marvin's voice was soft, barely perceptible. "I remember the ambulance out there, the paramedics trying to revive him, and then Ty getting off the bus, seeing his brother laying there. It was one of the saddest times in my life."

"Sad time," agreed Domino.

"Next year we went to high school, and the team kinda broke up after that," said Foogie. "We'd get together every summer and play, but it wasn't never the same."

"Never the same." Domino pointed at Foogie.

"Then"—Marvin pointed at Domino—"you starts in with your drinking."

"Yep." The slender man smiled. The high of the forty-ouncers had slackened, and his words emerged only with some effort.

"You was drinking every night, Olde English, drinking to get drunk, staying in your room." Marvin's tone stayed light, as if he was joking. "You turned into an old man in high school."

"Yeah, I did." Domino raised his head proudly. "But I *still* came out. I love my brothers, and that's enough." He looked around. "I *love* my brothers."

There was only one more big game, and that came during the Tigers' first year of high school. Instantly forming the nucleus of the Waller High varsity squad, the Tigers carried the team to the city semifinals against some now forgotten West Side school. The stakes were high: the city championship was to be played at Wrigley Field. It was a tightly played game, the score tied going into the last inning.

"They had men on first and third. Domino was pitching, and he starts to wind up." Marvin licked his lips, bringing an imaginary ball to his chest and looking in to the plate. Domino, whose memory for these events was cloudy, smiled vaguely at the ghost of his long-ago self, wondering what would happen next.

Marvin resumed the play-by-play. "He fakes to third, then he spins and throws to first, and we got the guy out. He's *out*! But then the umpire come in and tell us that we can't do that, that it was a balk and the run scored." His nostrils flared at the remembered anger. "We went off—I mean, we went *off*. We pulled a trick on them, and they weren't with it—and they tell us we're *cheating*! We had been playing *base*ball, we knew all the tricks in the trade, been doing that every day in practice—and they tell us we can't do that." He shook his head. "They won by one run."

After a pause Marvin went on. "The next year most everybody went their own way. Pretty soon they had even messed up our old field at Seward Park, moving the backstop over to the other side and laying down all this bullshit dirt. There used to be light brown dirt, *real* dirt. Now they got this stuff that look like dried mud—I mean, they messed our field *up*."

They talked a while longer, about other fields, other teams they had beaten, old rivalries. Then Domino raised his head. Something Marvin had said had caught his attention.

"The ground . . ." He paused, swallowing. "The ground on that field we had was smooth and hard. I mean, I still got *bruises* on me from when we played." His old teammates turned to look, but Domino's eyes and hands were on the table, the tips of his skinny fingers moving lightly over the smooth brown plastic.

"We played hard, I mean we played *hard*. I got to give it to these brothers—we played hard ball. *Hard* ball, man. People out there today, man, these cats don't know how we played. We was little-bitty guys, and we was playin' *hard ball*. . . ." His voice trailed into a cough, then silence.

"I wouldn't want to have growed up nowhere else," Marvin said after a moment. Domino turned and nodded vigorously, as if his teammate had completed his own thought exactly.

"I wouldn't wanna be *no*where else except *right here*." Domino's palm slapped the table.

"They cut out the shooting," said Foogie, "and everything be good here again, like it was."

They went on to piece together the fates of their old teammates. Gym Shoe, the base-stealer, was in prison for burglary. Melvin, their gospel-singer coach, was in prison for breaking and entering. Smiley, the stocky backcatcher, was serving a two-year sentence for involuntary manslaughter. Touché, a slick-fielding third baseman, was in jail for violating his probation. Ty, LeRoy's quiet brother, had a good job with CHA maintenance. Don, a wiry outfielder, drove city buses, and Randy, Don's brother, worked in an optical lab.

The Tigers were gone, but children had come to take their place. Ty had two boys in the new league who were fine players, and Smiley had four, one of them a pint-size pitcher who could throw as well as anybody. Nobody knew whether Gym Shoe or Curtis or Glenn or Don or Touché or any of the other players had children who played ball, or whether those children played in the new Little League. But probably they did.

On Saturday it rained so hard that puddles bloomed in the base paths. The championship was rescheduled for Sunday at three.

FOUR

Maurice awoke early on Sunday. Moving quietly so as not to wake his brother, he went to the kitchen and pulled the cartridge from the refrigerator door tray, then turned on the TV and cued up Nintendo Bases Loaded 2. The screen flickered, and the set began to hum.

Maurice's game-day rituals hadn't changed since the beginning of the season. He still ate Kix and wore his Charlotte Hornets T-shirt (although in a slight alteration he had begun ironing the shirt), and he still played Nintendo. If he played well in Nintendo, he would play well against the Ewes. Of course, there had been other signs as well. At the end of practice on Friday, Coach Bill had asked him who should be the starting pitcher in the championship game. Maurice hadn't hesitated. "Me."

Bill had looked him over, and Maurice had looked back. They both knew that Freddie had a better arm, and that Jalen was probably better in the clutch. But Bill had surprised him.

"Okay." He put his big hand on Maurice's right shoulder and shook it lightly. "You'll start."

Now, Maurice sat a few inches away from the television, the early-morning light glowing through the sheets that hung over the windows, the pale blue glimmer from the TV lighting up his face, his fingers fluttering over the control board as he reared and fired to the computer-controlled batters. *Click-click*—strike one. *Click-click*—strike two. *Click-click*—strike three. If things went like this, the Kikuyus would beat the Ewes easily. Then again, Nintendo batters were busters.

A few blocks away, in Louis's bedroom, the X-Cons were playing the Sky Men. It was a classic LBL matchup—the Sky Men surging ahead with their superior speed and skill, the X-Cons clawing their way back with rough tactics made easier by uneven officiating. The crowd suspected that the X-Cons, known for their corrupt practices, might have paid off the referees, but as usual, nothing could be proven.

With time running out and the score 101–71, Sky Men leading, one of the X-Cons went up for a game-winning thirty-two-pointer. He never made it. One of the Sky Men, a promising young guard named John, had cleverly planted a smoke bomb in the ball. When the X-Con attempted the required bounce off the head, the ball exploded, smoke got in his eyes, and time expired.

"Sky Men win! Sky Men win!" The commentator leaped on his bed, bouncing so high that his fingertips seemed to brush the ceiling.

Alonzo and J-Nice headed for the Memory Playground early on Sunday. Alonzo, still reveling in his long fly ball against the Mandinkes, gave J-Nice a batting lesson.

"You got to be *quick* with your *wrists,* like I am," he said, grabbing the bat from the smaller boy. "Bein' quick make you dangerous, and then you can whack the high cheese."

"*Dange*-russ." J-Nice wiped his nose.

"Yop. And when you get the high cheese, up in the wheelhouse, you got to turn on it, use your body. Home-run hitters like me, they whack it with their whole bodies."

J-Nice nodded. Now that school had started, he and Alonzo were spending less time together. They didn't see each other much during the day, since they were in different grades, and sometimes when Alonzo was walking with his friends in the halls, he would pretend not to notice J-Nice. But when they got back home, onto the Memory Playground, they were friends. One day Alonzo showed J-Nice a postcard that he was sending to his father. On the front was the skyline of Chicago. On the back Alonzo had written about how the Kikuyus were in the championship and how Alonzo had whacked three homers against the Mandinkes in the semifinals. He had signed it "Your son, Alonzo."

"Step back," Alonzo ordered. "I'm fittina show you my home-run swing."

Alonzo began a slow-motion swing, his left foot lifting and then striding, his head tilting back, his long arms extending until the tiny barrel of the toy bat reached the center of the X that marked home plate.

"*Boom!*"

FIVE

Warm-ups went quickly. The Kikuyus looked tight, nervous; they were aware of the large crowd gathering behind the backstop. Though Saturday's rain and wind had pressed the field smooth, the Kikuyus' infield missed more than its share of Coach Kevin's warm-up grounders, raising catcalls from the shorties. The Ewes, in contrast, looked cool and collected in their royal blue jerseys. Their coach, Charles Hudson, stood wearing a black "X" hat and an imperturbable expression.

"No sweat." Coach Bill clapped to his players. "Don't worry about them. Let's go."

But the Kikuyus were worried, and with good reason. Not only were they facing the defending champions, the same team that had annihilated them 22–2 earlier in the season, but the weather had conspired against them as well. Had the game been played on Saturday as scheduled, the six-innings-per-week pitching rule would have forced the Ewes to go with their second-best, Big O, whose sidearm stuff was eminently hittable. But Sunday marked the start of a new week, and that meant that Lemon, the hard-throwing ace who had shut the Pygmies down in the semis, was available to pitch the entire game. As he strode out to take his warm-up tosses, the Kikuyus' hopes flagged.

"That ain't fair!" Rufus's eyes brimmed with tears. "He pitch against the Pygmies—they *cheatin'*."

"Relax there, chief," Bill said. "It ain't over yet."

The crowd behind the backstop grew, drawn by the perfect, windless day. Generously built women, their Sunday hats pinned against the wind, stepped gingerly across Division Street on high heels. Three white-haired men, one of them toting a tall paper bag, set up bar in the bleachers. Young women in neon sweatsuits chatted behind home plate, small babies perched in their arms. Toddlers wandered about, sucking cola from barely opened cans. Four teenagers with their hoods up despite the heat stood like fenceposts along the foul line, accompanied by a troupe of Little Cobras, one of them leafing through a thick wad of paper-towel money. More children were everywhere, climbing on the backstop, thumbing the water fountain to spray one another, throwing rocks at the passing El train, scrabbling in the dust for a foul ball.

Maurice and Rufus's mother, of course, was there, in her lawn chair. Other parents stood nearby—Harold's father, Calbert's mother with French Fry, Jonathan's mother, Jalen's father, and Demetrius's mother and his girlfriend. They stood watching intently, their forearms pressed against the chain link.

In the dugout stood an older man with snowy hair and a face that bore more than a passing resemblance to Joe DiMaggio's.

"Dad," Bill was saying, "watch this kid Freddie. He's got an incredible arm."

His parents' divorce had finally gone through, and Bill had invited his father to the game. It was the first time they had been together in quite a while, and Bill seemed a little distracted. During warm-ups he had sneaked several glances toward the dugout to see whether his father was watching.

"Not bad." Bill's father nodded at Freddie and lit a cigarette. "He's not bad at all."

Then it was time. The Kikuyus, as the team with the worse record, would bat first.

"All right, guys, bring it in." Bill knelt and put out his hand. The players gathered and put their hands on top of his. Bill looked around the circle, trying to make eye contact with every player. Most of them were looking away, distracted in their nervousness.

"Let's be positive, let's support each other, and let's have a little fun out there. Now, on three, I want to hear 'Kikuyus.' One . . . two . . . three . . ."

Sixteen voices rose at once.

"*Kikuyus.*"

Freddie, bouncing on his toes, swung at the first pitch and grounded back to Lemon for the first out. Jalen waved Rude Dude past three straight pitches. Then Maurice, waggling his bat anxiously, swung at the first two pitches and missed.

"Fan him, Lemon," shouted someone on the street.

"We gonna lose," announced Jalen.

"Come on, Reese," Mary yelled to her son.

On the next pitch, Maurice hit the longest shot of his life, a massive shot to dead center that spun out and hung like a golf drive, and which would have rolled to the backstop of the other diamond had it not struck the pitcher's rubber there. By the time the outfielders tracked down the ball, Maurice was rounding third and the Kikuyus' dugout was in chaos. Parents pounded the fence; Mary was out of her chair, pointing at the ball and shouting, "Look at that! Look at that!" The coaches nodded to one another, pretending that they had expected as much. Maurice returned to the dugout, trying unsuccessfully to contain his emotion. Kikuyus 1, Ewes 0.

With two out and two on in the bottom of the first, a grounder scooted under Harold's glove and past Louis in right field for a three-run homer.

"No problem, Maurice, no problem." The Kikuyus' coaches clapped and shouted. "Get 'em next time."

In the bottom of the second, with the bases loaded and the score still 3–1, Big O whacked a long fly ball to center field. Freddie, whom Bill had put there for his speed, raced backward and leaped, and for a moment it seemed he would make a spectacular catch. But the ball flew an inch or two beyond the tip of his glove, and kept going, and it was 7–1, Ewes.

"Yeah, baby, yeah." Charles Hudson clapped, still unsmiling.

"Rally, rally, the pitcher's name is Sally," the shorties chanted.

"Maaaaaaaan!" Jalen yelled.

It was never close again. Inning after inning, Lemon mowed through the Kikuyus, giving up only a triple by Jalen, a ground-ball homer by Harold, and a scattering of singles. Maurice threw as hard as he could, but the Ewes were swinging well, and by the fourth inning Bill had brought in Freddie. Things didn't improve. When the Kikuyus came up for their final at-bat, the score was 16–3 and the dugout was silent. The coaches, knowing better than to cheerlead, focused their attention on upset players. Freddie, distraught after bouncing out to the pitcher for the third time, wiped his eyes on Bill's shirtsleeve. Rufus, angry after being taken out of the game so Jonathan could play his two innings, sat leg against leg with Cort. Steve sat with Maurice, whose cheeks were still sticky with tears. Everybody was waiting impatiently for the game to end. After all, they had gone farther than anyone had expected. As the players reminded any shorty who teased them, they still would get their trophies.

Then, with one out, the Kikuyus staged the beginnings of a rally. Jonathan walked, and Demetrius did the same.

With men on first and second, Rassan came to the plate. The dugout began to stir.

"Come on, Rassan," shouted Maurice, sniffing. "Whack his junk."

It was fitting that small, wiry Rassan was at the plate now. In the few weeks in which he had been on the team, he had impressed everyone with his hustle and willingness to learn. He evaded easy classification—too fast and coordinated to be a Buster, too small and inexperienced to be a Home-Run Hitter. So both groups treated him equally well, and everybody liked him. When he took a mighty swing and missed for strike one, the noise from the dugout grew louder.

"Rip a shot now, Rassan," shouted the coaches, picking up on the enthusiasm. "Wait for your pitch, and nail it."

Rassan lined the next pitch over the shortstop's head and into left field.

Though it was the Ewes who shortly would be throwing their caps and mitts and forming a roiling, dancing, taunting mass of blue, chanting "Back to back, back to back!" and leaping about with parents and posing for pictures, the Kikuyus cheered Rassan's hit as if it had won the game. They rattled the fence and howled his name as if they knew this would be their last chance to yell.

"Man, Rassan's gonna be good next year," Maurice kept saying after the game. "You see the way he whacked Lemon's junk? He's gonna be *good*."

Ten minutes later the Kikuyus stood in their dugout, the dust of the Ewes' celebration coating them like a light rain. A smattering of complaints and cries could be heard, but for the most part the players seemed content, and a little relieved, to have it all over with. Some were even cheerful. Calbert, apparently not cognizant of the final score, hauled his little brother into the dugout to meet everyone and announced that French Fry would be the team's official mascot next year. Alonzo shook the Ewes' hands with a slight smile on his face that said he had fooled them all.

The celebration died down, and the coaches packed up the gear. Steve and Cort loaded the bats and gloves into the bags; Brad made a few final scratches in the scorebook; Kevin collected the uniforms in a nylon mesh bag as the kids changed into T-shirts and shorts. Bill was turned away from the field, engrossed in quiet conversation with his father. They talked about where to go to dinner, and Bill's father asked him whether he had time in the next week or so for a round of golf up in Skokie, where they used to play when Bill was younger. Bill said that sounded fine.

When the coaches shouldered their various bags and were ready to go, they found that most of the players had disappeared. After yelling for them, they were able to come up with only a few. The field and the street were thronging with shorties, and without their yellow jerseys, the Kikuyus blended in and were swept along in the tide.

SIX

The Kikuyus collected their trophies at the league banquet the following night, and almost a month passed before the team was together again. The occasion was the team party at Bill, Kevin, and Cort's place. The coaches met the players—accompanied by Maurice and Rufus's mother—at Carson Field around six, then drove them to their rehabbed North Side home.

"Y'all *better* have hamburgers." Jalen stomped up the stairs and looked around angrily. "Last time you took us out, all you had was a bunch of phony hot dogs."

"Relax there, chief," said Bill, smiling. "We got hamburgers, we got bratwurst, we got cheese, we got a basketball court up the street. It ain't phony."

"You *best* not be lyin'." Jalen's face contracted into his best glower. "Or I'm leavin'."

The coaches were struck by the appearance of the players. They looked different, older. During the season the players hadn't seemed to age, but a few weeks' absence had added years. Alonzo and Freddie had new close-cropped haircuts that enlarged their faces and lent them an air of inscrutability. Rufus's face looked leaner, more angular, trimmed of baby fat. Nathaniel, still tanned from his southern summer and filled out from his grandmother's home cooking, was a few inches taller. Jalen, somebody noticed, had sprouted an almost imperceptible fuzz on his cheeks. Maurice had finally gotten a haircut, a smart fade with a lightning stripe on the side. "They look like teenagers," Brad said incredulously. "When did that happen?"

Soon the kids had deployed themselves around the two-story house, Jalen and Freddie dunking socks in the Nerf hoop, Calbert and Louis watching a sports bloopers video, Maurice and Demetrius playing fetch with Hobey, Bill's black Labrador retriever. The coaches, along with Brad's girlfriend, Dianna, and Bill's girlfriend, Molly, and Mary, gathered around the barbecue on the back porch.

There was a lot of catching up to do. Maurice and Freddie were playing on a basketball team ("I can almost dunk, Bill," Maurice said, showing him a scrape on his hand. "See, I cut it on the rim"). Rufus had enrolled in an art class at Seward Park and had stitched several beanbags already. Most of Calbert's time had been spent in school, "gettin' straight A's and bein' the teacher's helper," while Harold proudly detailed how he had had to complete eighteen laps of the school grounds after calling the principal an idiot. Alonzo did him one better, however, saying that he had done 180 laps. "I take big steps," he said, winking. Jalen had decided to try out for his school's football team, and had been spending some time in the weight room ("Hey, *hey,*" said Bill admiringly, wrapping his fingers around the boy's wiry biceps), and Louis had been appointed cartoonist of his school newspaper. Mary had news as well: She was going back to Loyola, which she had left when she became pregnant with Maurice, to finish her accounting degree. "I'll take the train, and my momma will take care of the kids," she said. "I just hope I can remember some of that math."

Life had changed for some of the coaches, too. After some uncertainty, it appeared that Bill would keep his job. "I still don't have any idea what I want to end up doing," he said. "But at least it's a paycheck." Cort, a few credits short of his divinity degree, was trying to set up a work-study program in which he would help Bill Seitz establish a scholarship fund for the league. With only a few weeks of golfing weather left, such a move would perhaps delay his attaining a PGA teacher's card, but Cort didn't mind much. "If this thing works out, it could be great," he said. "I work with the kids, get my credits, and I can get my card next summer."

The night went by quickly, and before long it was nine o'clock. "Hey, hey, settle it down," Bill said as he attempted to sweep the team together in the living room. This accomplished, he pulled out a lumpy shopping bag and began the awards ceremony. The trophies weren't much—a new baseball inscribed, in Cort's graceful handwriting, with the player's name and award, each carefully chosen to avoid any value comparisons. Alonzo got the Golden Spikes, Freddie got the Cy Young, Rassan got Rookie of the Year, Harold got the Babe Ruth Award, Nathaniel was Best Traveler. The kids liked them and held them gently in their palms, careful not to smudge the ink.

"It's been a great year," Bill concluded. "I know we're going to miss a few of you next year, but we hope you'll come back and help us coach. Maurice"—he nodded toward the boy—"has already said that he'll come back. I hope the rest of you—Demetrius, Harold, Louis, Otis—come back, too." Bill cleared his throat. He was never much for speeches.

"I'll come back, to kick your white ass." Harold cackled, and everybody smiled, for different reasons.

"Hope you do, Harold."

There was one more item of business. The tutoring program, administered through a Cabrini group, the Community Youth Creative Learning Center, would start the following week, and tutors and pupils had to be paired up now. Some of the coaches had tutored the previous year. Bill explained the program in case anyone was unfamiliar with it: every Monday night, from seven to eight-thirty, until the end of the school year.

Slowly, twosomes started forming. Kevin and Louis decided to work together, and they even made plans to go to Milwaukee to see an architect friend of Kevin's and his computer-aided–design business. Steve, whose Blazer drew several suitors, settled unexpectedly on Calbert. Dianna approached Alonzo, who, with several other offers, said he'd get back to her the next week. Freddie decided on Cort. Molly and Demetrius exchanged phone numbers. Brad shambled up and, tugging on his Royals cap, asked Harold what he thought about working together. "Get rid of that Hooptie and get a real ride"—Harold crossed his arms and tilted his head—"and I *might* think about it."

Bill and Jalen eyed each other across the room. Jalen hadn't been considered eagerly by anyone. Too much of a headache, one coach said. The two old adversaries stared at one another until finally Jalen cracked.

"Okay," he warned, "but you *better* take me out for pizza after every time!"

Finally it was time to go. The kids had school the next day, and the coaches had work. There were a few casual words of thanks, a few shouted good-byes to their hosts, and then the children were racing one another toward Steve's Blazer, fighting to be able to ride in it. There was not room for all of them, however, and as they elbowed for those precious seats, the coaches yelled and told them to cool it, to calm down.

Standing on the steps watching the commotion, Mary turned to a coach. "They started up again," she said. "Yesterday I was looking out my window and saw some boys, maybe fifteen or sixteen, running with guns, shooting at one another. I think they was Vice Lords and Cobras, but I don't know. I wish I knew what it was all about. Then I could go out there and tell them to quit."

"Yeah," said the coach, not knowing what else to say.

Fifteen days later that feud would end, when a seven-year-old named Dantrell Davis was shot and killed by a sniper as he made the hundred-foot journey from his home in 500–502 West Oak to Jenner Elementary School. He was the fifth child from Cabrini, and the third from Jenner, to die violently in 1992, but his death, perceived as more poignant than the others, quickly became a national symbol of inner-city problems. It was reported on the front pages of *USA Today*, *The New York Times*, the *Los Angeles Times*, and *The Boston Herald*, as well as on network news and *60 Minutes*, and in hundreds of newspapers, magazines, and television programs. Dantrell's killing, mentioned by then presidential candidate Bill Clinton, became a clarion call for public housing reform, and catapulted Cabrini-Green into the living rooms of America, at least for a few nights. The furor resulted in the bricking up of several Cabrini buildings, including the Castle, and greatly increased security in the highrises, in the form of metal detectors, lights, security guards, and the retention of Public Housing North Special Functions Division.

Less attention was given to the matter of Dantrell Davis's alleged killer, a thirty-three-year-old Army veteran and sometime Little League umpire named Anthony Garrett. After his arrest, Garrett signed a confession—later recanted—stating that he had been aiming at some teenagers who had been shooting at him earlier, and had accidentally hit the boy. The coaches who knew Anthony were shaken to the core. *Him?* The guy who had kept the kids so strictly in line, who seemed the kind of strong role model they so badly needed? He must've lost it, just snapped. But others were less surprised.

"Who knows why he did it," said a dispirited Al Carter the morning after the shooting. "It's just one of those things, man, just one of those things."

Now, finally, the Kikuyus got into cars. Some of them had to ride in buster cars, and though they complained about it for a moment, they didn't really care. Once you were moving, the car wasn't important. Riding was all that mattered. The little squadron pulled away, heading south, back to the projects, and as they accelerated into the dark streets, a dozen small hands could be seen sticking out of the windows, trying to capture the air.

ACKNOWLEDGMENTS

 Thanks to Laura Yorke for her editorial guidance, to Todd Savage for his research assistance, and to Marshall Sella, Laura Hohnhold, Donald Katz, Ed Marciniak, and Jane Isay for their ideas and counsel. Thanks to the tireless David Black for his work in honing this project, and to Mark Bryant and Larry Burke of *Outside* magazine, who granted me the leave of absence to pursue it. Thanks to Anna Jardine for her sharp eye in copyediting, to Eric O'Connell, whose perfectly rendered photographs provided the basis for the hardcover jacket illustration, and to Beeb, my mother-in-law, for her close and accurate readings of the manuscript.

In addition, I am of course greatly appreciative of the dozens of people in Cabrini-Green who gave unsparingly of their time and energy. Among them are Officers Dennis Davis, Eric Davis, William Felke, and James Martin of Public Housing North; Officer Ken Charles of the 18th Police District, Charles Price of the Chicago Housing Authority, Juris Strautmanis and Richard Moore of Edward Jenner

Elementary School, Tommie Johnson of Demicco Youth Services, John Raffetto of the Chicago Park District, and Dr. Charles Holmes; the others are far too numerous to name here.

Finally, I thank the Kikuyus players, their families, and their coaches for their generosity and, moreover, for their lasting friendship.

MORE THAN FRIENDS
Barbara Delinsky
The Maxwells and the Popes are two families whose lives are interwoven like the threads of a beautiful, yet ultimately delicate, tapestry. When their idyllic lives are unexpectedly shattered by one event, their faith in each other — and in themselves — is put to the supreme test.

"Intriguing women's fiction." — *Publishers Weekly*

CITY OF GOLD
Len Deighton
Amid the turmoil of World War II, Rommel's forces in Egypt relentlessly advance across the Sahara aided by ready access to Allied intelligence. Sent to Cairo on special assignment, Captain Bert Cutler's mission is formidable: whatever the risk, whatever the cost, he must catch Rommel's spy.

"Wonderful." — *Seattle Times/Post-Intelligencer*

DEATH PENALTY
William J. Coughlin
Former hot-shot attorney Charley Sloan gets a chance to resurrect his career with the case of a lifetime — an extortion scam that implicates his life-long mentor, a respected judge.

Battling against inner demons and corrupt associates, Sloan's quest for the truth climaxes in one dramatic showdown of justice.

"Superb!"
— *The Detroit News*